The Heresy of Monasticism

alba house

A DIVISION OF THE SOCIETY OF ST. PAUL
STATEN ISLAND, NEW YORK 10314

The Heresy of Monasticism

James A. Mohler, S.J.

The Christian Monks:
Types and Anti-types

An Historical Survey

Nihil Obstat:
    Edward Higgins, O.F.M. Cap.
    Censor Librorum

Imprimatur:
    Joseph P. O'Brien, S.T.D.
    Vicar General, Archdiocese of New York
    February 5, 1971

The nihil obstat and imprimatur are official declarations that a book or pamphlet is free of doctrinal or moral error. No implication is contained therein that those who have granted the nihil obstat and imprimatur agree with the contents, opinions or statements expressed.

ISBN: 8189-0183-7

Library of Congress Catalog Card No. 76-148683

Designed, printed and bound in the U.S.A. by the Pauline Fathers and Brothers of the Society of St. Paul, 2187 Victory Blvd., Staten Island, N.Y. 10314 as part of their communications apostolate.

# Acknowledgments

G. Allen and Unwin, London, for quotes from *Monks and Civilization* by J. DeCarreaux.

Archabbey Press, Latrobe, Pa., for quotes from *The Rule of St. Benedict* by P. DeLatte.

Basil Blackwell Oxford, for quotes from *The Desert a City* by D. Chitty.

Catholic University of America Press for quotes from the *Fathers of the Church Series*, R. Deferrari, ed.

Wm. B. Eerdmans Publishing Co., Grand Rapids, for quotes from *A Select Library of Nicene and Post-Nicene Fathers*, P. Schaff and H. Wade, editors.

Epworth Press, London, for quotes from *The Evolution of the Monastic Ideal* by H. Workman.

Harvard University Press, Cambridge, Mass., for quotes from the *Loeb Classical Library*.

Oxford University Press for quotes from *Ireland, Harbinger of the Middle Ages* by L. Bieler.

Paulist / Newman Press, New York, for quotes from the *Ancient Christian Writers* series, J. Quasten et al, eds., and *The Monks of Qumran* by E. Sutcliffe.

Talbot Press, Dublin, for quotes from *Irish Monasticism* by J. Ryan.

World Publishing Co., New York, for quotes from *The Essene Writings from Qumran* by A. Dupont-Sommer.

ontents

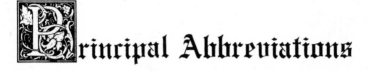

Principal Abbreviations

ACW	*Ancient Christian Writers,* eds. J. Quasten et al. Westminster, Md., Newman Press.
CC	*Corpus Christianorum,* Series Latina, Tournai, Brepols.
CSEL	*Corpus Scriptorum Ecclesiasticorum Latinorum,* Vienna.
DACL	*Dictionaire d'archéologie chrétienne et de liturgie,* H. Leclercq et H. Marrou, eds., Paris, Librairie Letouzey et Ane.
FOC	*Fathers of the Church,* R. Deferrari, ed., New York, Fathers of the Church, Inc.
LCC	*Library of Christian Classics,* Philadelphia, Westminster Press, J. Baillie, J. McNeill, H. Van Dusen, eds.
Loeb	*Loeb Classical Library,* Cambridge, Mass., Harvard University Press.
NPNF	*A Select Library of the Nicene and Post-Nicene Fathers,* Second Series, P. Schaff and H. Wade, eds., Grand Rapids, Wm. B. Eerdmans Publishing Co.
PL,PG	*Patrologiae Cursus Completus,* J-P. Migne, ed., Paris.
SC	*Sources Chrétiennes,* H. De Lubac et J. Daniélou, eds., Paris, Cerf.

# Introduction

hurch and monastic officials are alarmed at the current drop in vocations and at the increasing defections from convents and monasteries. Empty novitiates, seminaries, and cloisters dot the land. To try to stem the exodus there has been a frantic spurt of activity: vocation campaigns, up-dating of rules, moving of houses from the country to the inner city or to university campuses where the action is.

In all of this, no doubt, Christian secularism has played a part with its world-centered, man-centered Christianity stressing God's immanence over his transcendence. Existentialism with its emphasis on the individual person here and now pushed eschatology into the background, although the recent theology of the future has revived it. Freedom of the individual over commitment to a cause is another current trend.

Today's flight from the monastery to the world parallels in

many ways that of the Reformation. And as the reform churches continued many monastic traditions, while rejecting others, so today's church rebels bear many monastic characteristics, basically a lay heresy, anti-institutional, anti-clerical, prophetic and reforming.

All through the history of monasticism, the initial prophetic founding spirit has waned by the third generation, with new reforms growing up to replace the old. This happened in Egypt, Palestine, Gaul, Italy, and Ireland. Sometimes the very monastic renunciation led to an unhealthy corporate wealth. Far removed from the poor communes of the beginning, the monasteries grew into wealthy estates with vast lands and revenues.

We hope in this work to outline briefly the early history of Christian monasticism, but not without first seeing some of the glorious prototypes such as the Buddhist Samgha and the Jewish monks of Qumran. Both of these illustrate some of the basic principles of monasticism, namely, an attempt to live a religious life in a perfect, intensified, and usually communal manner, often hoping to recapture the lost spirit of their founder which has been diffused by some foreign influence.

Certainly the Christian heresy of monasticism started in this fashion. Christianity of the fourth century had lost its primordial eschatological dynamism. When persecution ceased and Roman protection ensued, the Church became soft and complacent, with the clergy becoming government officials. At first lay Christians fled to the desert as hermits to pursue sanctity in the caves or other isolated places. As their numbers increased, communism soon developed with rules of which Pachomius' is a prime example. Although it was to become largely a cenobitic movement, Christian monasticism never lost its yearning for the solitary.

Though Egyptian monasticism rather quickly tapered off, it always remained as the mythological prototype of the Christian monks. Either Monastic founders visited the desert fathers personally as Basil, Jerome and John Cassian, or read about them as Augustine, Columban, and Benedict. New founders emphasized the communal and the moderate, although the Irish monks tended more towards Egyptian severity.

Christian monasticism always remained basically a lay heresy, although there were periodic atttempts to organize the clergy into communistic life. Often apart from and sometimes at odds with the church of the bishops, the monks' motto was "Avoid women and bishops." The monastic heresy generally remained orthodox although some of its exaggerations were at one time or another condemned by episcopal synods, for example, Pelagianism, Monophysitism, and some outmoded Irish customs. But, in general, the communist rule helped towards a moderation of the idiosyncracies of the hermits and Benedict's stability curbed the monastic wanderlust.

The history of monasticism seems to be cyclic with its greatest successes in apocalyptic and eschatological times such as the barbarian invasions and most recently the cataclysm of World War II, with a dropping off in more prosperous eras.

Is the monastic ideal still valid for today's Christians in these generally prosperous times? The Second Vatican Council, stressing the lay church in the world, has forced many religious to ask themselves: would I not be better off living as a good Christian layman in the world? Oddly enough, this was exactly how Christian monasticism started, namely, with pious lay families expanding, taking in others, writing a rule, etc. This was true with Basil, Augustine, Melania, Paula, the Irish clan monks, and others. Benedict's rule is based on the Christian family with the abbot as the *bonus et diligens pater familias*.

So what is the difference between a good Christian family in the world and a lay monastery? Perhaps not as much as one might think. The monastic separation of the sexes plus a life-long commitment so that the monk will never be emancipated to marry and become a *pater familias*, but remains perpetually a *filius familias* are obvious differences.

There has always been a basic urge in monasticism to flee the world of sin and strife for some mythological other world of peace and tranquility, an eschatological utopia, whether at Qumran, the deserts of Egypt, the Isles of Lérins or Iona. This unending search for the idyllic desert isle, the mythological, the transcendent is deep-rooted in man. Recent trends in the Hippie movement, Zen Buddhism, transcendental meditation, astrology and the eschatological theology of the future bear this out. If these spirits continue, they could well spell the end of secularism with modern man seeking an escape outside of his present world whether in drugs, Nirvana, or astrology.

There is a similarity in monasticism, namely, the eschatological search for tranquility, *apatheia,* prayer and union with God, away from the cares of business, family, strife. In fact, the entrant begins an entirely new life, leaving his past life behind as at Baptism.

We have called this book *The Heresy of Monasticism* not in the modern pejorative sense, but rather in its root meaning of an option, choice, way of life, or sect. In this sense the early Christians were a Jewish "Way" or heresy. Christian monasticism is sometimes called the church (*ekklēsia*) of the monks, a lay church alongside of and sometimes opposed to the church of the bishops. In later times in the West, especially after Gregory the Great, the church of the monks was protected from bishops and secular rulers by the Pope of Rome. In turn, they gave him their allegiance and the long association of monks and papacy often benefited both.

Our hope is that in this study of the first centuries of the Christian monastic heresy along with its Buddhist and Jewish counterparts we may find some lasting values to further the development of monasticism and its younger brother religious life in their existential situations today.

Special thanks to Fr. James Mackin, S.J. and the John Carroll University library staff for their kind and efficient help.

Thanks also to Fr. Raymond Schoder, S.J. of Loyola University, Chicago, for the photos and to Miss Ryn Gates, Cleveland, for the maps.

The Heresy of
Monasticism

1. I Take Refuge In the Samgha

(Buddhist Admissions Formula)

he ascetical spirit is a quality or virtue peculiar to no particular religion. There seems to be a basic self-understanding in every man by which he recognizes in himself and in others evil tendencies which he tries to overcome by denying himself illegitimate and even legitimate pleasures, striving for peace and tranquillity. Since this is impossible to achieve in the daily turmoil of business, family, and ephemeral worldly cares, he pursues it to some distant isle or within a monastic enclosure. Although this escape often is sought individually, man's social nature prompts him to group together with others of similar bent for mutual encouragement. Often a solitary will attract disciples, leading to some type of communism.

1

Ascetical practices are found in most religions, indicating the universality of the trend. For example, we see it early in India and the East, whence it moves Westward to Judaism and Christianity. In this chapter we hope to see some of the Buddhist ascetical and monastic trends which built upon even earlier Indian culture.

Buddha was born in Lumbini near the Nepal-Indian border either in 624, 567, 466 B.C. Scholars disagree. He was of the Sakya clan and although his given name was Siddhartha, he was called Gautama. At age 29 he went to study under the ascetic Yogis who trained their students in a religious rule, Vinaya. Gautama and his fellow disciples sought the solution to the problem of evil in the world with its misery, sorrow, sickness, death, war, destruction.

Not satisfied with yoga, Gautama tried living as a solitary ascetic for seven years. Emaciated and frustrated, he concentrated on meditation to gain insight into his previous lives and find the true way of deliverance from the vagaries of the world. It was while meditating in the lotus position under the bodhi tree at Bodhgaya that he experienced his great enlightenment.

He was anxious to tell others of this primordial event, especially his five former companion ascetics, relating his path through meditation to insight, enlightenment and Nirvana. The root meaning of Nirvana seems to be "blown out" as a lamp, that is, one may only achieve enlightenment by first extinguishing all his desires. All suffering (Dukkha), he related, has its origin in desire (Tanha), a yearning for infinite existence, pleasure or success. It is only by the conquering of our desires that we can overcome suffering, through the eight-fold path of right views, right intent, right speech, right conduct, right means of livelihood, right endeavor, right-mindfulness, right meditation.

As his disciples increased, Buddha sent them on missionary journies to help others, showing them compassion. When a man was ordained as his disciple, he repeated the three-fold formula: "I take refuge in the Buddha, I take refuge in the Dharma and I take refuge in the Samgha." Buddha by no means pioneered groups of ascetics in India for mendicant holy men had always been a part of the tradition there. Although initially Samgha (community) included all of Buddha's followers, it was to become synonymous with the monks (*Bhikkhus*).

In order to enter Samgha, one first had to leave the world (*Pabbajja*), taking instructions and vows. But it seems the vows were not life-long so that those who find that they do not have a true vocation can return to the world, where if they cannot achieve Aratta (perfection), can hope for it in a future rebirth. With its egalitarian Dharma, (Law, Doctrine, Scripture), Buddhism was a rejection of the Brahmin caste system. The lack of grades and distinctions, fundamental to any family life, was to become the hallmark of Western monasticism, as well. The essence of Dharma is Buddha's enlightenment, law and community.

Although in the beginning the monks travelled abroad, living in peace in forests and caves, as their numbers increased, they adopted a form of communal living. Over the years the proportion of monks to laity has generally been small, although there have been times and places where a large number of the male population were monks or where it was normal for a young man to spend a year or two as a novice or monk.

In a sense the monks are the only true Buddhists, for to them alone is given the opportunity to lead the highly spiritual life away from the world in which Nirvana could hope to be attained. The Mahayana Buddhists, however, claimed that a layman could also be a first class Buddhist (*Bodhisattva*).

When Buddha died, there was a crisis among his monks. One monk, named Subhadda, felt relieved to be out from under his authority. At an assembly of the monks, Kassapa the Great suggested that the Dharma (Law) and the Vinaya (Discipline) be recited lest they be forgotten. At the request of the monks, Kassapa chose as members 499 Arahats, that is, those who had traversed the eight-fold path to Nirvana.

Once the monks became established in monasteries, the early more democratic atmosphere when monks and laity mixed freely, gave way to a monastery-orientated life of Theravada Buddhism with its holy ones (*Arahats*) seeking perfection on the way to

Nirvana, whereas the lay community existed for the support and encouragement of this spiritual elite.

From Buddha till the third century B.C. a number of councils and sects developed with different interpretations of Buddha's teachings. Oral traditions were codified into the Pali Canon, monastic rules (*Patimokkha*) many of which were adapted from Brahminism.

The steady growth of Buddhism in the early centuries was largely due to the proselytizing monks. In the beginning Buddha hoped that his Samgha would exist side by side with the political Samgha. But in the reign of King Asoka (third century, B.C.), the expansion of the empire was used to promote Buddhism. Samgha became limited to monks and nuns supported by the government and so no longer dependent on the laity. As Buddhism spread and monasteries multiplied, laxity increased and different schools of interpretation arose.

One of the main themes of Buddhist monasticism was that of Nirvana. As envisioned by the monks, it was a release from the limitation of separate existence. Although Buddha refuted the existence of self as a permanent individual entity, he insisted that what one does in this life has an effect on one's future existences. The real for Buddha is more of a becoming than a changeless substance as in the Brahmin tradition. Basically Nirvana is the cessation of rebirth, the extinction of passions, and the replacement of suffering by bliss. There are two kinds of Nirvana: the first "with remainder," that is, the material and immaterial conditions of being (*Upadi*) remain and the cause but not the effects of reincarnation are destroyed. This is attainable in this life. The second type of Nirvana attainable at death is "without remainder," with a total extinction of conditions of life, destroying both the cause and the effects of reincarnation.

Control of Atman (*Self*) is necessary for Nirvana. Atman, the intangible supreme principle especially as manifest in the human soul, is the very root of attachment and desire. To begin with each monk must obey the basic moral precepts of avoiding the killing of any living being, stealing, unchastity, lying, alcohol—supplemented by the monks rules: namely, no eating outside proper times, no watching of displays, dancing, singing, or music, the use of garlands, perfumes, or oils, or high or wide beds, gold or silver. Controlling his earthly desires, the monk is free to move towards the intuition of his former lives and the mysteries of life and death, the contemplative way that Buddha had experienced beneath the Bodhi tree.

Along with celibacy and inoffensiveness, poverty constitutes a pillar of Buddhist monasticism. A monk was only allowed his robes, begging bowl, needle, rosary, razor, and water filter. Although originally his robes were made by hand from scraps of cloth and dyed a saffron color, later cloth was donated by the laity.

In the beginning the monks had no home, for they had left all worldly comfort to live in forests or wherever might be convenient. Although the Vinaya (Rule of Discipline) speaks of living in houses, convents or grottos as allowable, it also points out the dangers of this type of life. The monks obtained all their needs by humble begging. In the early days no money could be possessed, but with time the inevitable laxity allowed both money and property. The begging bowl was the talisman of Buddha's humility and poverty, as most of his statues attest. It was the custom of a Buddhist master to pass his bowl on to his disciples.

By their begging the monks could cultivate many virtues. Since they were fully occupied in meditation and the quelling of desires, the laity supported them. Far from being regarded as "free-loaders," the monks were the elite of the Buddhist society, for whom the rest of the Buddhists exist. Of course, not all of the laity equally recognized the superiority of the contemplatives, so sometimes the begging tours involved humiliations. And on occasion they had to accept poor or even forbidden foods without complaint. Indifferent to the vagaries of life, the monks learned to get along on very little. Although independent of the world, they lived in it. Subsidized by the laity, the monks were free to pursue Nirvana.

Celibacy was also fundamental to the monk's way of life, for the married man is tied down to family and world and so

cannot control his desires or seek contemplation. Also the monks
believed that the lower rapture of sexual intercourse and the
higher state of contemplation were incompatible. Chastity (*Brah-
macarya*) or the proper moral conduct of the holy man is of the
essence of monasticism. Thus any one who violated sexual abstinence is immediately expelled from the group. The monks
tended to look upon sexual intercourse as something below them,
even bovine. Holding women in disdain, they avoided all occasions of seeing, speaking or even thinking of them, a misogynism
reminiscent of later Christian monks.

Certainly a basic part of Buddhist monastic control of desire
is the denial of the instinct for sexual pleasure. It is true that
a measure of calm and tranquility is attained in the sexual union,
but it is a mere shadow of that achieved through meditation.
Marital intercourse has frequently been used by the prophets
and mystics as a weak image of the union between God and
man. Some later Buddhists such as the Tantra (800 A.D.) felt
that sexual life was not incompatible with monasticism.

The monks took no vow of obedience, for all are equal without any of the distasteful gradations of Brahma. Yet there was
always a respect for the elders and their spiritual maturity.
Buddhist monasteries are basically democracies with the head
monk as first among equals. Thus when problems of discipline
arise, the monks as a whole judge the case in their bi-monthly
conventions, assigning a proper penance. Expulsion was the
penalty for any of the four cardinal sins, namely, violations of
chastity, theft, killing, and falsely claiming supernatural powers.
The laity also keep a check on the conduct of the monks.

Inoffensiveness is a central theme of Buddhism as it is in
Jainism, both of which are looked upon as sixth century heresies
of Hinduism. At any rate, the Buddhist shibboleth of "no harm-
ing" may have been a reaction to the age of violence which preceded it. And it is interwoven with the doctrines of reincarnation
and compassion. As Conze writes,[1] by inviting other selves to

1. **Buddhism, Its Essence and Development**, New York, Harper, 1959,
p. 61.

enter our own personality, we break down the barriers built up by our innate selfishness. Through the centuries the compassion of Buddha and his followers had a great humanizing effect on all of Asia, even softening the fierce warriors of Tibet and Mongolia. Also there has been little religious persecution in Buddhism, but rather a toleration of many diverse schools of interpretation.

Although Buddhist nuns (*Bhikkunis*) were an early development, Buddha himself was reluctant to admit women into Samgha. When his disciple Ananda suggested it, Buddha responded,

> Women are soon angered, Ananda; women are envious, Ananda; women are stupid, Ananda. That is the reason, Ananda, that is the cause why women have no place in public assemblies, do not carry on a business, and do not earn their living by any profession.[2]

Legend has it that Buddha's aunt Mahapajapati was the first nun. Although Buddha frequently refused her request to join, she continued to hound him, cutting her hair and putting on the yellow robes. Finally he relented, agreeing to ordain her if she would follow the eight strict rules (*Garudhamma*), commanding deference to the monks. For example, "A nun even of 100 years standing shall (first) salute a monk and rise up before him, even if he is only just ordained." Buddha always felt that the presence of women in his order would be detrimental in the long run. "For just as houses, where there are many women and few men, are easily broken into by robbers, even so in the doctrine and discipline in which a woman goes forth the religious system will not last long."[3]

Especially in the beginning the monks had a close relationship

2. A. Coomaraswamu, **Buddha and the Gospel of Buddhism**, New York, Putnam, 1916, p. 162.

3. E. Thomas, **The Life of Buddha as Legend and History**, London, Routledge and Kegan Paul, 1960, p. 109.

with the laity, for as peripatetic beggars they had constant contact with them, influencing their lives by example and in turn receiving their necessities from the lay Buddhists. Conze [4] outlines a three-fold need that the monks fulfilled for the laity, namely, spiritual, mythological and magical. First of all, the laity need the monks to keep reminding them of the ultimate purpose in life. The monks, both by word and example, gave the people a window through which they could look out of their self-enclosed lives into the other world. An edifying monk, spiritual, kind, compassionate, detached from the things of earth, self-controlled and tranquil, gave the householders an ideal on which to model their lives. In certain places and times the rapport between the laymen and the monks was extremely close, since most of the men had either studied in the monastery or were former novices or monks who had returned to the world.

The mythological or other-worldly plays a large part in Buddhist thought. Buddhist faith is not an intellectual assent to stratified and abstract dogmas, but fundamentally a detachment from the world, a turning from the visible to the invisible. The laymen respect Buddha, Dharma and Samgha because they detect this spirit in all three.

Magical protection of crops depended upon ceremonies performed by the Buddhist priests, while fertility of soul and physical well-being of the people depended on the monks. Conze speaks of the necessity of the magical,[5] "If religion rejects the magical side of life, it cuts itself off from the living forces of the world to such an extent that it cannot even bring the spiritual side of man to maturity." In Buddhism as in many other religions, we find a paradoxical denial of self-interest alongside of a magical subservience to self-interest.

Less was demanded of the laity than of the monks. Lay obligations are summed up in the three jewels: "To the Buddha for refuge I go; to the Dharma for refuge I go; to the Samgha

4. **Buddhism, Its Essence and Development,** pp. 77ff.

5. Ibid., p. 84.

for refuge I go." Also they obeyed the five-fold commandment
against killing, stealing, illicit sex, lying, and the use of intoxi-
cants. But the laity were generally looked upon as second class
Buddhists.

Under King Asoka (third century, B.C.) the Mahasanghikas
relaxed the Vinaya rules, giving greater place to the laity. The
apotheosis of Buddha and the greater emphasis on Karma (action) leading to unceasing transformation in the wheel of trans-
migration were of greater interest to the laity. Less stress was
placed on Nirvana, Dharma and the meditation of the monks.
Moreover, literature and sculpture which were of more interest
to the people were produced.

When Asoka subsidized the monks, they lost their early spirit
of poverty, becoming well-fed, clothed, and housed, attracting
undesirables to the easy life. The monks now freed from begging
and the pursuit of the simple life removed from the world, spent
their days in a leisurely study of scriptures and learning. Now
the monks were independent of the laity, but when their subsidy
ceased, once again they had to appeal to the people for support.
And thus arose the Mahayana interest in the salvation of all.

Although Buddhist monasticism has undergone many revi-
sions, reforms and interpretations in many different countries
throughout the thousands of years of its evolution, yet it has
remarkably preserved its traditions intact, passed from one generation to the next and written down in the Pali canon. David
Pfanner has made a recent study of contemporary Theravada
Buddhist monasticism in rural Burma,[6] in which he describes the
interaction of monks and laity in the village of Mayin, Burma,
including about 700 people in 150 households.

The buildings of the monastic school where the monks live,
study and teach and where the laity come on the Sabbath are
apart from the village proper, indicating the Samgha separation

6. "The Buddhist Monk in Rural Burmese Society," in **Anthropological
Studies in Theravada Buddhism, Cultural Report,** Series no. 13, Southeast
Asia Studies, Yale University Press, 1966, pp. 77-96.

from the world. There are two village monasteries, one each for
the strict and moderate observance. Both contain novices and
ordained monks who rank in seniority.

The monks constitute about three per cent of the males of
the area; half of these are novices many of whom will not remain
in the monastery. Most of the villages in Burma have a monastery
or two. Although the monks are well fed and housed, their monasteries are of plain and simple construction. According to Buddhist tradition, the monks are entirely supported by the laity.
So each morning the younger monks and novices collect rice
in the village and some families send food to the monastery
besides. Also sometimes alms are collected for the monks, for
example, at the annual alms presentation and initiation ceremony.

The monks are highly regarded by the laity, using such
honorific titles as Pongyi (Great Glory or Great Holiness) or
Yahan (Perfect One). The monks are a people apart by their
dress, language, patterns of eating and social relations. They
can be easily spotted by their shaven heads and saffron robes
with their few possessions of begging bowl, needle, razor,
strainer and axe. Some of the modern monks also have sandals,
umbrella, pen, paper, books, and eye glasses. The monks may
accept any food offered by the laity unless it is expressly killed
for them. But they neither ask for anything nor thank the donor
for it is considered a privilege to have one's offering accepted
by a monk.

Besides the five precepts binding all Buddhists, the monks
observe their own regulations: not eating in the afternoon, not
participating in or witnessing of shows, not using perfumes,
high beds or seats. The rules for ordained monks are contained
in the 227 precepts of the Patimauk, a section of the Vinaya.
Expulsion is still the penalty for violations of chastity, the taking
of human life, stealing, and false claims to supernatural powers.
Although today's monks do not observe all 227 regulations, they
faithfully keep the ten precepts, though some (Thudhamma)
may attend musical entertainments. That the monks are faithful

to their rule is attested by the great reverence which the faithful have for them.

The monks come from all social levels and must be twenty years of age or older, with consent of parents, debt-free, healthy, and possess the eight prerequisites of bowl, needle, etc. Since most of the males of the village have studied in the monastery as boys, they know the life and its requirements. Almost half of the men of the village were at one time novices and fourteen per cent were formerly ordained monks. It is not at all unusual for a man to remain in the monastery for several years and then return to life as a layman, although the more common practice is to remain as a novice or ordained monk for a short time and then return to the world. While in the monastic state they are excluded from roles in business, farm or family.

As across the world in other religions, so there has been a recent drop in ordinations of Buddhist monks. The main obstacle seems to be the difficulty in keeping the vows whose infraction might mean a retrogression in the life cycle, namely, a rebirth in a lower state or in hell. Moreover, the traditional discipline such as the enforced seclusion, lack of evening meal, and celibacy are irritating to modern young orientals. The monks spend most of their day studying and teaching with a little formal prayer such as the reciting of the Pali stanzas morning and evening.

On the Buddhist sabbaths the monks hold a service for the people, some of whom keep the monastic precepts for the whole sabbath, remaining in the monastery till dusk. "A monk for a day." The coming together in the monastery to feed the monks or to hear the law is the commonest form of service. This can be on a holiday, a child-naming, or a death. One group of monks (*Thudhamma*) makes charms and amulets to protect from evil spirits, showing some affinity with animism.

The rapport between the monks and laity is rather formal with little contact with women. Rarely do the monks visit the homes of the people except for the daily food collecting and on the occasion of a death in the family. The monk's relationship

to the layman is as a teacher and pupil with laymen showing
due reverence to the monk at all times. As Pfanner notes,[7]

> More than any other role in Burmese society, the role of the
> monk is associated with the cognitive, moral, and transcen-
> dental values.... A life dedicated to personal salvation or
> enlightenment through adherence to a monastic code and
> a rejection of personal or material attachment in the world
> of the laity.

Monks are poor, humble, continent, austere, self-abnegating, re-
nouncing the world to achieve enlightenment by way of Samgha.
The greater a monk's years of service, the greater his Karma
(merit) and so more reverence is due to him. Although the
increasing secularization of Burmese society and the restriction
of the monks in secular affairs has limited the monk's role and
increase of secular education has meant a lessening of monastic
influence in this area, yet modern Buddhist monks reflect an
amazing continuity over the thousands of years of Samgha. And
it argues well that despite a present low in vocations due to
current secularism, they will persevere.

Besides the southern Theravada Buddhists of Ceylon, Burma,
Siam and Cambodia with their stress on the monastic road to
Nirvana, the northern Mahayana school also has thrived with
a universal appeal of the heart and intuition over against the
more intellectual approach of the Theravada. While the goal
of the Theravada is the attainment of Arahatship or self-salvation,
Mahayana renounces this in order to aid all men on the road
to salvation.

Zen is a popular form of northern Buddhism. Starting in
China in the sixth century A.D., it spread to Japan and in modern
times throughout the world. Hoping to find enlightenment in the
world rather than withdrawing from it, Zen permeates all activities from art and gardening to Judo.

In Buddhism today the Samgha still plays a strong role,

7. "The Buddhist Monk," p. 90.

though in the eyes of many its influence is waning due to increasing secularization and a greater stress on lay spirituality. Yet in the monastic samghas, whether the spiritual retreats of Theravada or the training colleges of Mahayana, the monk is basically a teacher by word and example to the layman. Even in today's world Buddhism would be but a shadow without the third jewel, Samgha.

2. In the Wilderness Prepare the Way
(Is. 40:3)

Although asceticism has not been a central theme in the history of Israel, nevertheless, from time to time we find ascetic individuals such as Samuel or Elijah and groups such as the Rechabites, descendants of Jonadab son of Rechab (ninth century, B.C.), who abstained from wine and lived frugally in tents up to the time of Jeremiah (Jer 35), and the abstinent and hirsute Nazirites (Jg 13:7; 16:17; Am 2:11; 1 Mc 3:49; Acts 18:18).

A. The Qumran Monks

In the apocalyptic period, 200 B.C. to 200 A.D., arose certain heresies or sects showing ascetical qualities, namely, the Pharisees, Essenes, Therapeuts, Baptists and Christians. Most desired to lead a more perfect way, removed from corrupting elements

15

whether they might be foreigners, sinners, etc., and avoiding all impurities to make their bodies worthy to come in contact with sacred objects (Lev 10:9; Nb 6:3; Am 2:12; Jg 13:14; Ex 19:15). They fasted, prayed, studied Torah, and had their own special rules of conduct. The Qumran people bear some semblance to later Christian groups in the same area.

In 198 B.C. Antiochus III, the Seleucid king of Syria took Palestine from the Ptolemies and began a thorough Hellenizing. But the Hasidim rose up in opposition, joined by the Maccabean revolt of 166. Jonathan Maccabee, appointed High Priest by the Seleucid king Alexander Balas, seems to have introduced practices not acceptable to many of the Jews. He may well have been the Wicked Priest spoken of in the Qumran scrolls.

During the corrupt reign of Jonathan arose the famous Teacher of Righteousness, who organized some of the Hasidim who were now split from the Maccabees. He objected strenuously to Jonathan's temple innovations and calendar changes. This was about 150 B.C. *The Damascus Document* (DD 1:11-12) comments: [1] "He raised them up a Teacher of Righteousness to lead them in the way of his heart to make known to the last generations what He would do to the last generation of traitors."

His first followers included twelve laymen and three priests. After a two year preparation, they separated themselves from the traitors, fleeing to the desert at Qumran on the shores of the Dead Sea, as Isaiah commanded, to make way for the Lord (Is 40:3).

And when these things came to pass for the community in Israel at the appointed times, they shall be separated from the midst of the habitation of perverse men to go into the desert to prepare the way of "Him" as it is written "In the wilderness prepare the way.... Make straight in the desert a highway for our God" (Is 40:3) (*Scroll of the Rule* SR 8: 12-14).

1. Qumran quotes are from A. Dupont-Sommer, **The Essene Writings of Qumran**, Cleveland, World, 1962.

The messianic eschatological call of Isaiah was the talisman not only of the Qumran monks, but of the Christians as well. The Qumranites called their desert retreat "Damascus" (Am 5:27).

The Teacher of Righteousness was neither a prophet nor messiah, but rather an interpreter of the prophets, a priest and teacher. Persecuted by the Wicked Priest, the monks fled Qumran in 145, but were allowed to return by Simon in 140. In their desert retreat the monks not only hoped to escape the wickedness of Jerusalem, but also pursued a most perfect observance of the Law of Moses and strict levitical purity. "To seek God with (all their heart) and (all their soul) (and) do what is right and good before Him, as He commanded by the hand of Moses and all his servants the prophets" (SR 1:2-3).

They will love what He has chosen and hate what He despised, practicing good works, truth, righteousness, and justice, avoiding a guilty heart, lust and all evil, obeying the precepts of God in the Covenant of Grace, united in the council of God, loving the sons of light and hating the sons of darkness (SR 1:4-11).

Their return to a strict observance of the Law paralleled that of the Pharisees who also grew out of the Hasidim.

Perhaps a few words of description of the Qumran monastery would be in order here. It is located on the shore of the Dead Sea, ten miles south of Jericho and fourteen miles east of Jerusalem, on a raised plateau between the cliff and the beach. Wadi Qumran just south of the monastery is the only source of water in the rainy season. The monks probably cultivated the oasis Ain Feshkha for food. The monastery itself measures about one hundred yards by eighty, with a large water system containing many cisterns and baths, a tower for defense, offices, kitchen, hall, pantry, scriptorium. The monks were self sufficient with their own pottery, bakery, dyer, stable, library, etc. There is a cemetery of 1,000 graves, covering the period of occupancy from 150 B.C. to 68 A.D. Average age seems to have been thirty-five years.

When the original band had become established at Qumran, others were attracted to join them. The *Scroll of the Rule* (SR 6:14-23), describes the admission procedures. The length of the postulancy varied according to how long the entrant's arrival preceded the general admissions date. Preliminary acceptance as a postulant followed an examination by the mebaqqer or overseer. If the applicant's conduct and intelligence are approved, he is admitted to the covenant. Promising to obey the Law of Moses, he is instructed in the rules of the community.

Admission as a novice depended on the favorable vote of the community. As a first year novice, he still kept his own property and had to support himself by a trade. This was a guarantee against "free-loaders." The first year men, still dirty with the corruption of the world, were not allowed in contact with the rest of the community, and could not even help prepare the meals lest the purity of the monks be endangered. Second year novices could help prepare the food, but not the drink. At the end of the first year there was another vote of the community on the novice's intelligence, his understanding and observance of the Law. Only after this approval are his property and wages handed over to the mebaqqer who inscribes the amount in a register, so that if he leaves the monastery, his money will be returned.

At the end of the second year a third vote of the community approves the novice as a full-voting member of the monastery.

When they join the Community, let whoever comes to the Council of the Community enter into the Covenant of God in the presence of all the volunteers, and let him undertake by oath of obligation to be converted to the Law of Moses according to all his commands, with all his heart and all his soul, following all that is revealed of it to the sons of Zadok, the priests who keep the Covenant and seek His will, and to the majority of the members of their Covenant, they who volunteer together for his truth and to walk in His will. And let him undertake by the Covenant to be separated from all perverse men who walk in the way of wickedness. (SR 5: 7-11) (See also Josephus, *War* 2:139-142).

This is the conversion of morals and loyalty to the Covenant which has been the essence of religious life from the beginning.

The Initiation Hymn sung by the new monks (SR 10-11) outlines more in detail their intention to lead a perfect life according to the Torah and the oral customs, including the praise of God day and night (*Berachoth* 4:1), the predecessor of the Christian office. God is blessed on rising, retiring, eating, in sorrow and happiness, etc. The feasts of the new moons and seasons are to be kept perfectly. Doing good, the new monk must avoid wickedness, lust, strife, anger against the penitent, deceit, baseness, uncouthness, and empty words.

He will show justice and kindness to the downtrodden, firmness to the fearful, discernment to the strayed, enlightenment to the bowed, meekness to the proud, humility to the base. But he does none of this alone. "For to God belongs my justification and the perfection of my way and the uprightness of my heart are in my hand; by His righteousness are my rebellions blotted out" (SR 11:2-3). He leans upon God as upon a rock. "For God's truth is the rock of my steps and His power, the stay of my right hand, and from the font of His Righteousness comes my justification" (SR 11:5). God has denied his righteousness, power and dwelling to those of the assembly of the flesh.

But God has given them as an everlasting possession to those whom He has chosen. He has granted them a share in the lot of his Saints, and has united their assembly, the Council of the Community, with the Sons of Heaven, and the assembly of the holy Fabric shall belong to an eternal planting for all time to come (SR 11:7-9).

Since the monk still belongs to wicked humanity, he can only be lifted up by the hand of God. And although he staggers, God's mercies are his salvation forever. His justice justifies the sinner, His goodness pardons his iniquities.

> Blessed be thou, O my God, who hast opened unto Knowledge the heart of Thy servant! Establish all his works in righteousness, and according to Thy loving-kindness to the elect among men, grant to the son of Thy handmaid that he may watch before Thee forever (SR 11:15-17).

Far from an arrogant asceticism, the Qumran monks displayed a dependence on Yahweh typical of the elect of Judaism.

The monks' poverty is essential to their common life. Having seen the corruption of riches, they insisted on community of property, although, as we have seen, the first year novices retained their possessions. Private property was also allowed in the camps. Initially a priest had charge of the community of goods, later a levite or even a lay mebaqqer.

Although originally the Hasidim were married, the Teacher of Righteousness seemed to favor celibacy or continence for his community of fifteen. Married Essenes lived in separate camps. What was the motive of Qumran celibacy or continence? Perfect levitical purity as in the temple? The approaching eschatological battle (War Scroll)? The fact that his family life divides a man's allegiance from the community? Practically speaking the smaller communism of married life is incompatible with the strict monastic community as at Qumran, although it worked out in the looser federations of the camps.

Philo in his *Apology for the Jews,* quoted in Eusebius' *Praeparatio Evangelica* (8:2),[2] defends the celibacy or continence of the Essenes.

> Moreover, they have avoided marriage, which they quite clearly perceived would be the only or the chief agent in

2. Quoted by E. Sutcliffe, **Monks of Qumran**, Westminster, Newman, p. 228.

breaking up their fellowship. Another was their quite excep-
tional practice of continence. For no one of the Essenes takes
a wife, because woman is a selfish creature and immoderately
jealous and clever at ensnaring a man's character and gain-
ing control by persistent exercise of her spells. For she practices flattering speeches and the other arts of playing a part
as if on a stage. And when she has enthralled eyes and ears,
and these, as subordinate faculties, are quite deceived, she
ensnared the master faculty, the mind. If children should
be born, she is filled with pride and boldness of speech.
Whereas previously she hinted with false dissembling, now
she speaks out with emboldened insolence and shamelessly
insists on actions which are all inimical to fellowship. For
a man either in bonds of a woman's love charms or by
natural instinct preoccupied with the care of children, is no
longer the same towards other men. He has imperceptibly
become another man, no longer free, but a slave.

Philo's misogynism is echoed in later monastic writings. But
the fact is ever present, namely, that a woman's charms have
lured many a monk away from the cloister.

The Qumran monks promised to obey the community code,
and Monastery officials and the whole assembly of the monks
enforced this. Originally the Teacher of Righteousness vested
authority in the priests. Later a more democratic spirit reflected
changing structures of the Jerusalem Sanhedrin. The general
assemblies of the monks were the chief means of governing
(SR 6:8-13). Priests took precedence, followed by the elders and
then the rest of the monks. Questions of law, property, admissions, promotion, expulsion, accusations and trials were handled
by the congregation.

The government of the community at Qumran and in the
camps was modeled on that of the Jewish state with the community council paralleling the sanhedrin.

The mebaqqer in charge of all the camps shall be aged
between thirty and fifty years, having mastered all the secrets

of men and all the tongues which their various clans speak.
The members of the Congregation shall enter at his command, each in his turn. And for everything which a man has
to say, let him say it to the overseer concerning every dispute
and judgment (DD 14:9-12).

In the camps a learned priest was mebaqqer ruling over groups
of ten. If such a priest was not available, a levite or possibly
even a layman of learning took over.

He shall instruct the Many in the works of God and shall
teach them His marvelous deeds and shall recount before
them the happenings of former times .... And he shall have
pity on them as a father of his children and shall carry them
in all their despondency as a shepherd his flock. He shall un-
loose all the bonds which bind them that there may no more
be any oppressed or broken among his congregation (DD
13:8-10).

Parallels to the later Christian episcopal can easily be detected.
The mebaqqer has over-all charge of admissions, examining and
instructing the neophytes, in charge of business transactions.
In the camps he accepted at least two-days' wages a month from
the working members, setting aside a portion of this for the
widows and orphans, the sick and elderly, fugitives, virgins and
old maids. Offenses against the Law are reported to him so that
he can give a proper punishment.

Violations of the Law or community regulations in the camps
were tried by the local sanhedrins of ten elders, four priests and
six lay, who are well versed in the Law and rule. Witnesses
were required according to Jewish Law and the punishments
enforced by the mebaqqer. At Qumran the erring member was
judged by a sanhedrin of all the professed monks.

Since the monks of Qumran were dedicated to the perfect
observance of the Law, they sometimes went to extremes in
their enthusiasm. For example, on the Sabbath not only was no
work allowed, but no talk of work, no cooking, drawing of water,

opening of sealed vessels. It seems that they were not even allowed to answer nature's call on the Sabbath, perhaps because it involved digging a hole (DD 10:14-18) (Josephus, *War* 2, 8, 9).

The strictness of the rule was backed up by a strong penal code, with punishments ranging from a mulcting of food for ten days to banishment from the community. For example, if one interrupts the words of another, ten days; sleeping in the assembly, thirty days; laughing stupidly and loudly, thirty days; calumniating a fellow monk, separation from the community for one year; murmuring against the institute, expulsion (SR 6:24 - 7:25).

Purity of life was almost a fixation in the community, for they had fled the impure Hellenizers of Jerusalem. Moreover, they were careful to keep impure novices and delinquent members from an unhealthy contact with the pure monks. They bathed frequently especially after work and before meals, insuring a daily purity and necessitating many water reservoirs and channels and bathing places. These lustrations at least implied a continuing repentence and conversion to the ways of righteousness by the Holy Spirit, so that one who was unrighteous and unclean was removed from the community and its lustrations (SR 3:1-11).

They not only kept the Law perfectly, but studied it day and night (SR 6:6-8), making copies of the Torah and other documents in their scriptorium. Their writings, paralleling intertestamental literature and Christian works, were filled with angelology with the good angels Gabriel, Ariel and Raphael opposing the evil spirits of Belial (*War Scroll* WS 9:15-16). Messianism and eschatology were other common themes.

The Qumran monks were strictly an eschatological community. In fact, they had fled to Qumran on Isaiah's advice (40:3) to await the Messiah in the desert. The last days are here, in which God has raised up the Teacher of Righteousness "Whom God placed in (the House of Judah) to explain all the words of His servants the Prophets, by (whose hand) God has told all that will befall His people and (the nations)" (*Habakkuk Commentary* HC 2:8-10) (DD 1:11-12). The Messiah was to come forty years after the Teacher of Righteousness' death and the eschatological war of the Sons of Light against the Sons of Darkness would last for forty years. Yet the prolonged delay in the consummation brought the inevitable laxness into the community (HC 7:10-14).

The Messiah will be a lay prince (Nasi) of David, yet the priests will take precedence at the messianic banquet. There the High Priest, the religious head of the community, will be at the side of the Messiah, the political head, as Aaron and Moses, Zadok and Solomon, Joshua and Zerubbabel. Although both the High Priest and the Messiah are anointed, only the latter is called the Messiah (SR 9:10-11). So the Qumran people were anxiously awaiting the Messiah. This is reflected in the preaching of John the Baptist who was probably a member of the community.

One of the main concerns of the monks was the illegal manner in which the temple sacrifices were being made under Jonathan (*Temple Scroll* TS). Moreover, they resented the new solar-lunar calendar, preferring to follow the older solar calendar of the *Book of Jubilees*. The Wicked Priest, probably Jonathan, persecuted them for not changing. The problem of isolated monks following ancient calendars would come up again with the Christian Celtic monks in the sixth and seventh centuries after Christ.

The monastic order at Qumran consisted in prayer, work, bathing, vesting in their white habit, then eating. This process seems to have been repeated both in the morning and in the afternoon. The meals were simple including bread and must. Besides mealtime the monks also gathered for common prayers and community assemblies. Josephus describes the daily life of the Essenes (*War* 2:128-133),[3] which probably resembled that at Qumran.

Before the sun is up they utter no word on mundane matters,

3. Loeb Series, **Josephus II**, H. Thackeray, Tr., Cambridge, Mass., Harvard, 1962-1965, pp. 373-375.

but offer to him certain prayers, which have been handed down from their forefathers, as though entreating him to rise. They are then dismissed by their superiors to the various crafts in which they are severally proficient and are strenuously employed until the fifth hour, when they again assemble in one place and after girding their loins with linen cloths, bathe their bodies in cold water. After this purification they assembled in a private apartment which none of the uninitiated is permitted to enter. Pure now themselves, they repair to the refectory as to some sacred shrine. When they have taken their seats in silence, the baker serves out the loaves to them in order, and the cook sets before each one a plate with a single course. Before meat the priest says a grace, and none may partake until after prayer. When breakfast is ended, he pronounces a further grace. Thus at the beginning and at the close they do homage to God as the bountiful giver of life. Then laying aside their raiment, as holy vestments, they again betake themselves to their labors until the evening. On their return they sit down with them. No clamor or disturbance ever pollutes their dwelling. They speak in turn, each making way for his neighbor. To persons outside the silence of those within appears like some awful mystery. It is in fact due to their invariable sobriety and to the limitation of their allotted portions of meat and drink to the demands of nature.

What relationship did the Qumran sect have to contemporary Jewish heresies? The prevailing view of scholars is that they were Essenes, a Jewish heresy described by Josephus, Philo, and Pliny the Elder. The monk companions of the Teacher of Righteousness were an offshoot of the Hasidim as also were the Pharisees. So they had much in common with the Pharisees, emphasizing levitical purity and resisting corrupting foreign influences. Both used the name, rabbi. But the Qumran interpretation of the Law was much stricter than that of the Pharisees. Modern attempts have been made to show similarities between the Qumran people and the zealots, Samaritans, Baptists, and Christians.

Documents similar to those at Qumran have been found in the zealot fortress at Masada. Did some of the monks flee there in 68?

The Christian heresy may well have been influenced by Qumran. John the Baptist was probably a member as well as some of his disciples. It is possible that Jesus, John's cousin, visited the monastery at least as a guest. He certainly was in the area. Moreover, there is a long period of his life of which we are in complete ignorance. As Gaster points out,[4] early Christians and the Qumran community used the same Hebrew name, 'edah, and had the same term for their legislative assemblies. The Essene mebaqqer resembled the Christian episcopal. Moreover, the *Scroll of the Rule* and the *Damascus Document* bear resemblances to early Christian manuals of discipline such as *Didache* and *Didascalia Apostolorum*.

The Qumran theme of the war between the Sons of Light and the Sons of Darkness can be found in John's writings. Besides dualism, discernment of spirits, enlightenment, rebirth, eschatology, messianism, angelology, all Qumran themes are found in Christianity. It is likely that some Essenes recognized Jesus as their long-awaited Messiah and became his disciples.

The Qumran monks were dispersed by the Roman army in 68. Anticipating the attack, they hid their precious library in caves to be discovered 1900 years later. And although ruthlessly tortured by the Romans, they refused to disobey the Law. Those who escaped may have fled south to Masada. Some may have joined with the Pharisees or the Christians.

The Qumran monks in their hidden lives by the Dead Sea illustrate many traditional qualities of monasticism. First of all, their keen desire to escape from the world of ordinary men where the Law is only imperfectly observed and where there was constant danger of the corruption of Gentiles and sinners. After two years of testing, the renunciants were accepted into the community, giving over their property and marriage rights in view of the proximate eschaton. But when the Messiah's advent was delayed, they slipped into laxness, but, nevertheless, the

4. **The Dead Sea Scriptures**, Garden City, Doubleday, 1964, p. 41.

community lasted over 200 years. John the Baptist's asceticism, eschatological message, and even his baptism may have been Qumranian in origin, but perhaps a later development.

B. *The Therapeuts*

Another contemporaneous sect of Jewish monks were the Therapeuts, described by Philo in his *On the Contemplative Life*. They lived near the Mareotis Lake, not far from Alexandria. Whereas the Palestinian Essenes were more concerned with the active life, the Greek-influenced Therapeuts are strictly contemplatives, and so do not have any specific work assigned to them as the Essenes did. Nor do they share a common monastery as at Qumran, but live in their own houses. Also while the Qumran community was male, the Therapeuts had both male and female members. And, in general, their lives were more severe with long hours of prayer and strict fasting.

Philo writes of a community with which he probably had personal acquaintance. But was this an isolated group? "This kind exists in many places in the inhabited world, for perfect goodness must needs be shared both by Greeks and the world outside Greece. But it abounds in Egypt in each of the nomes as they are called, and especially around Alexandria" (*On The Contemplative Life*, 3).[5] If the Therapeuts were as numerous as Philo claims, it is hard to understand why they were ignored by contemporaneous authors.

Eusebius (HE 2,17) and Jerome (*Church Writers*, 8) thought that Philo was writing of very early Christian monk converts of Mark — poor, ascetic, virgin, studying Scriptures, and celebrating common feasts under a president. Indeed, the Christian monks of Eusebius and Jerome's time resembled the Therapeuts and may have inherited some of their traditions. But no modern scholar would admit that Philo's Therapeuts were Christians.

The monks of the Mareotis Lake are called Therapeuts,

5. Quotes from Loeb Series, **Philo IX**, F. Colson, tr., Cambridge, Mass., Harvard, 1941.

writes Philo, because they heal (*therapeuo*) those who come to them, especially those afflicted with moral illnesses, "Oppressed with grievous and well-nigh incurable diseases, inflicted by pleasures and desires and griefs and fears, by acts of covetousness, folly and injustice and the countless host of other passions and vices" (2). Indeed, their concern for sinners reminds one of their contemporary Essene mebaqqers (DD 13:10) and of Jesus of Nazareth, not to mention the later Christian monks.

The Therapeuts' name can also be interpreted by their worship (*therapeia*) for their whole lives are devoted to the worship and service of the one, true God.

Their life is primarily dedicated to contemplation, the *Bios Theōretikos* so idealized by the Greeks. But they rather seek the self-existent God, who is better, higher, and more primordial, and certainly more personal than the Good, the One or the Monad of the Greek philosophers. To free themselves for contemplation of the one, true God, the Therapeuts leave all their property, giving their lands, homes and businesses over to the care of relatives and friends and flee the worldly city. Also they freed themselves from the bonds of marriage. Although there were female Therapeuts, they were kept strictly segregated from the men.

In their colony on the shores of the Mareotis Lake, the Therapeuts live in simple houses, each of which has a consecrated room called a sanctuary (*semeion*) or closet (*monastērion*), set aside for meditation on Scriptures and other holy works which they do from sunrise to sunset, praying at morning and evening. They take nothing into this room either for food or drink or for the needs of the body, but only the Law and the Prophets and whatever else aids piety and knowledge (25), interpreting the Scriptures allegorically and writing hymns. On the Sabbath all meet in the synagogue, both men and women, but separated by a high wall. The senior (*presbytatos*) and the most knowledgeable gives a sermon (30-32).

Their fasting is extraordinary, not eating anything at all till sunset, since contemplation should be in the daylight, while the needs of the body should be cared for in the dark (Platonic?). Some go three or six days without food. Yet even when they eat on the seventh day it is only a simple fare of bread and water. Their clothing is frugal, a thick skin in winter and a linen shirt in summer (34-39). Their simplicity in food and dress contrasted sharply with the luxuries of the times.

On the eve of Pentecost all meet in their white robes. Standing together, they pray to God that their feast may be acceptable and proceed according to His will. Then they recline in order of seniority. Women, mostly aged virgins, share the feast. "They have spurned the pleasures of the body and desire no mortal offspring, but those immortal children which only the soul that is dear to God can bring to the birth unaided because the Father has sown in her spiritual rays enabling her to behold the verities of wisdom" (68).

At the feast, the men recline on the right and the women on the left. Standing by are specially chosen young deacons. "For it is not just any free men who are appointed for these offices, but young members of the association chosen with all care for their special merit who as becomes their good character and nobility are pressing on to reach the summit of virtue" (72). Bread and water are served, but no wine, for just as a priest abstains while sacrificing, so these men for their whole lives, for wine produces folly, and meat — desire (74).

The president (*proedros*) discusses a question dealing with Scriptures in allegory. The monks applaud. Then the president sings a hymn, the others following in turn. Next comes the meal of leavened bread served with salt mixed with hyssop (75-82). Afterwards there is a vigil with singing, men and women alternating, then together till dawn when all face East, stretching their hands to heaven and praying for bright days and increase of knowledge of the truth and power of keen-sighted thinking, a practice similar to the Essenes (*War* 2:148). Then they depart for their private sanctuaries.

The Therapeuts are followers of the monastic ideal, leaving the world with its cares and sin, keeping to their monasteries where they live in contemplation.

Citizens of heaven and the world, presented to the Father and Maker of all by their faithful sponsor Virtue, who has procured for them God's friendship and added a gift going hand in hand with it, true excellence of life, a boon better than all good fortune and rising to the very summit of felicity (90).

It is the conversion of morals, the excellence of life, which along with God's friendship is the reward of monasticism.

The eschatological apocalyptic spirit of the times is reflected in both the Qumran monks and the Therapeuts and also the Christians. Christian asceticism owes much to its predecessors and the eschatological Christian monks of the fourth and fifth centuries bear many characteristics of the Jewish monastic traditions.

3. They Had Everything In Common
(Acts 4:32)

What evidence of asceticism is there in the Christian heresy of the first century? Certainly asceticism was in the air. We have seen the Qumran monks and the Therapeuts; and the Pharisees were everywhere with their strict observance of the Law, ritual purity, fasting, prayers and almsgiving. The Baptists in the Jordan valley were a rigorous lot.

Jesus of Nazareth was not unaffected by this *zeitgeist*. His own life and teaching probably reflected the Pharisees more than any other Jewish heresy. But this is to be expected since they were the dominant sect in Palestine at the time. But Jesus did not follow their fasting and purifications and drew their criticism for this.

Following his cousin John into the desert, Jesus was bap-

31

tized, fasted and prayed. Then when John was imprisoned, Jesus
spread his kerygma to Galilee, taking some of John's disciples
with him and gathering others. "The last days are here. Repent
and believe in the good news and be baptized." Jesus had a
small group of companions, as other contemporary rabbis. With
his headquarters at Capharnaum, he traveled up and down Galilee, preaching, healing and loosing the bonds of sinners. In this
latter aspect he was not unlike the Therapeuts and the Essene
mebaqqers. Jesus' invitation to discipleship implied a giving up
of home and property, and family (Mk 1:16-20; Mt 4:18-22;
Lk 5:1-11), although we often find Peter and his friends back
home in Capharnaum fishing. Perhaps the "leaving" applies to
the missionary journeys, which later meant a complete abandon-
ment of Galilee. There is some evidence of Pharisaic missionaries
of the period (Mt 23:15).

Jesus' advice to the rich young man to sell his goods, give
to the poor and to follow him (Mk 10:21; Mt 19:21; Lk 18:22)
was to become the hallmark of Christian monasticism. Were
Jesus and his companions really the proto-types of the Christian
monks? They lived a peripatetic, but frugal existence, depending
on the charity and hospitality of friends. Jesus instructed them
in the ways of prayer and virtue. Yet compared to the Qumran
monks, the Therapeuts and even the Pharisees, it was a moderate
way of life.

After Pentecost the Christians in Jerusalem seemed to have
led a life of voluntary community of goods, at least for a while
(Acts 2:44-45; 4:32, 34, 35, 37).

And all who believed were together and had all things in
common. And they sold their possessions and goods and
distributed them to all, as any had need. And day by day
attending the temple together and breaking bread in their
homes, they partook of food with glad and generous hearts,
praising God and having favor with all the people. And the
Lord added to their number day by day those who were being
saved (Acts 2:44-47).

Many Church Fathers such as John Chrysostom, Eusebius, Jerome and Augustine consider these early followers of Christ as the first Christian monks. Although they met in prayer and eucharist and had a voluntary community of goods, the rest of the time was spent in normal family and business activities. Perhaps more than any other group they resembled the Essene camp under its mebaqqer and council of elders to whom they donated a portion of their wages for the care of widows and orphans and who supervised admissions and the general conduct of the members.

Although monasticism as we know it was not practiced by the early Christians, the seeds of it were there. The life of Jesus as that of his cousin John was a model of chastity, poverty, and obedience to the Father. He pursued solitude to pray every chance he could. Yet neither Jesus nor his disciples ever sought to flee the world on a permanent basis as the Qumran monks did. Rather his temporary retreats set the stage for further apostolic work.

There is no direct evidence of a common practice of virginity in the nascent church despite the example and counsels of Jesus and Paul. Mention is made of Philip's four virgin prophetess daughters (Acts 21:8-9). But by and large, except for the Qumran people and the Therapeuts and some rabbis celibacy or continence were not a part of the Jewish tradition.

Were the counsels of Jesus given only to certain followers or rather to all? When the rich young man refused Jesus' offer, did he, therefore, cease to be a member of the elite, or did he cease to be in any way a follower of Jesus? Perhaps he was being called to be an apostle. At any rate, the so-called evangelical counsels do not seem to have been practiced in a special way by any small group of elite Christians, at least in the beginning, outside of the Jerusalem custom mentioned in Acts. Rather poverty as a detachment from the inordinate use of goods seemed to apply equally to all. It was only later when Christianity became lax and Romanized, losing its initial fervor, that groups of Christians broke off to form an elite church in the desert.

The prayer habits of the early Christians followed those of the synagogue (Qumran SR 10; *Berachoth* 4:1), which in turn mirrored the fixed temple hours of prayer and sacrifice morning and evening. The prayers consisted largely in psalms, the Shema, and the eighteen benedictions (*shemoneh 'esreh*). For example, the Great Hallel (Ps 112-117)and also Ps 120-136 were recited at the ninth hour. By the third century the Christians were praying six times a day: night prayers, morning prayers, terce, sext, none, and evening prayer. Perhaps because of persecution and the proscription of daytime gatherings, evening prayers became popular including vigils, vespers and lauds. Midnight was a sacred hour to the Christians as it had been for the Jews, for this is the hour when the Messiah will come (Ps 118/119). The rabbis embraced their wives on the Sabbath vigil, signifying the union of heaven and earth, God and His Shekinah. Christian spouses purified themselves with the moist breath of the Holy Spirit following intercourse, and then knelt in prayer at midnight (*Apostolic Tradition*, 32). After the Peace of Constantine (313) all Christian prayers became public. And when monasticism arose in the fourth century, it fostered the prayer customs, inherited from Judaism.

Eschatology played a large part in Christian asceticism as it had in the very foundation of Christianity and its predecessors at Qumran, who were expecting the imminent coming of the Messiah. When Jesus preached the approaching eschaton, many believed. Although the urgency of the eschaton became of less importance during the second century, it was always taught by some Christian sects. Martyrdom, virginity, asceticism and monasticism are all products of Christian eschatology. The world must be denied because it will end shortly. Virginity is especially eschatological for there is no sense in bearing children so close to the end. From time to time a prophet such as Montanus would predict the exact date of the coming of the New Jerusalem.

Cyprian in his letter to Dimitrianus (252) took a rather

gloomy view of the times, namely, that the world was on the way down hill towards its final consummation.

> The world tells its own tale and in its general decadence bears adequate witness that it is approaching its end. There is less rain in winter to encourage the growth of seeds; springtime is not now so enjoyable or autumn so fruitful; the quarries, as if from weariness, give less stone and marble, and the gold and silver mines are already worked out; the land remains untilled, the seas lack pilots, and the armies are without men; there is less innocence in the courts, less justice in the judges, less concord between friends, less artistic sincerity, less moral strictness. Do you think that anything which is in a decline can be as vigorous as it was originally? .... Everything in these days is rushing to its doom and is affected by the general debility(3).

And the barbarian invasions would add to the portentuous prediction.

Obviously with such a view of life, the martyr, anchorite, ascetic and virgin who rejected the moribund earth seemed to have the answer to it all. Breaking with family, home and culture, they fled to a world of eschatological asceticism, fighting as athletes to bring their bodies under subjection for the final contest. Virginity and continence played a large part in the picture. But the difference between orthodox and heterodox asceticism was precisely this. Matter, body, flesh, sex, are not intrinsically evil for the orthodox, but rather weakened by original sin and certainly of less importance for the eschaton.

Although examples of virginity are few in the beginnings of Christianity despite the teaching and example of Jesus and Paul, as time passes we find it more and more — first, in the heterodox eschatological heresies as the Marcionites, Montanists and Encratists, some of whom would demand it of all Christians. Tertullian spoke of large numbers of Montanist *spadones* and virgins living in Carthage by the end of the second century. Living in their own homes, sometimes wealthy, honored in the liturgy, their big temptation was pride. Both Tertullian and Methodius of Olympus praise virginity in imitation of Christ.

Christian virgins were to be seen in Smyrna and Corinth in the second century, walking in the liturgical processions behind the clergy and in front of the widows. Ignatius of Antioch had to warn them against their occupational hazard, namely, excessive pride in their calling (*Polycarp* 5:2).

Wandering prophet ascetics were quite common by the third century. Frugal, peripatetic, without family, home or country, they appear to act independently of the resident episcopal and are honored as the high priests in *Didache* (10-13). In fact, when they disappear from the scene, the bishops seem to adopt some of their prerogatives. Although Christian ascetics, both male and female, grew in number during the second century, as yet they were not on an organized basis. No doubt eschatological expectations spurred virginity as they had at Qumran and Corinth.

Cyprian of Carthage in the middle of the third century had a group of virgins that he watched over, ranking them only after the martyrs (*The Dress of Virgins*) for they will receive the royal reward of heaven. Receding from all carnal concupiscence, they dedicate themselves to Christ in a spiritual marriage. And if they renege, they are adulteresses (c. 20), to be punished by excommunication and penance. Although Cyprian's virgins are not bound by rules of poverty, they should refrain from worldly ostentation.

Virginity was also popular in Syria and Palestine in the third century. Two anonymous letters to virgins survive from this period, describing virginity not only as a means of personal sanctity, but also liberating the ascetic for the apostolate. Often the virgins or celibates were itinerant. When they stopped at the home of an ascetic or one of the faithful, they were asked to give a sermon or lead the community in Scripture or prayer. Visiting the orphans and widows, healing the sick, driving out evil spirits, they remind us of the wandering prophet-apostles of the *Didache*, though no mention is made here of the Eucharist (*Letter Two* 4:2; 5:11; 7:3).

Although this is not yet monasticism, it could be the very beginnings. After all, it is not till we get to Benedict that the gypsy monks are tied down by the vow of stability. The male wanderlust not only infected the ascetics but also the clerics until held to their dioceses by church law and a imperial edict.

There were dangers to this foot-loose existence and the ascetics had to be on guard lest they lose their modesty, gravity and piety (*Letter Two* 4:2; 5:1; 7:3), and be careful not to give scandal. Probably the warnings against false prophets in *Didache* (11:7-12) could apply equally to these wandering ascetics. It seems that although these prophetic figures were loners, they were, nevertheless, drawn to the homes of their fellow ascetics, gradually forming a class apart from the rest of the faithful who were busy with the daily affairs of family and business. Eventually they will form families or monasteries. At present they remind us of the early wandering ascetics of India and the East.

The first letter to the Syrian virgins warns sharply of the dangers of the life, for example, the too close association of the male ascetics with the consecrated virgins, eating and drinking together, gossiping under the pretext of reading Scripture, etc. (L 1, 10-). Although most of the virgins were chaste, holy, and mortified, some may have been attracted to the life temporarily out of laziness, vain glory or the hope or raising some ready cash through begging (L 1, 11:2-4).

The close association of the male and female ascetics usually, as today, started out on a high plane of spiritual conversations, or offered or requested guidance. An increasingly common practice was that of the spiritual marriage between two ascetics. It was found also among the clerics. Their utopian hopes that their marriage would remain only a spiritual union were based on a misguided angelic view of human nature. The Council of Nicaea (can. 3) was to forbid this arrangement. Ascetics and clerics had been known to mutilate themselves to insure the spirituality of the union (can. 1).

One thing that the early history of Christian asceticism brings home is that it is most difficult when practiced alone, or with one of the opposite sex. The early ascetics became the anchorites and hermits of the third and fourth centuries, in flight from civilization to the desert, mortified and prayerful, in contrast to the active, itinerant way of the earlier ascetics. Yet even the lonely hermits drew followers and often developed cenobia.

What sort of commitment to their way of life did the early ascetics and virgins make? There must have been some sort of promise or oath. The honor given to the virgins would seem to presuppose a promised dedicated life. Did they serve for a period of time as the Roman Vestals who retired at thirty-six? Cyprian and later Augustine took a dim view of those who abandoned virginity for marriage. However, Methodius of Olympus, although recommending perpetual vows in his *Banquet,* nevertheless, maintains that if a virgin has not the courage to remain faithful, she may marry.

The conversion of Egypt aided greatly the advance of Christian asceticism. Dating from the time of St. Mark, Egyptian Christianity first centered in Hellenistic and cultural Alexandria. By the end of the second century Pantaenus a former Stoic had founded a catechetical school there. Since many of the early converts were of the intelligentsia, Greek-speaking, cosmopolitan, favoring religious syncretism, they inclined towards the Gnostic, Neo-Platonic and Neo-Pythagorean. Shrines at Alexandria and Memphis honored both Greek and Egyptian Gods.

Christianity entered Egypt during this syncretistic era. So Christ was accepted as one savior among many as Dionysius, Mithra or Osiris, or as a sage by the Gnostics along with Paul, Homer, Plato and Pythagoras. As the Christians adopted Egyptian customs such as embalming the dead, there arose a mixture of rites and sects including the Gnostics, Marcionites and Encratists. In the next two hundred years the whole of Egypt would be converted with the gospel being preached to the Copts of upper Egypt by the end of the third century. Lacarriere points out [1] that the conversion of the fellahin to Christianity corresponds to the revolt of the Copts against Diocletian with both the Christians and the Copts allied against pagan imperial Rome.

1. **Men Possessed by God,** Garden City, N. Y., Doubleday, 1964, p. 44.

These were the "last days" prompting Christian ascetical flight to the desert.

Up in Alexandria theologians such as Clement and Origen were influenced in their views on asceticism by the semi-Stoic idea of life as a progress (*prokopē*). Life is a battle, a gymnasium, an *askēsis* in which we destroy sin to climb to God. As Greek philosophers became Christian, the emphasis turned to *theōria*, in which contact is had with the absolute through the intuitive intellect (*nous*). To many this Greek approach seemed foreign to the gospels and Paul. Owen Chadwick writes: [2]

> St. Paul or St. John, Hermas or even Irenaeus could not conceive the Christian life in terms of progress towards a goal because they believed that the goal had already through God's acts been reached, the kingdom had come. The eschatological event, though its consummation was in the future, was also a present fact. The Christian had died to sin, he could be described as righteous, saintly, perfect.

As the Church grew she became more realistic, since it soon became clear that her members were not always holy. Baptism did not make people into angels. Then the Church became more of a post-baptismal training ground for heaven. And the Christian ascetic came to the fore, although Paul's "good fight" was a fore-shadowing of this.

As the Church moved farther away from Jesus, it lost some of its eschatological urgency. From an eschatological society of saints, it became a sanctifying and training society. The average Christian now no longer possessed the kingdom nor the messianic banquet, but the Church must train him to reach this in the future. For example, we see this in the increasing liturgical stress on the confession of post-baptismal sins, reconciliation, and the medicinal Eucharist. Those who engaged strenuously in this fight were professional ascetics, a class apart from ordinary Christians.

2. **John Cassian,** Cambridge, 1950, pp. 77-78.

Some of these were the Christian Gnostics of Alexandria, the predecessors of the monks. Clement wrote of them, describing their struggle for a likeness with God through charity and chastity. The true Gnostic approaches *gnōsis* of God by triumphing over his vices and passions (*apatheia*). For Clement the *gnōsis* sometimes seems to be intellectual, at other times the whole man is involved, including both the Christian virtue *agapē* and the Stoic *apatheia*. The whole life of the Christian is in pursuit of the *gnōsis*.

Clement's Christian Gnostic, though not ordained, was thought to have presbyterial gifts, "Not being ordained by men, nor regarded righteous because a presbyter, but enrolled in the presbyterate because righteous" (*Stromata* 6:13). Clement distinguishes his orthodox Gnostic from the heterodox. "For us, then, he alone is a Gnostic, who has grown old in the Sacred Scriptures, maintaining the apostolic and ecclesiastical rectitude of doctrines" (*Stromata* 7:16). Clement's gnostic minister, seeking perfection in the knowledge of God, seems to be of the charismatic order as the prophet-teachers, confessors, and later the monks, indicating a two-fold ministry in third century Alexandria, namely, the official episcopals and the charismatic gnostics, types of the later churches of the bishops and monks.

Origen developed Clement's gnostic teaching into a system of spirituality. If he had been born a hundred years later he surely would have been a monk of the desert. As a youth Origen had led a strict ascetic life, even going the limits of self-castration. In his austerity he sold his library, limited his sleep, food and clothing, spending his time in the study of Scriptures.

Origen praised virginity, ranking the virgins behind the martyrs (*Homily* 2 *on Numbers* 10). The ascetics must guard the body, keeping it under subjection in order to maintain virginity. Yet it is imitation of the humble Christ that makes Christian virginity superior to the continence of the pagan philosophers (*Commentary on Romans* 6). He compares the Christian vow of virginity to that of the Nazarites which was for three or four years (*Homily* 11 *on Leviticus* 9) (*Homily* 17 *on Joshua* 15).

Origen is strong for mortification, purifying the soul in order to free it for contemplation. His interior road to perfection, stressing sin, virtue, demons, fasting, *apatheia,* prayer and contemplation was carried on by men like Evagrius and John Cassian.

Although asceticism had been in Christianity from the beginning, as it had a place in Buddhism, Judaism and among the Roman Stoics, it was still largely an informal affair with the spiritual athletes either living at home or wandering the countryside, doing good, visiting the sick, consoling sinners.

The virgins followed the martyrs in dignity, indicating that their ascetical privations were looked upon as a kind of self-martyrdom. After the Edict of Milan, 313, and the subsequent patronage of Christianity, martyrdom ceased, except during the reigns of heretical emperors. Now the virgins and ascetics came into their own as "white" martyrs, assuming the top echelons of the charismatic church, inheriting many of the privileges of the martyrs, for example, presbyterial honors and the guidance of sinners.

Although earlier persecutions had driven some ascetics into the desert, it was the Constantinian church with its corruption and secularization, which encouraged a large scale flight to the wilderness.

Constantine did all in his power to make the Christian religion official, building basilicas, presiding over the Council of Nicaea as the Defender of the Sacred Canons, giving privileges to the clergy. The new peace gave rise to the golden age of the fathers as the educated middle and upper classes adopted the now politically safe and "in" religion. The empire did not become Christian over night, but retained many pagan practices. In a sense Christianity is now worse off than it was before, for then the small local churches could keep alive the primitive apostolic tradition. Now mixed with paganism and Roman politics, Christianity seemed to be losing its pristine fervor. As the Hellenizing of the Seleucids and Jonathan had driven the Teacher of Righteousness and his disciples to the wilderness of Qumran, so the Romanization of Christianity was to force Christians to retreat to the deserts of Egypt, forming a heresy or church of lay monks outside of the state church of the bishops. Not till the Council of Chalcedon (451) did the bishops gain a measure of control over the monks.

Approval of Christianity by the emperor in many ways proved worse than the persecutions, especially when he interferred with church government, appointing bishops and giving them civil status in the *Cursus Honorum*. Some of the emperors as Constantius gave approval to the heterodox Arians, while persecuting the orthodox. The Church was to pay dearly for government patronage as it would do all through its history. The emperor could use his divine prerogatives to direct or persecute the Church as he saw fit. In general, the empire kept to its pagan ways of slavery, political despotism, high taxes, lawlessness, moral corruption.

Paradoxically along with the corruption of the decadent empire, or perhaps reacting to it, we find a certain sense of spirituality growing in three great contemporary religions, namely, the worship of the Great Mother, Isis and Serapis, and Mithra. All had a spirit of sacrifice, a sense of immortality and mysticism. Moreover, renunciation and asceticism held an important place in their mores. They practiced a certain penitential abstinence, preparing the worshiper to approach the Gods or to be initiated into the sacred mysteries.

Chastity was associated with the priesthood of Vesta and Isis, the latter requiring a life long dedication to asceticism and chastity. Forty-two temples of Serapis in Egypt may have had groups of priests living in some sort of cloister, although this is disputed among scholars. Mithra seems to have had bands of ascetics and companies of virgins. Asceticism was in the air. And as the religions of India, Egypt and Greece demand sexual abstinence of those who participate in the liturgy, so the Christians abstain in preparation for their initiation rites and eucharistic banquet.

The fourth century seems the opportune time for the beginning of Christian monasticism. Christian ascetics were escaping from sin city to the desert of God. It all began in Egypt which had a tradition of monasticism going back to the Therapeuts. Basically monasticism from the beginning has been built on the desire to escape from the present world of sin and death into the world of the eschaton. Perhaps it is man's inner idealism, which drives him to seek happiness in far distant places, away from the evils of his present life. Christians also wanted to duplicate the ideal eschatological communities of early Christians, even though the archetype may have been embroidered over the centuries.

Actually the corruption of the Roman empire led to two simultaneous invasions, the barbarians from the north charging in wave after wave across the weakened Roman defenses and the Christian monks fleeing the corrupt cities and churches to build their own in the desert. Both were headed on a collision course, eventually to meet in Europe where they gave birth to the Christian Middle Ages.

4. Call the Young Men Together and Dwell With Them

(*Palladius*, Lausiac History LH 32:1)

hristian monasticism began in Egypt with the solitaries and indeed the word *monos* indicates a man living by himself, although gradually the word was adopted for the semi-hermits and cenobites as well. The Egyptian desert solitaries trained themselves as athletes through *askēsis*.

A. Antony, the Anchorite (251-356)

Although Antony was not the first Egyptian solitary, he was one of the most famous and is rightly called the father of Christian monasticism. It was his biography, written in Greek by Athanasius and translated into Latin by Evagrius of Antioch, that, more than any other single work, spread Egyptian monasticism to the West.

45

Antony, an unlettered Copt from the village of Coma in middle Egypt, was rather typical of monks and hermits of middle and upper Egypt, who tended to resist the more intellectual gnostic trends of the monks of lower Egypt. Born in 251, Antony early showed virtues which would come to fruition in his later life. He was a loner, perhaps even anti-social, preferring to remain at home rather than playing with companions his own age or going to school. One day while attending church, he heard the call of Christ to the rich young man, "If you would be perfect, go sell what you possess and give to the poor, and you will have treasure in heaven; and come, follow me" (Mt 19:21). So at age twenty he sold the farm which his parents had left him, reserving a portion for the support of his sister.

Again he heard the gospel message, namely, that the God who cares for the birds of the air and the lilies of the fields will watch over those who love him, "Therefore, be not anxious about tomorrow, for tomorrow will be anxious for itself. Let the day's own trouble be sufficient for the day" (Mt 6:34). Giving the rest of his money to the poor and placing his sister in the charge of some pious women, he was now free to devote his life to asceticism under the guidance of a holy old man living near Qeman.

This was the custom of young ascetics from the beginning, namely, to study under a master or guru in order to learn the principles of the spiritual life, prayer and fasting. After a while Antony left to strike out on his own in the Libyan desert, seeking shelter in an abandoned tomb carved in the side of a mountain. He stayed there till he was thirty-five, fighting off sexual and other demons. Perhaps to be even farther removed from the world, he crossed the Nile to the right bank to live in an abandoned fort. This was the Outer Mountain at Pispir. Placing large rocks by the door to keep out intruders, he lived there for twenty years of asceticism. As his fame spread, many visitors came, some out of curiosity, others with a genuine desire to imitate him. When his disciples became numerous (c. 305), they pulled down the rock wall in order to avail themselves of his counsel. By word and example Antony became the father of many monks discoursing on the monastic life, asceticism, temptations of demons, prayer, discernment of spirits.

Antony's Discourse to the Monks (*Life of Antony,* LA 16-43)[1] is perhaps the first rule proposed to an embryonic monastery. In it he tried to buoy up the monks, discouraged with the ennui of the desert asceticism and weak from the attacks of the demons.

The Scriptures are really sufficient for our instruction. Yet it is well for us to encourage each other in the faith, and to employ words to stimulate ourselves. Be you, therefore, like children and bring to your father what you know and tell it, while I, being your senior, share with you my knowledge and my experience.

To begin with, let us have the same zeal, not to give up what we have begun, not to lose heart, nor to say, "We have spent a long time in this asceticism." No, beginning over each day, let us increase our zeal. The whole of man's life is very short measured by the ages to come, so that all our time is as nothing compared to eternal life. And in the world everything is sold at its worth, and like value is bartered for like. For scripture says: "The days of our life have seventy years in them; but if in the mighty they are eighty years and more, they are labor and burden." If, then, we live the full eighty years, or even a hundred, in the practice of asceticism, we shall not reign the same period of one hundred years. But instead of the one hundred we shall reign forever and ever. And although our striving is on earth, we shall not receive our inheritance on earth, but what is promised us in heaven. Moreover, we shall put aside our corruptible body and receive it back incorruptible.

The baubles of the world are trifles compared to eternal glory.

1. S. Athanasius, The Life of S. Antony, ACW 10, pp. 33-57.

Rather we should concentrate on possessions we can take with us: prudence, justice, temperance, fortitude, understanding, charity, love of the poor, faith in Christ, meekness, hospitality.

To receive the promised reward, one must persevere in asceticism without any turning back, even though the demons constantly try to dissuade him from the path. Prayer and discipline bring the gift of discerning the good and bad spirits.

A vision of the holy ones is not turbulent for "He shall not contend, nor cry out, neither shall any man hear his voice" (Mt 12:19). But it comes so quietly and gently that instantly joy and gladness and courage arise in the soul. For with them is our Lord who is our joy, and the power of God the Father. And the thoughts of the soul remain untroubled and unruffled, so that in its own bright transparency it is able to behold those who appear. A longing for things divine and for things of the future life takes possession of it, and its desire is that it may be wholly united to them if it could but depart with them. . . .

On the other hand, the attack and appearance of the evil ones is full of confusion, accompanied by crashing, roaring, and shouting: it could well be the tumult produced by rude boys and robbers. This at once begets terror in the soul, disturbance and confusion of thoughts, dejection, hatred of ascetics, indifference, sadness, remembrance of kinsfolk, and fear of death; and then a desire for evil, a disdain of virtue, and a complete subversion of character (LA 35-36).

Momentary fears should not disturb, but prolonged fears are from the devil. Although the devil rejoices in weakness, when stoutly confronted, he weakens.

During the persecution of Maximin Daja, the desert solitaries wanted to go to Alexandria to console the confessors in prison and even if possible join the ranks of the martyrs. Taking a group of monks to Alexandria, Antony was detained by the police.

But when the persecution ceased, the people did not want to let him go back, so great was his reputation.

Besieged by pilgrims and people seeking solace, Antony determined to flee to a distant place (c. 312). So joining a caravan of Saracens on the way to the Red Sea, he accompanied them for three days until they came to Mt. Qolzoum, the Inner Mountain, still known today as Dêr Mar Antonius. There was a spring there and a small grove of date palms. Antony's disciples soon searched him out, giving him tools and seed to grow a garden there. To this day there exists the Coptic monastery of Deir El Arab. Facing East, Antony had a view across the Red Sea to Sinai. Periodically he returned to Pispir to visit his disciples.

About 340 Antony allowed two of his disciples, Macarius and Amatas to join him at Qolzoum. As the word got around, pilgrims flocked to his Inner Mountain, including Greek philosophers and even Arians, whose arguments he resisted. Many greats conferred with him including Athanasius and Paul the Hermit. In 354 or 355 shortly before his death, Antony went to Alexandria to confront the Arians. Pagans and Christians alike rushed out to greet the holy old man, but he soon returned to the desert for he felt like a fish out of water in the towns (LA 53).

Returning to Qolzoum to die, he asked that his burial place never be revealed. He left his few possessions to his friends, a sheepskin and a cloak to Athanasius, another sheepskin to Serapion, a hairshirt to Macarius and Amatas. Antony died in 356 at the age of one hundred five. His monastery at Pispir produced many giants including Hilarion of Gaza, Macarius the Elder of Scete, Amoun of Nitria and Paul the Simple.

Athanasius wrote Antony's life which within a generation was known all over the empire inspiring all with the simple lesson of renunciation by which peace and victory over Satan can be obtained. Both his personal influence on men like Athanasius and his indirect influence through his *Life* have earned him the title of the father of Christian monasticism.

Some in reading the mythological account of his life, ask whether Antony was a real person. Certainly Jewish, Greek,

Egyptian and even Christian literature used myths liberally. In fact, any religion which deals with the marvelous past and the hoped for ideal eschaton must use mythology. As much other religious literature, the lives and stories of the desert fathers were embroidered for propaganda purposes.

Certainly Antony's life had a historical nucleus. Athanasius probably wrote it during one of his two desert exiles (359, 366). But this is not a biography, rather aretology or an edifying dissertation popular in pagan antiquity and portraying an ideal. Lacarriere [2] writes that the principal literary forms found in the *Life of Antony* may be seen also in the lives of the sages of the previous centuries, for example, the *Life of Apollonius of Tyana* by Philocrates (third century) and the *Life of Pythagorus* by Iamblichus (fourth century). As the sages, so the Christian saints control the elements, dispel plagues, perform marvels, etc. Many of Antony's visions and demons parallel Egyptian descriptions of the trip of the sun god through the land of the dead, Am-Duat. The *Life of Antony* served as a model for future Christian lives as Jerome's *Life of Paul of Thebes* and Sulpicius Severus' *Life of Martin*.

Although Antony is generally considered unlettered, a number of letters under his name are addressed to his disciples and to high government officials. His fame had spread so wide that even emperors wrote to him. Writing to various monasteries, perhaps through a disciple, he encouraged the monks to persevere for they were tempted to weaken in their vocations and return to the world. He also constantly warned them of the dangers of Arianism. The monk should above all know himself for this is the prerequisite of knowing God. In his first letter he outlines the work of the spirit in the monastic vocation, inspiring either directly, or indirectly through meditation on Scriptures or as an atonement for an evil life. Since the monastic life is basically a battle against Satan, the beginner must arm himself under the guidance of the Holy Spirit, purifying his passions and keeping his body under subjection.

2. **Men Possessed**, p. 53.

As we have seen, many of the desert hermits had fled the cities and the church of the bishops. Nevertheless, Pope Athanasius, when exiled by the Arians struck a rapport with his fellow escapees, the solitaries. He and Antony became great friends. When the need arose, Antony and his fellow ascetics would return to help the city church in its battles against persecution and heresy. Seeing the need of a liaison between the bishops and the monks, Athanasius appointed Ammonas, a disciple of Antony, as bishop of Oxyrhynchus to supervise the monks of the area.

Although Antony did not found cenobitism as we know it, he did encourage the hermit and anchorite life. Whereas the hermit lived alone in the desert, the anchorite was usually closer to civilization. Antony practiced both at different times in his life. Yet even in his time the beginnings of cenobitism were evident, as disciples gathered around the solitaries. Perhaps the principal reason why the anchorite life did not last, eventually giving way to communism, is that man is basically a social being. "It is not good for man to be alone" (Gn 2:18). The solitaries could only rarely make it on their own without developing hallucinations and idiosyncracies. So difficult is this on man's nature, that it is still reserved as the most cruel of prison punishments. The ascetics soon found that the wild imaginations and severe temptations of the lonely life were mitigated by the comforting companionship of fellow ascetics. The common life, moreover, gave ample opportunities for humility and charity.

B. Pachomius the Cenobite (292-346)

A contemporary of Antony, Pachomius is generally considered as the founder of Christian monastic communism. As we have seen, there were communal tendencies among Antony's and other hermit's disciples. At Schenesit the ascetic Palamon directed such a colony, which Pachomius was to join in 314. A pagan from Latopolis in the Thebaid, Pachomius was drafted into the Roman army at the age of twenty during Maximin's last war against Licinius (312-313). As the draftees were being transported down the Nile, they were locked in the prison at Luxor to keep from escaping. Impressed by the local Christians who brought them food, Pachomius inquired about the meaning of Christianity and prayed that if he were released, he would spend the rest of his life serving God. When Maximin was defeated, Pachomius returned to the Thebaid, settling in a ruin near Schenesit, where he led a simple life, cultivating beans and date palms and helping the poor and travelers. Pachomius was the first of a long line of soldier ascetics which would include such greats as Martin of Tours and Ignatius of Loyola.

The Coptic lives have Pachomius living as an ascetic before his baptism and for three years after in a small temple of Serapis near the river. According to Ammon, when Pachomius decided for the solitary life, heterodox groups such as the Meletians and the Marcionites sought his membership, but, warned in a dream, he resisted.

Instead he went to Palamon the hermit, who instructed him in fasting, vigils, and prayer, clothing him in the schema, and training him in the Antonian tradition. One day when Pachomius had wandered far in search of wood, he came upon the deserted village of Tabennesis on the banks of the Nile near where the river forms a bend north of Thebes. A small voice told him to stay there and build a monastery. His mentor, Palamon, helped him build a small cabin (monē) there, but when Pachomius' brother John arrived, they disagreed on the size of the monē. Soon some anchorites living in the area came to visit Pachomius, erecting cabins nearby. Although they began to share meals and expenses, they did not want to give up their independence to form a community. By 315 Pachomius had a small group of disciples, who would eventually number in the thousands.

There was an emphasis on manual work at Tabennesis. The monks worked in the fields, gardens, offices and at trades such as baking, carpentry, tailoring, etc., the hours of labor alternating with hours of prayer and lectures on Scriptures. The aim of monastic work was two-fold, namely, to avoid idleness which is the root of discouragement and to contribute to the support of the monastery. A popular slogan against "free-loading" brethren was "If a monk will not work, let him not eat." The monks lived in the same house with their fellow tradesmen so that carpenters lived in one house, gardeners in another, etc.

When Tabennesis proved too small for the growing number of monks, Pachomius found it necessary to start satellite communities, beginning at Peboou not far away. Gradually a rule was formulated to guard the Pachomian traditions.

Pachomius welcomed all postulants and even those who had led culpable lives could be received under certain conditions. But escaped slaves who still owed allegiance to their masters were not to be accepted. The postulant who appeared at the monastery gate was made to wait a few days to test his sincerity. When he begged the brethren for admittance, they would respond by jostling and pushing him to see how he would take it. Then the monk gatekeepers instructed the neophyte for a few days; finally invested with the monastic garb, he is led into the monastery. There was no novitiate as such nor vows, although the new monks were expected to keep the rules, living in common with no private property and avoiding contact with women.

The transition from the free-wheeling solitary life to that of the cenobium was not easy for many monks and their wander lust drew them out to far distant places. Pachomius stressed obedience as essential to the cenobite life. The fierce independence and self-sufficient ways of the hermits and the road-runners left them little opportunity for humble submission and when they joined a cenobium they often found the transition all but impossible.

Pachomius was particularly worried about the chronic griper who undermined the community spirit. Griping has always been a healthy psychological outlet for communistic groups from the family to the army and monastery. But too much is too much. Pachomius said that if a monk had to be corrected five times for griping and still refused to reform, he should be sent to the infirmary as a sick man.

During his lifetime Pachomius remained the abbot general of his monasteries, living initially at Tabennesis, then at Peboou. Eventually he ruled over 7,000 monks with 1,300 at Tabennesis and 200 to 300 at the lesser foundations. In order to avoid a power struggle after his death he appointed Petronius as his successor. Over each house of monks, carpenters, gardeners, etc., was a subordinate *praepositus*. The individual houses took weekly turns at running the day to day affairs of the monastery with the *hebdomadarius* calling the monks to prayer, reciting parts of the office, relaying orders of superiors, etc.

The monastic synaxes were at dawn, noon, before evening meal, before retiring, and at midnight, and consisted of psalms, Scriptures and prayers, basically the liturgy of the Word, with the anaphora celebrated on Saturdays and Sundays. Any one coming late for the synax had to untie his cincture and incline before the altar to be corrected by the superior. No giggling or whispering was allowed during the synax and the monks had to be properly dressed in cowl and cloak. When going and returning, they meditated in silence on the Scriptures.

The Saturday and Sunday Liturgy was led by a visiting cleric or else the monks went to the local church. Although Pachomius respected the clerics, he was reluctant to have his monks ordained. As DeCarreaux observes,[3] "With a high degree of good sense he feared that their superiority over the ordinary brethren might lead to false pride, envy, jealousy, and contention, all of which were the perdition of the monasteries." The monks from the beginning had been a lay heresy and were to guard their lay character jealously through many future generations.

The monks were instructed by their abbot and the superiors of the houses on the principles of the spiritual life twice a week on the fast days, Wednesday and Friday. Also the abbot gave three catecheses a week, one on Saturday and two on Sunday. The monks also read the Scriptures and discussed spiritual points among themselves.

In general, they were to keep from contact with the world, although they were allowed to visit a sick parent or attend a funeral if accompanied by a companion, but they were not to bring any worldly news back to the monastery. Some monks

3. **Monks and Civilization**, London, Geo. Allen & Unwin Ltd., 1964, p. 74.

were allowed to sell the products of the monastery in the town and sometimes went all the way to Alexandria by boat.

As we have seen, work was demanded of all the monks. In the beginning they helped out on local farms with Pachomius acting as a general manager, providing food, shelter and clothing for the monks. He even carried their noon meal to them in the fields, and as the number of monks grew, he had to buy an ass to transport the food. When the work day was finished, some of the more rambunctious brethren climbed on the ass, with others running alongside, galloping back to the monastery, leaving the poor superior to carry the food vessels back home alone. But Pachomius could only tolerate these high jinks for so long before laying down the law.

Besides the farm work, some monks wove mats and baskets out of rushes, while others practiced the trade that they had known in the world. They either worked in silence, or sang psalms. Daily work orders were given by the chiefs after the morning synax. Econome had charge of the material things of the monastery. For example, they took special care to see that not too much food was prepared lest it spoil in the intense heat. Individual monks rendered account of their production to their local chief, who, in turn, reported to the head econome at Peboou, who was the chief buyer and seller, usually in the village market, but sometimes in Alexandria.

The monks came together in the refectory for meals twice a day at noon and night. It was a simple vegetarian fare. Some of the monks might refrain from one meal, while others ate in their cells. Palladius (LH 32:11) has them coming in at different hours, for example, 6, 7, 8, 9, 11, or later. Some only came every second day, depending on their strength and self-discipline.

At the signal of the *hebdomadarius,* all the monks go to the refectory dressed in their melote and cowl, but without sandals or cloak. There they eat in silence with their heads covered by their cowls. Any one guilty of loud talking or laughing stood up to the end of the meal. Late comers return to fasting. When they leave the refectory, the monks are given *dulciamina* in sufficient quantity for three days. In general, the fare was frugal:

bread, beans, soup, fruit, cheese. Meat and wine were forbidden, but probably were rare items in the fellahin diet any way.

Penances were given for various offenses against the rule, ranging from fasting on bread and water, temporary separation from the community, to a stay in the infirmary, blows, exclusion and dismissal.

As Pachomius' movement spread to other monasteries (ultimately nine for men and two for women), it became necessary to formulate a rule. It would seem that Pachomius, as many other religious founders, wrote his rule piecemeal as problems came up and customs developed. His successors added to it in a similar manner. Palladius (LH 32:1) describes the mythological origin of the rule, written on a brass tablet and presented to Pachomius by an angel in his lonely cave. "You have successfully ordered your own life. So it is superfluous to remain sitting in your cave. Up! Go out and call all the young monks together and dwell with them."

"You will let each one eat and drink as suits his strength; and divide up their tasks in accord with their respective strengths, and not hinder any one from fasting or eating. Assign the more difficult tasks to the stronger ones who eat, and assign lesser tasks to those who are weak and ascetic. Make separate cells in the cloister and let there be three monks to a cell. Meals, however, should be taken by all in one house.

Let them not recline at full length, but let them take their rest sitting down on their coverlets thrown over the backs of chairs. At night they may wear lebitons. Let each one have a coat of worked goatskin: they may not eat without it. On Saturday and Sunday when they go to communion, they may loosen their girdles and go in with the hood only."

He fashioned cowls for them which were without hair as a child's and he ordered a brand in the form of a cross to be added in purple.

He arranged them in twenty-four groups, and to each group he assigned a letter of the Greek alphabet, beginning with alpha, beta, gamma, delta, and so on. When he asked questions or carried on the community business, he would ask the prefect: "How is the Alpha section? How is the Zeta doing?" Or again: "Give greetings to Rho." They followed a special meaning which was given to the letters: "To the simple and less worldly you shall assign the iota; but to the more difficult and headstrong, the chi." And so he fitted the letters to each order according to their state of life and disposition; but only the more spiritual ones knew the meaning of each symbol.

On the tablet was engraved: "A strange monk of another monastery may not eat or drink or stay with them unless he is really on a journey. And one who has come to stay they do not receive into the sanctuary for a period of three years. When such a one has performed the more laborious works, however, he is received, but only after a three year period.

When they are eating, let them cover their heads with their cowls, so that a brother may not perceive his neighbor chewing. Nor should one talk while eating or cast his eye from his own plate or table."

He commanded that they pray twelve prayers each day and twelve at lamp-lighting time, and that at all-night devotions they say twelve prayers, and three at the ninth hour. When the group was about to eat, he commanded them to sing a psalm in addition to each prayer.

When Pachomius objected to the angel that the prayers were too few, the angel said: "I arranged it this way so that even the little ones might keep the rule and not grieve. Now those who are perfect need no rule of life, for they have offered themselves entirely to the contemplation of God in their cells. I have made rules for such as may not have true knowledge, so that they may fulfill the duties of their station in life, like house-servants and so enjoy a life of complete liberty." [4]

Palladius' version is a shortened form and not the later more complex rule translated by Jerome. Notice the stress on moderation and toleration of the weak ones.

Although Pachomius' rule was composed over the years and added to as occasion demanded, the myth of the angel and the brass tablet give him a certain stature as the Coptic Moses. This is a perfectly normal use of myth, namely, to give status or authority to a way of life by claiming it had been revealed by God or an angel, etc. Pachomius' rule as seen in Jerome's version was probably not formalized till after the first generation and contains numerous repetitions and additions.

Pachomius' rule was the prototype of Eastern and Western monastic rules. Originally in Coptic, it was translated into Greek, then Latin by Jerome in 404-405. Basil used it. It influenced the *Regula Vigilii* (Gaul fifth century) and the *Regula Tarnatensis* (sixth or seventh century). Benedict and Caesarius of Arles knew it.

Pachomius' institutions and rule played a large part in the spread of cenobitism to Ethiopia where we find a version of the rule, down the Nile and on to Rome via Athanasius (340-346), and into Palestine, Asia Minor and Gaul aided by Jerome's translation and the zeal of men like John Cassian.

Meanwhile another type of Christian monasticism was developing from Lycopolis to the Mediterranean. A hybrid between the anchorite and the cenobite, it reminds one of the Therapeuts of the Mareotis Lake. Indeed, Eusebius and Jerome seem to have confused the two. Nitria and Scetis were the main centers. At the time of Palladius and Rufinus (fourth to fifth century), there were 5,000 monks in the area, some living singly, others in pairs or in threes.

The deserts of Wadi Natrûn are sixty miles south of Alexandria and fifty miles north of Cairo. The soda lakes there provided natron which the Egyptians used for embalming the dead.

4. **The Lausiac History**, LH 32, ACW 34, pp. 92-94.

As the saltpetre cleanses the dirt from soiled clothing, so it can remove man's sins, the ascetics believed. As the lakes rose and fell with the seasons, they left weird natron encrusted shapes along the shore. It was a dangerous place, plagued by lack of food and water, robbers, quagmires and crocodiles.

One of the first ascetics to inhabit the desert of Nitria was Amoun who left his wife, home and the world in 325 soon to be followed by disciples who lived in huts or hollows, fasting, praying and watching. Most were simple peasants who interpreted both Scriptures and the whole spiritual life in a literal manner. At the east end of the Wadi Natrûn and ten miles south were cells hollowed in the ground. Macarius the Younger went to one every lent, practicing severe penance, such as standing motionless in the desert for twenty days and going naked into the bug-ridden swamp for six months as a punishment for slapping a mosquito. The Cells in Nitria were far enough apart that the solitaries could not see each other. But on Saturdays and Sundays they all gathered in the church for the liturgy. If one of the monks was missing, they went to his cell to see if he was sick.

Near the Nitria church were three palm trees with a whip hanging from each, one for back-sliding monks, one for attacking robbers, and one for robbers who happened by. Attacking bands of brigands were a constant danger to the monks. The sinner is tied to the appropriate trunk, offering his naked back to the strokes of the lash. Near the church also was a hostel for pilgrims and travelers. We know how popular were the pilgrimages to see the monks of the desert. Some guests stayed two or three years or more. Although the first week was free, after that they had to work for their keep, either in the garden, kitchen, making linen, etc.

The main church at Nitria was served by eight presbyters of whom the eldest presided at the Eucharist while the others stood silently by. The lay monks sang the psalms and meditated privately in their cells, but came to the main church for the Eucharist. This type of monasticism combined contemplative advantages of the solitary with the social values of the cenobitic life. The Palestinian laurae operated similarly (LH 7).

Two days' journey south of Nitria is the desert of Scetis. Macarius the Elder, a pneumatophore who left his wife and home, was the first to settle there, a cherubim showing him the way. It is a terrible place with foul smelling water. When disciples came to settle in the nearby rocks, Macarius with his companion Separion went to study under Antony at Mt. Qolzoum (340-360). After he returned, he would frequently retreat farther into the desert to avoid the crowds of tourists, seeking *apatheia* and prayer by day and night. Many humble ascetics came to Scetis — besides Serapion, Moses the Ethiopian, a former brigand and John the Small, the famous dry stick waterer.

C. Shenoute of Atripe (348-466)

Before Pachomius died in 346, he appointed Petronius to be his successor, but he lived only two months, to be succeeded by Horsiesi under whose leadership Pachomian monasticism spread. In 350 Horsiesi appointed Theodore as coadjutor to help settle some difficulties that had arisen, especially an attempt at secession. It seems that satellite monasteries had adapted the rule of Pachomius to fit their own needs without consulting the head abbot at Peboou.

One of these was the monastery of Abbot Bgoul near the village of Atripe. Today it is called the "White Monastery" (Deir el Abiad). It is a large rectangular block constructed of white limestone from the ruins of a local temple. Inside are the monks' houses, with two cells in each. A large meeting hall, infirmary, hall of catechesis, offices, kitchen, bakery, bread room, church and garden are within the thick walls.

Bgoul had given his small group of monks a rule distinct from that of Pachomius, reforming and developing the monastic traditions. Whereas Pachomius had measured his rules according to the strength of the monks, later abbots tended to be more severe against a growing laxness, for example, some limited the meals to one a day.

Shenoute succeeded his uncle Bgoul as abbot of Atripe, continuing to pursue the monastic ideal. Many pressing needs of the monastery were met; for example, a well was dug, garden planted, and workshops built. The work of the monks plus the donations helped make the monastery self-sufficient.

Shenoute made his monks sign a profession of their moral conversion which they recited before the brethren in church. The signed and witnessed profession was kept in the monastery archives:

> I promise before God in this holy place, as the word that my mouth promises is my witness. I do not wish to stain my body in any manner. I do not wish to steal, I do not wish to take false oaths, I do not wish to lie, I do not wish to do evil secretly. If I transgress that which I have promised, I do not wish to enter into the kingdom of heaven, for I see Him, God, before whom I have pronounced the formula of the covenant. Let Him annihilate my soul and body in the gehenna of fire, for I will have transgressed the formula of the covenant that I have pronounced (DACL 2:3116).

Notice that there is no mention of the classical promises of poverty, chastity and obedience, although these were implied in the communistic pursuit of perfect morality. The renunciant promises to lead a good moral life, not unlike the moral conversion of Samgha, Qumran, Evagrius and Benedict.

Shenoute's written profession of faith is the first evidence we have of formal monastic promises or vows. Evidently earlier anchorites and cenobites indicated their willingness to begin their new life by going to the place of retreat, showing sincerity of intent and being accepted by the community, and signified a change of mind by withdrawing from the monastery.

Shenoute was stricter than his predecessor, and even early in his career there is evidence of insubordination. As the number of his disciples grew, he had to erect new buildings, for example, a church and a convent. As is usual in the early biographies, the number of monks is probably exaggerated. Thus Besa says that Shenoute had 2,200 monks and 1,800 nuns under his care. But his congregation probably did not extend beyond the mount of

Atripe and its environs. Besides the central monastery, there were satellite communities, provisioned by the general econome with bread, beans, clothes, etc. The main buildings and offices such as the church, bakery, cellar, weaver, etc. were in the central establishment, while the lesser houses concentrated more on agriculture. Besa tells of a gardener who was in charge of furnishing beans to the brothers living on the mountain, in caverns or in hermitages. They all gathered in the central monastery four times a year. Shenoute himself retired to a hermitage for five years and his monks did not mind this one bit.

The Pachomian plan has evolved. Thus now monks trained in the common life are returning to the hermit existence, yet still keeping in contact with the mother house. Whereas Pachomius saw in the cenobium the culmination of monastic excellence, Shenoute sees in it a period of transition and formation to prepare mature souls to reach for the more austere and ascetic solitude of the anchorites.

Yet many Pachomian customs were retained. For example, at Atripe the functions of the *hebdomadarii* of Tabennesis were taken over by the "Brother Servants" who had charge of the more important services of the gate and infirmary. Also teams of bakers, laborers, etc. worked under their proper superiors. Prayer at Atripe was similar to that of Tabennesis with synaxes in the evening, night, morning and noon. Arriving at the church, the monks kneel, prostrate themselves on the ground, reciting the invitatory psalm. At the signal, each arises, makes the sign of the cross, recites the Sunday prayer, asking for the fear of the Lord and pardon for committed faults. At another signal, the monk signs his forehead and sits to listen to the reading of the holy Scripture from the ambo, sometimes followed by a hermeneutic discourse. Then all meditate on the scriptural reading and return to their cells in silence. This is basically the liturgy of the Word, the central worship of the lay monks. On Sundays the Eucharist is offered solemnly by visiting clerics in the monastic church, with a large number of the faithful assisting. The whole church is brightly lit with lamps and candles on Saturday night and Sunday.

As in most monasteries, so at Atripe are found both observant and mediocre monks. Jealousy, squealing, leaving without permission, overfamiliarity with externs, a longing for the delicacies of the infirmary — a paradise dreamed of by whining monks, hoping to be admitted under some psychosomatic pretext even though they are as healthy as camels. Some keep back part of their earnings to give to relatives and friends.

Though the Coptic labor-gang bosses were noted for their severity to their fellahin underlings, Shenoute was not to be outdone. He ordered blows at the slightest provocation; in fact, some monks are reputed to have died under his lash. In a letter to a mother superior he recommends how many blows are to be administered on the offending nuns. Shenoute is presented as a severe ascetic in his *Life* by Besa. And he was as hard on others as he was on himself. There is evidence that he did not run a happy ship for he is constantly shouting and threatening against insubordination, the bonhomie of Pachomius replaced by intransigence. Eventually this became almost pathological. Ruling by terror, he gave strokes for the lightest offenses.

The aim of all of this seemed to be an absolute physical unity in the monastery including absolute and immediate obedience to the bell, identical motions in prayer, etc. Even the making of bread was outlined in detail to insure uniformity. Spiritual unity militated against any personal property or even the use of "my" or "mine." Any lighthearted laughter or gaiety was rubbed out by the whip.

Shenoute even used false visions to achieve his ends. For example, he dressed up a peasant in fine robes, telling the simple fellahin monks that it was David himself come to read the psalms. He claimed to have seen the angels and his *Life* records frequent conversations with Jesus. In all of this it should be remembered that Shenoute was the leader of the anthropomorphists, whose whole aim in the spiritual life was to see God and Jesus physically.

Shenoute extended his reign of terror outside of the monastery walls, sometimes leading groups of monks to tear down pagan temples. This was a great outdoor sport of the Coptic monks.

Egypt's 8,000 years of temple and priestly tradition did not give in easily to the Christians who thought of the pagan ways as stupid and idolatrous, especially the combining of human and animal dieties. Shenoute not only destroyed temples, breaking statues and beating up the priests, but also confiscated the temple treasuries. But despite the raids, Isis was still worshipped in Egypt well into the fifth and sixth centuries.

At other times Shenoute rescued the persecuted from loan sharks and civil magistrates, even serving as a local judge himself as occasion demanded. Moreover, he seems to have been a leader in the renewal of the Coptic church especially in its victory over the Origenists in Alexandria (400). Later (431) he accompanied Cyril of Alexandria to the Council of Ephesus. Shenoute's monastic reforms were less well received and he never achieved the popularity of Antony, Pachomius, or even Evagrius. His strictness and violence never had the appeal to weak human nature that Pachomius' moderation had.

D. Evagrius the Pontic (345-399)

In 382 the deacon Evagrius came to Melania the Elder's monastery on Mount Olivet near Jerusalem in flight from an adulterous love affair in Constantinople. The son of the chorbishop of Ibora in Pontus, Evagrius was chosen as a lector by Basil and ordained deacon by Gregory of Nazianzus. When he resigned his bishopric of Constantinople in 381, Gregory left Evagrius to his successor Nectarius as an aid in the refuting of heresies.

Held in high honor by the city for his brilliance, Evagrius, in a moment of weakness, fell in love with a married woman of high social standing. And although he knew his enemies would make much of it, he could not bring himself to break off the affair. Foreseeing in a vision the soldiers of the emperor taking him prisoner, he promised an angel to leave the city. So he set out for Jerusalem where he met Melania, the mother of Roman monasticism in Palestine. But he soon fell back into his old ways.

When he fell ill, Melania promised him health if he would agree to become a monk.

So Evagrius set out for Nitria where he lived for two years and then fourteen years in the Cells, eating but a pound of bread and a pint of oil in three months. He wrote a lot and seems to have served as a scribe, penning gracefully in the oxyrhynchus style. After fifteen years of struggle, his mind seemed so purified that it could receive the gifts of knowledge, wisdom, and the discernment of spirits.

To bring his body under subjection he sometimes went to extremes. For example, when he was bothered one night by the sex demon, he stood naked till dawn in a cold well. Since it was winter time, his flesh froze. Through similar hard penances he tried to keep his carnal desires in hand. But on his death bed he admitted that it was only during the last three years of his life that he was free of the sex demon.

Evagrius continued to write. Following the Origenist line, he is, nevertheless, an original thinker and founder of the science of Christian spirituality. Christianizing the Stoic *apatheia,* a quelling of the passions derived from eastern asceticism, he classified the eight evil *logismoi* as the basis of the so-called seven capital sins. Evagrius was the first Egyptian monk to write extensively on spirituality and asceticism. But unfortunately few of his writings survive in Greek, due to the condemnations of Origenism at the second council of Constantinople (553). However, some of his works remain in Latin, Syriac, Armenian, Arabic and Ethiopian translations and some pseudonymously under the names of Basil of Caesarea and Nil of Ancyra. He wrote in aphorisms, a type of wisdom literature, inaugurating the popular spiritual centuries.

Evagrius' *Antirrhetikos* includes selections from Scripture against the eight tempting spirits that challenge the monk, namely: gluttony, adultery, avarice, despondency, irritability, accidie, sloth, arrogance. Analyzing how the demons tempt, he then gives scriptural quotes to combat the attack. This is meant to be a guide for beginners still struggling against Satan. He also wrote his *Monachikos*: the first part, *Praktikos,* gives one hundred sayings for simple anchorites; the second half, *Gnostikos,* contains fifty sayings of Antony, Macarius, Athanasius, Serapion and others for the more advanced. Besides his *Mirror of Monks and Nuns* and *Gnostic Problems,* Evagrius probably wrote *On Prayer,* although some attribute it to Nil of Ancyra.

Evagrius entered into the Alexandrian synthesis of Greek philosophy and religious thought going back to Philo. Clement and Origen had followed this tradition with the life of a Christian as a battle or game in which he fights as an athlete (*askētēs*) trained for victory. The aim was *gnōsis* of God, allied with Christian *agapē* and Stoic *apatheia.* Origen had used Aristotle's distinction between the active and contemplative life, but considered them as complementary with the active ascetical life aiding *theōria.*

Evagrius, however, tended to look upon the two lives as rather successive and distinct. The ascetic started out in the active or practical life and for these beginners he wrote his *Praktikos* and *Antirrhetikos.* For the contemplatives advanced in the spiritual life he wrote his *Gnostikos* and *Gnostic Problems.* Moreover, Evagrius adds a monastic hue to Origen's way of perfection, stressing virtues, vices, vigils, prayer, apathy, the goal of the practical life leading to *gnōsis* and *agapē.* Jerome detested Evagrius' use of Origen and accused him of either making the soul a stone or God (L 133:3).

Apathy is a stripping of worldly desires reminding one of the *gnōsis,* which at its high peak is *theologia,* a knowledge of the Triune God, filling the whole mind, in a state of pure prayer. Since God is necessarily simple, the mind cannot approach Him while complex with various ideas, thoughts and desires. To attain this state of pure prayer the mind must be completely naked (*gymnos, psilos, kōphos, alalos*), expelling all thoughts. Thus the mind comes to a complete standstill, without passions, thoughts or images, so that it shines like a sapphire (*Cap. Prak.* 70), filled with the Holy Spirit and in a state of *anaisthēsia.*

Evagrius' spiritual ladder leads through virtue, apathy, agape, *gnōsis* of God in nature to the *gnōsis* of God in Himself. The intellectual exercise of Evagrius' ladder led the anthropomorphists to accuse the Origenists of turning Christianity into a philosophy.

The spiritual life for Evagrius was a higher state of light and love in which the soul delights in the *gnōsis* of God, constantly thinking of God and united to Him in love. For Evagrius, one in a true state of charity could not possibly love a worldly object more than the divine *gnōsis*.

Prayer for Evagrius is contemplative and the habitual state of a perfect soul. The true wise and spiritual soul, the man of prayer seeks constant union with God, talking with Him as a Father, having removed all passionate thoughts (*On Prayer* OP 54). To attain perfect prayer the ascetic has to work for a progressive control, blotting out all thoughts, preoccupations, tendencies, inclinations, memories, the soul dominating nature and producing a calm and self-possession which leave him completely open to grace.

The spirit must blot out all cares, imaginations, concupiscence and impatience. A person attached to his earthly desires easily loses patience and finds it most difficult to pray. "If you are armed against anger, you will not be bothered by concupiscence for it furnishes the material for anger and it troubles the intellectual vision, corrupting the state of prayer" (OP 27). Sins against charity also militate against prayer. "Prayer is the bud of kindness and patience" (OP 14). "If you want to pray as you should, do not inflict sadness on the soul. Otherwise you run in vain" (OP 20). Humility and temperance also are prerequisites for prayer (OP 31, 121).

The demons never allow the man of prayer to rest. "The devil is extremely jealous of the man who prays, he uses every trick to destroy his intention, continually reminding him of stirring business ventures and exciting him with fleshy desires to impede his good progress towards God" (OP 46). The devil is never satisfied. If defeated the first time, he keeps trying again (OP 47). The demons hate prayer. But all their temptations can be of some avail provided that one resists them.

The aim of Evagrius' patience, love, apathy is not so much prayer as *gnōsis,* illumination of the soul, knowing God better. Although this is a free gift of God, nevertheless, man can dispose himself for it. The Lord will not give his *gnōsis* to the man who keeps himself in a state of constant titillation of worldly desires and distractions. Only to the apathetic and tranquil will the grace of God illuminate with the *gnōsis* of the Trinity.

As carnal desires detract from the practical ascetic, so for the advanced contemplative any simple thought offers a distraction. As the passions are turned back by virtues, thoughts are conquered by spiritual *gnōsis* and a grand light appears to the spirit at the moment of prayer, the intellect penetrating into this light without form, which is called the place of God, for God dwells there.

Evagrius' Origenist approach to prayer, combining Neo-Platonic, Christian and Stoic elements was popular especially in lower Egypt. However, it was not without its enemies. We have already mentioned Jerome's attack (L 133). Also the relatively uneducated anthropomorphist and pious Coptic monks despised Evagrius' Hellenistic cerebral approach to prayer. They taunted him that in his own country he might well have become a bishop, but here in Egypt he was just an ordinary monk like the rest of them.

Within a few days of Evagrius' death in 399, Pope Theophilus of Alexandria condemned the anthropomorphists in a pastoral letter in which he favored the intellectuals of Nitria and the Cells. The letter was not well received in Scetis where the old monk Serapion cried out "They have taken away my God, and I have none that I can hold now, and know not whom to adore or to whom to address myself." It seems that some of the monks felt that they could see God physically.

But the anthropomorphists, probably under the leadership of Shenoute of Atripe, were not to be done in so easily. With murder in their eyes, they marched on Alexandria, forcing the wiley Theophilus to reverse his field, condemning the Origenists and chasing them from Egypt. There was a great battle in Nitria in which the Origenists were defeated. Four of their leaders called the Tall Brothers escaped with 300 monks to Sythopolis in Palestine and sought the help of John Chrysostom in Constantinople (400-401). John Cassian and Germain left Egypt about the same time for Constantinople and Gaul.

Evagrius' influence has been great in mystical and ascetical theology, despite the eclipse of his thought due to the condemnation of Origenism at Constantinople II (553). Palladius stayed with Evagrius and admired him. John Cassian and Germain visited the Cells when Evagrius was there. And although Cassian does not mention Evagrius by name, his work depends on Evagrius with certain modifications to fit the western mind. Evagrius also influenced Byzantine thinkers such as: John Climacus, Hesychius, Maximus the Confessor, Dortheus, Simeon the New Theologian and also various Syrians, Nestorians and Monophysites.

E. Concluding Remarks on Egyptian Monasticism

In general, the monastic flight to the deserts of Egypt seems to be a national movement. Except for the more educated Greek and Syrian monks of Scetis and Nitria, the majority of the ascetics were Coptic speaking fellahin, simple, uneducated, biblical literalists, anthropomorphists with a keen desire to see God physically. Their motives for seeking out the desert were not always the highest, fleeing persecutions, tax-collectors, army recruiters, slave owners, police, etc. However, among them also were many who fled the vanities of the world for a closer union with God. Indeed, there is a parallel between the escaped outlaws and the desert ascetics for both reject contemporary society and both are called anchorites with the same rebel connotation.

This is basically a Coptic movement and so in opposition to the Greek and Roman culture of the north. Unfortunately most of the accounts of the monks have come down to us in Latin or Greek by non-Copts such as Jerome, Palladius, Rufinus or John Cassian. But the great monks such as Antony, Pachomius, Shenoute, Macarius, etc. were largely Copts. Their strong Coptic traditions of a future life served as a foundation to their eschatological way. Moreover, their simple rugged fellahin lives had prepared them well for the rigors of the desert. For example, most of the fellahin slept on the bare ground and ate a simple fare of dry bread and lentils. Some, no doubt, bettered their social condition by joining the monasteries. Communism, either religious or political, has always appealed to peasants as a way of improving their social status.

We have seen earlier Egyptian ascetic traditions in the Therapeuts of the Mareotis Lake. And although attempts to link the Christian monks with the cloistered priests of Serapis (*katochoi*) have been unsuccessful, the general ascetical spirit of the times was the zeitgeist in which Christian monasticism was born.

Starting as anchorites and hermits living isolated in caves or huts, the Christian ascetics soon attracted disciples. Thus arose forms of common life, with community prayers, meals, work, protection from robbers, etc. This is basically a lay movement, at least in part a rejection of the ecclesial-government establishment in Alexandria. Clerics, reluctantly accepted into the monastery, were equivalently laicized, since to preserve their clerichood would be to introduce repugnant gradations into the classless society. The monks were men of action, even standing up to church and government officials when the need arose. Living isolated in the deserts and existing with little formal education, they were cut off from new developments in doctrine and law and so were suspicious of new trends from the philosophical schools of Alexandria and new episcopal canons from the church of the bishops.

Monastic communism got a firm start with Abba Pachomius and soon spread to all parts of Egypt and eventually to the whole empire. Alexandria, cosmopolitan center that it was, attracted many varieties and many nationalities of monks including solitaries, cenobites, and road-runners. When they caused trouble, which sometimes was frequent, the government attempted to keep them out in the deserts. But city monasticism grew. From the gates of the city convents and hermitages ranged along the highways to the desert and the sea.

In general, each cenobium was independent, a lay *ecclēsia*, although we do find families of monasteries as in the Pachomian system. Though the monks guarded their freedom jealously, they were to suffer increasing pressure from councils of bishops and emperors. In spite of the dominance of communism after the first generation, Egyptian monasticism never lost its love for the solitary, the lonely undistracted quietude of the desert kept as a mythological ideal amidst the mixed blessings and hardships of the cenobium.

The essence of Egyptian monasticism was the conversion of morals. In this *metanoia* a new life was begun and it often followed baptism. Everything in the past was left behind including family, friends, property, imperfections and sins. The new monk promised to lead a life of perfect morals, with daily synaxes, Saturday and Sunday Eucharist, instructions by the Father, manual work, fasting Wednesday and Friday. Did this daily life differ radically from that of a good Christian family of the time? Probably not, for the communism of the family parallels that of the monastery, with common property, obedience to the father, and celibacy for the children until they come of age. Obvious differences are the separation of sexes and the admission of those outside the family circle into the cenobium. The separation of the sexes generally involved a convent of nuns living nearby. The problem of mature men and women leading the lives of children or slaves in the monastic family has always been with the movement. The same paradox is, of course, encountered in the natural family.

Slaves were attracted to the monasteries. The freed ones had little other means of support, while escaped slaves sought refuge from their masters. The flight of the slaves to the desert caused consternation in the fourth century ecclesial-government establishment. In a slave-based economy, the upper class owners and rulers feared a collapse of the system. The council of Gangra (340) took action against Eustathius and his monks who were persuading slaves to join the monastic life. And the Emperor Valens (fourth century) decreed that the monks return all escaped slaves to their rightful owners, although some abbots continued to defy this especially in cases where injustice had been done.

Most chroniclers of the history of monasticism cite large numbers of monks in Egypt during the fourth and fifth centuries. But we must allow for a certain amount of embroidery. For example, Pachomius was supposed to have 7,000. Jerome claimed that 50,000 were present at the annual general meeting of the Pachomian monks. Serapion was said to have 10,000 under his jurisdiction. Probably most monasteries did not include more than 200-300. But in remote places the number of monks probably exceeded that of the non-monks.

The chroniclers frequently describe the lives of the desert fathers as a paradise. And, indeed, the anchorites attempted to become as innocent as Adam, by the elimination of all vices and passions. To carry the analogy further, some of them went around nude, receiving their food from an angel or a bird. The lions and crocodiles obeyed them. The desert was not only a restoration of the original paradise, but also an anticipation of the future one. In a sense, the monks lived both before and after history, that is, removed from the temporal world of sin, living in the presence of Christ whom they saw physically and conversed with. Indeed, their desert lives paralleled his with similar miracles such as walking on the water and even the raising of the dead.

The deserts were also filled with angels and devils. The angels were guardians, companions, messengers sometimes in angelic form at other times in human guise. When the monk died the good angels carried his soul to heaven to meet the saints.

The science of demonology was advanced by the desert monks. We know that both Jesus and the Qumran monks encountered desert demons. Did the lonely life of the hermits leave them more open to hallucinations? The wide open spaces and endless sand dunes lend themselves to mirages and visions as any traveler can attest. The dust devils appeared to the solitaries as animals, naked women, or little black people. A notable lessening of temptations or hallucinations came in the cenobitic life, which is a more natural and social existence. But a case certainly can be made that demons do inhabit lonely and far out places and that they delight in tormenting the isolated and unprotected.

The monks' temptations are probably not all due to errant imagination.

The monks were basically misogynists, going out of their way to avoid women. One of their slogans was: "Avoid women and bishops." Neither marriage nor procreation had a place in the eschaton. But sexual passions sometimes sought other avenues of release. Thus beardless boys were kept away to lessen the danger of pederasty. And some monks, bothered by technicolor visions, returned to the sailors' brothels in Alexandria. As with other men, sexual delights were the most frequent temptations of the monks. Rare was the monk who did not experience them in a prolonged manner. Indeed, their very continence escalated their appetites. Frequent conferences of the fathers treat of the problem, for example, Cassian's discourses on concupiscence (4), chastity (12), and wet dreams (22). To combat temptations some stood naked in cold wells or rolled in the thorn bushes. Ideally the monk should aim for an angelic apathy in which his sexual passions would be completely dead to any stimulation. For example, Simeon of Salus had such control that he could even deal with courtesans unharmed. And a certain Serapion and a virgin to prove that they were dead to the world, took off all their clothes and paraded in the buff through the streets of Rome.

Discouragement and ennui (accidie) were occupational diseases of the monks. Usually attacking around noon when they were hungry from long fasting and fatigued after heavy labor and hot from the noonday sun, this is the midday devil who made the monks restless, desiring to visit and talk with the brethren, or to go to far distant monasteries where conditions were better. A solution was often found in hard work and prayer.

The everlasting battle of the monks against the desires of the flesh through fasts, vigils, penances, prayer and work led them towards the paradise of tranquility which the Stoics and Epicureans had vainly hoped for in their dreams of *apatheia*. The Christian ascetic was constantly in anxious pursuit of contemplation, stillness, quiet, silence, loneliness, peace (*hēsychia*). In a sense the desert could be the ideal place for the search, its endless hori-

zons, silent calmness, and deep nights, lack of distractions leading to contemplation and union with the one God.

As the Egyptian monks' fame spread throughout the empire,
it became a "must" for pious and curious Christians to make
a tour of the monasteries and the huts of the solitaries. Egypt
with its mystery, monuments and mummies had always held a
certain fascination for the Romans. The Egyptian cult of Isis
became popular in Rome around the first century before Christ.
When Rome became Christian and Christian ascetical life grew
in Egypt, the fascination increased. As Lacarriere writes: [5] "The
miracles attributed to the anchorites — who walked on the waters,
halted the sun in its course and raised up the dead — attracted
to Egypt crowds of Greeks and Romans who thought of themselves as pilgrims, but who were in fact nothing but tourists in
search of Christian marvels in succession to pagan marvels."

But many came for reasons other than mere idle curiosity,
for the monks did have a reputation for sanctity. Moreover, they
continued the tradition of their predecessors, the Therapeuts, as
healers and counselors par excellence. So those sick of body and
mind traveled great distances, seeking relief from their burdens,
hoping to absorb some of the peace of the desert fathers into their
own troubled souls.

And the monastic spirit spread. When Athanasius brought two
monks with him to Rome in 340, the wealthy women went wild,
setting out on tour with their retinues of slaves. When they returned, they often set up communities in their homes or palaces.
Male ascetics also made the tour. Among the famous pilgrims
who helped spread the monastic movement by their writings and
foundations were: Basil, Rufinus, Palladius, Melania, Paula,
Jerome, Germain and John Cassian, Aetheria, Postumian, Hilary
of Poitiers, Eusebius of Vercelli, and of course, the great Athanasius himself.

The piety and mortification of the monks was as a magnet
drawing pilgrims from all over the empire. Many monasteries
had hostels where the travelers could stay a week, a month or

5. **Men Possessed**, p. 37.

longer. Some traveled around quite a bit as Germain and John Cassian, while others stayed on permanently as monks. Both in Egypt and in Palestine there were monasteries representing many nationalities. For example, Jerome translated Pachomius' rule for Latin-speaking monks in Egypt.

Monasticism was the zeitgeist of the fourth and fifth centuries. It was "in." Perhaps its novelty (good news) made it attractive. As a lay movement it attracted pious Christians not at all interested in the *Cursus Honorum* of the clerical ladder, the *homo religiousus* rather than the *homo politicus*. Perhaps, too, in a decadent and soft Christianity, idealistic young people, disillusioned with the church of the bishops, were searching for a better way to follow Christ. They saw in the desert heroes the successors of the martyrs.

The apocalyptic barbarian invasions forced many wealthy Roman Christians to flee with their slaves and money to the East or South, founding monasteries and convents in the Holy Places. This was a help in spreading monasticism in Africa, and Palestine.

But the freshness of the first generation of the Egyptian monks was fading.[6] The condemnation of the Origenists had sent many to Palestine (400). The devastation of Scetis by the barbarian Mazices in 407-408 was looked upon by the older monks as the judgment of God on their laxity. Many monks were killed, while others fled. By the third generation the teachings and practices of the early desert heroes had been committed to writing and put away in cupboards. Moral decay ate away at the Scetis foundations recalling the predictions of Macarius the Egyptian, "When you see a cell built near the Marsh, know that the desolation of Scetis is near. When you see trees, it is at the doors. When you see boys, take up your mantle and withdraw" (*Life of Macarius* 5). Isaac, priest of the Cells, also warned against the admission of boys, "Don't bring boys here, for four ecclesiae have become desolate in Scetis because of boys" (*Life of Isaac* 5).

6. See D. Chitty, **The Desert A City**. Oxford, Basil Blackwell, 1966, pp. 65ff. This section depends on Chitty.

There had been little mention of pederasty in the first generation. When some monks whispered about Carion's young son Zacharias, the boy immersed himself in the natron lake till he was disfigured for life. Later Paphnutius sent away the youth Eudaemon, saying, "I allow no woman's face to stay in Scetis, because of the warfare of the enemy" (*Life of Eudaemon*).

With the decline of the third generation came a great urgency for writing down the mythologized lives, legends and sayings of the early fathers of the desert. For example, the fifth century *Apophthegmata Patrum,* Palladius' *Lausiac History,* and Rufinus' *History of the Monks.*

In conclusion, we have seen the two natural divisions of Egypt: the upper with its Coptic Pachomian cenobitism and the lower with its semi-hermits, many of whom were Greek-orientated. Egyptian monasticism spread by pilgrims, writings of the Fathers, and exiled monks, passed to Asia Minor, Palestine, North Africa, Rome, Gaul and Ireland. Even though Egyptian monasticism lost its first fervor, it always remained the mythological prototype against which future monks would continue to measure themselves. Today, except for scattered ruins, there remain only four active monasteries including about 150 monks in the Wadi Natrûn and two monasteries on Mt. Qolzoum.

5. Soldiers of Christ the King

(*Basil*, INTRODUCTION TO THE ASCETICAL LIFE)

A. *Origins of Monasticism in the East*

he spirit of monasticism spread quickly from the deserts of Egypt throughout the empire. With the efficient Roman mail service and travel, the word got around fast. Pilgrims and tourists flocked to Nitria, Scetis and the Thebaid. As monasticism spread it adapted to new environments, sometimes mitigating the rigors of the Egyptians, at other times taking on new and strange twists of self-immolation.

Early asceticism in Asia Minor before the influx of the Egyptian influence bore monastic traits although not always orthodox. For example, the Montanists in Phrygia wanted to impose their

4

rigors on all Christians. Eustathians, Euchites and others sprang up in this area. The Council of Gangra (340) tried to limit some of the ascetical exaggerations such as the teaching against marriage, dividing families, making women dress like men, etc.

At an early date the monastic spirit of Egypt spread to Palestine via Hilarion, a disciple of Antony and to Mesopotamia by Mar Awgin, a follower of Pachomius. The *monazontes* of the Eastern church, spoken of by Athanasius and Aphrahat, seem to be neither hermits nor cenobites, but peripatetics.

After he left Egypt, Mar Awgin went to Nisibis, in Persia, building a monastery in the mountains there sometime between 336-345. Aphrahat (fourth century) in his *Sixth Demonstration* tells of a primitive monasticism, where solitaries lead ascetical lives within the Christian community. Their new lives of piety began with Baptism. If the newly baptized proves satisfactory, he enters the ranks of the solitaries or B'nai Quāmā, to practice celibacy, poverty, fasts, vigils. There probably was a gradual development of these scattered ascetics into full fledged cenobia of the latter half of the fourth century and the fifth century.

As in Egypt, by the third generation, abuses had crept in among the monks. For example, Aphrahat had to warn the monks and virgins to stay apart:

> If any man who is a monk or a saint, who loves the solitary life, yet desires that a woman, bound by monastic vow like himself should dwell with him, it would be better for him in that case to take (to wife) a woman openly and not be made wanton by lust.... It is just and right and becoming, that even if a man should be distressed, he should continue alone (Dem 6:4).

Nestorian synods of the fifth century warn sharply against the Pharisaism of the monks. They should keep to their monasteries in remote places and not be found in the cities and not seek to avoid the jurisdiction of the bishops, presbyters or *periodeutae*. Also there should not be a too easy interchange between monks and nuns. These monks seemed to live a semi-hermit life parallel to that of lower Egypt and which soon would spread to Palestine.

Monasticism soon came to Armenia by Daniel the Syrian and his disciples, Schagita and Epiphanius. Narsis, the great Katholikos of Seleucis, organized the anchorites into a form of cenobitism. Inspired by Basil of Caesarea, Armenian monasticism was to become a great missionary and literary force in the Eastern Church.

As in Egypt, so the monasticism of Syria and Asia Minor placed the solitaries on a high plane. But the lonely life not only attracts the eccentric, but also tends to exaggerate his idiosyncracies. The oddities of the eastern anchorites are well known and far outshine any individualities of the Egyptian solitaries. First of all there were the stylites living on pillars, the most famous of whom was Simeon (389-459), and the dendrites living in trees. Others sought absolute immobility for long periods of time under the hot sun. The *boskoi* ranged through the fields, eating grass. Some had heavy stones chained to their feet. Another never turned West. Others went around naked as Adam. Needless to say, though motivated by a spirit of asceticism, these exaggerations bordered on the heterodox.

B. *Basil of Caesarea* (329-379)

Basil, the founder of Byzantine monasticism, was to bring sanity and moderation to the movement. Born in 329 in Caesarea in Cappadocia, he came from an illustrious family, most of whom are honored as saints. Besides his grandmother Macrina and parents, Basil and Emmilia, most notable were his sister Macrina and brothers Peter of Sebaste and Gregory of Nyssa. Really the ascetical lives of Macrina and Basil were a continuation of their strong Christian family life. In fact, Macrina and her mother turned the family home at Annesi into a monastery after the death of her father and her brother Naucratius. Her younger brother, Peter, remained at home, eventually becoming the com-

munity econome. Besides Macrina and her mother and family
slaves, other pious women began to come from Cappadocia and
Pontus to join them.

Basil's father sent him to study in Constantinople and Athens
where he met a fellow student Gregory of Nazianzus. On his return home he gained fame as a rhetorician. But his sister worried
lest he become puffed up with pride. When his brother Naucratius, who had been living as a solitary near the family home at
Annesi, suddenly died, Basil awakened to the real values of life.
Imitating his sister's renunciation, he was baptized and determined to follow the ascetical way. Writing to his spiritual mentor,
Eustathius of Sebaste, in 375 (L 223), Basil explains his feelings:

> After I had wasted much time in vanity and had spent nearly
> all my youth in the vain labor in which I was engaged, occu-
> pying myself in acquiring a knowledge made foolish by God,
> when at length, as if aroused from a deep sleep, I looked
> upon the wonderous light of the truth of the gospel and saw
> the futility of the wisdom "of the rulers of this world who
> are passing away." Having mourned deeply my piteous life,
> I prayed that guidance be given for my introduction to the
> doctrines of religion. And before all else, I was careful to
> amend my ways, which for a long time had been perverted by
> my companionship with the indifferent. Accordingly having
> read the gospel and having seen clearly there that the greatest
> means for perfection is the selling of one's possessions, the
> sharing with needy brethren, the complete renouncing of
> solicitude for this life, and the refusing of the soul to be led
> astray by any affection for things of earth, I prayed to find
> some one of the brethren who had chosen this way of life,
> so as to pass with them over life's brief and troubled
> waters (3).[1]

Amending his ways, Basil sought the conversion of morals with

1. Basil's letters and ascetical quotes are from FOC, vols: 9, 13, 28.

the aid of like-minded brethren, which is the very fundament of monasticism.

But he first made the grand tour of Egypt, Libya, the Thebaid, Palestine, Syria and Mesopotamia, visiting the monks and solitaries, admiring their abstinence, fasting, work, nocturnal prayer, their scorn of hunger, thirst and cold. He admired especially Eustathius who was to be his spiritual guide for fifteen years and who influenced his monasticism to a very great degree, visiting Basil at Annesi frequently. Although eventually they split up over Trinitarian differences, Basil always admired Eustathius' asceticism.

Probably with Eustathius' encouragement, Basil determined to found a monastery on the banks of the Iris across from his sister's convent home at Annesi. Basil loved the spot and described it enchantingly. It seems to have been a sort of garden farm, inaccessible to ensure solitude. There was a small green plain fronting on the river, a backdrop of forests. The narrow pass leading to the monastery was surmounted by high summits, commanding excellent views of the river. Mother nature had made the place a paradise, with singing birds, jumping fish and smiling flowers (L 14).

Gregory of Nazianzus, Basil's friend and fellow monk for a while, did not share his enthusiasm. In contrast he saw cold, foggy bottoms with high crags cutting off the warm sun. The stream contained more rocks than fish and the small rocky garden patch could not even produce a few beans. The house was cramped, poorly roofed, cold, often without enough bread. If it had not been for charitable neighbors, the choice would have been between death by starvation and death by cold (L. 4). Obviously Gregory was not happy there and did not stay long. But his letter along with Basil's gives a good contrast between the idealist superior's report and that of the realist monk. Though Gregory's gripes were written at least partially with tongue in cheek, his friend Basil may have agreed in principle for we find him returning to clerical duties in Caesarea in 362,

only to flee to his retreat once more in 364-5 when he had
a falling out with his bishop.

In his travels Basil had observed the hermits and the cenobites of the desert. He readily saw the problems of living alone,
namely the lack of opportunity for charity plus temptations to
pride. Basil was repelled by their record-breaking fasts which
seemed more for themselves than to achieve a spiritual purpose.
He found the Pachomian cenobites more to his liking, but felt
that their monasteries were too large, veritable cities over which
the abbot was the administrator. Rather the monastic house
should be small enough that the superior could be a father to
his monks.

Our Lord gave example of his humility by washing the feet
of his disciples. If the monk lives alone, whose feet will he wash?
And how can he give service to others, be the last among many,
be patient or kind to his neighbor? "How, moreover, in a solitude,
will that good and pleasant thing be accomplished, the dwelling
of brethren together in one habitation which the Holy Spirit
likens to ointment emitting its fragrance from the head of the
high priest?" (Ps 132, 133) (Long Rule LR 7).

Basil best explains the purpose of his monastery in the preface
of his Long Rules (LR):

> Since by God's grace we have gathered together in the Name
> of our Lord Jesus Christ — we who have set before ourselves
> one and the same goal, the devout life — and since you have
> plainly manifested your eagerness to hear something of the
> matters pertaining to salvation, I, for my part, am under obli-
> gation to proclaim the justifications of God.... Since, more-
> over, the present is the most opportune time and this place
> provides quiet and complete freedom from external disturb-
> ances, let us pray together that we may provide our fellow
> servants their measure of wheat in due season, and that you,
> on your part, may, like fertile soil, receive the word and pro-
> duce in turn the fruit of justice, perfect and manifold as it is
> written.

The life of Basil's monastery was similar to other foundations of the time, with prayer, psalms, study of scripture, and manual work. The monks wore simple dress with a tunic and cloak and slept on a plank or mat. Food was frugal, largely bread, salt, herbs, and water.

Basil's instructions to his monks are concerned primarily with the interior life and his approach reminds one of Origen whom he had studied with his friend Gregory of Nazianzus. With the soul purified of affections, interests, opinions, it can renew itself easily. Freed from the distractions of the world, the monk can pursue the spiritual life in peace.

For Basil the monk is a soldier of Christ the King:

Where is Christ, the King? In heaven, to be sure. Thither it behooves you, soldier (of Christ), to direct your course. Forget all earthly delights. A soldier does not build a house; he does not aspire to the possession of lands; he does not concern himself with devious, coin-purveying trade. "No man, being a soldier of God, entangleth himself with secular business; that he may please him to whom he hath engaged himself" (2 Tim 2:4). The soldier enjoys a sustenance provided by the king; he need not furnish his own, nor vex himself in this regard.

By royal edict, a home lies open to him wherever there are subjects of the king. He is not required to toil at building a house. On the open road is his tent and he takes his food as necessity demands; water is his drink, and his slumber such as nature provides. Many are his marches and vigils; his endurance of heat and cold, engagements with the foe, the worst and greatest of perils; often, perchance, death itself — but a glorious death followed by rewards and a king's gifts. His life is toilsome in war; in peace it is joyous. The prize is valor, the crown awarded to him who has lived nobly in righteousness, is to be endowed with sovereignty, to be called the king's friend, to stand at his side, to receive his salvation,

> to accept honors from the king's own hand, to be eminent
> among the king's people, and to play the mediator for his
> friends without the court in whatever they desire (Basil,
> *Introduction to the Ascetical Life*).

The monk as a soldier completely dedicated to God goes back
to the Hebrew concept of the holy war in which the soldier is
totally committed, observing perfect continence until the final
victory (c.f. 2 Sam 11:1-20). Moreover, the Qumran monks' life
of poverty, celibacy or continence and obedience was not un-
related to their all out war against the Sons of Darkness
(c.f. War Scroll). Even the Roman Soldiers of lower ranks
were forbidden the *ius conubii* and in the fifth century were
not allowed to take another's lease or assume other obligations
for "They should be busy with their military service and not
with other people's affairs" (Code Just., 4, 65, 31).

So the Christian monks under their abbot, Christ's lieutenant,
completely separated from family and business, fight Satan, sin
and evil through asceticism and prayer, counseling, healing and
teaching others by word and example.

Many came to join Basil's army in his monastery on the banks
of the Iris. He was very careful on new admissions. The whole
community was informed about the newcomer, but there seems
to have been no formal novitiate as such. Extra precautions were
taken if some one only wanted to try out the life for a time
(Short Rule SR 97). Also the children from the monastery school
who wanted to become monks were put off till they could reach
a mature decision (LR 15). Married men were accepted with
the consent of their wives, although it seems there were excep-
tions to this (LR 12). Also freed slaves were welcome and even
escaped slaves provided that their masters had been unjust
(LR 11).

At the profession of the new monk church authorities should
be present (LR 15). Was the monastic commitment perpetual?
Basil answers:

> Surely every one who has been admitted to the community

and then retracted his promise should be looked upon as a
sinner against God, in whose presence and to whom he
pledged his consent in pact. But "If a man shall sin against
God" says the scripture, "Who shall pray for him?" (1 S
2:25). For if he has consecrated himself to God and has after-
ward turned aside to another mode of life, he is guilty of
sacrilege, by having committed the theft of himself and stolen
an offering made to God. The brethren are justified in never
again opening the door to these persons, even if they should
apply for shelter on some occasion when they are merely in
transit. The apostolic rule clearly directs us to avoid every
disorderly and undisciplined person and not to associate
with him in order that he may be put to shame (2 Thes
3:14)(LR 14).

Although Basil looked upon the monastic commitment as perpetual, one could return to the world for a good reason as Gregory of Nazianzus seems to have done when he became fed up
with the life. If a monk has been treated unjustly by his brethren,
and he cannot obtain redress, he may freely leave. However, if he
withdraws out of fickleness, he should try to cure this, otherwise
he is to be spurned by the brethren (LR 36).

As all monastic founders, Basil soon found a need of a rule.
It seems that he and Gregory of Nazianzus drew up a set of regulations in 358-59 showing Eustathius' influence and serving as
a basis for his later instructions, the Long Rules (LR), delivered
in 362-365. His Short Rules (SR) were composed later when he
was bishop of Caesarea. Basil wanted a sane balance of work
and prayer so that the interior spirit would be preserved. At an
early hour the monks rose to praise God and sing hymns. At
sunrise manual work began, alternating with prayers and hymns
and a study of Scripture. Besides the early morning service,
office was sung at terce, sext, none, at the end of the work day,
night fall, and midnight (LR 37). Although he recommended
that the monks work at a trade, it should not become a business
requiring frequent trips into town. The monk should work principally for his own needs and those of others (LR 42). There

seem to have been two classes of monks, the peasants who did manual labor and the aristocrats who did intellectual work.

Religious poverty for Basil did not mean giving one's goods to the monastery, but rather a gradual self-despoliation (LR 9). Keeping nothing for himself, the monk continues to manage his property or confides it to a trustee, gradually distributing this or that amount to the poor or to a good work. This gradual despoliation may have been an insurance against a future return to the world. Ideally the monk should be without possessions, but Basil is realistic, allowing the monks to receive income from properties which would help in the support of the monastery or aid the poor.

Obedience is of the essence in Basil's house. The brothers should obey promptly without discussion and murmuring. Any one refusing to obey should leave the monastery. Whereas in the beginning the superior ruled, later the Rule, the voice of the founder was the top authority to which even the superior was subordinate. New superiors were elected by the heads of neighboring monasteries (LR 43). After a trial run, they are to be accepted by the brothers (LR 43). The superior should rule by example rather than by word, leading all in the imitation of Christ (LR 43). He has the authority to punish erring monks and to assign them tasks, aided by his subordinates such as the cellarer and steward. Moreover, he should consult with the senior monks who also served as confessors and as a grievance committee for the monks (LR 48, SR 119). Confession of the younger brethren to the elders was a custom taken from Egypt (LR 26, 46; SR 229).

Perhaps following customs of Asia Minor ascetics, Basil advised his men to neglect their personal appearance:

> The humble and abject spirit often manifests itself by a gloomy countenance and a down cast eye, a careless appearance, unkempt hair, and soiled clothes, so that we by mere chance portray in ourselves these characteristics that mourners adopt designedly... (L 2).

Also this personal neglect may have been a reaction for the over-concern of the world for external appearance, to the neglect of the interior life.

A top rhetorician, Basil never lost his interest in education when he became a monk. He seems to have been the first monastic founder to link the ascetical life with the education of the laity. Christian fathers were happy that their children could receive a classical education and at the same time learn the fundamentals of their religion. At the time Christian education was largely a family affair with parents catechizing their children in Scripture, liturgy, and morality while they attended the state schools for the classics.

Some parents sent their children to Basil's monastic school with the hope that they would become monks. But, as we have seen, Basil never accepted them without extreme caution (LR 15). The young students did not mix with the monastic community, but lived in separate houses, coming together with the monks only for spiritual exercises. In no way were they required to keep the monastic rule. Some of the well-educated monks gave the children a religiously orientated education, with readings taken from holy Scripture and sacred authors. "In this way joyfully and with a relaxed mind, they will achieve their aim without pain to themselves and without giving offense" (LR 15). Moderate punishments were given for scholastic laxity, but more severe chastisements for vicious acts (LR 53). For example, a glutton, gossiper, bully, or liar should be condemned to silence or put to eating dry bread. Those who were studying a trade under an artisan could remain with him during the day, but had to return to their companions at night (LR 15).

The association of monks with education we have seen with the Buddhists. Basil's alliance began a long educational tradition in Christian monasticism. For example, in the West the monks were the main educational force right up to the founding of the universities in the Middle Ages.

Consecrated bishop of Caesarea in 370, Basil fought heresies with the help of Pope Damasus of Rome and Athanasius of Alexandria. At times he seemed to lean over so far to reconcile heretics, that he was accused of falling into error, but he was defended by Athanasius in two letters. Even as bishop, Basil continued to rule and increase his monks, collecting the isolated *monazontes* into monasteries, regulating their prayer, psalmody and work, and building a great cenobium and hospital in Caesarea. Basil was the prototype of the monk bishops, who, starting out as lay ascetics, were often called because of their learning, virtue and celibacy to rule in the church of the bishops.

Basil had a great influence on the growth of monasticism from the fourth century on, not only through his rules, but also by his other ascetical writings. Gregory of Nazianzus, Jerome, and Rufinus quote him freely. Rufinus, arriving in Italy in 397 from the East translated Basil's rules into Latin for Urseius abbot of Pinetum, editing the Long and Short Rules into a book of 203. John Cassian, Sozomen, Justinian and Benedict refer to him. Benedict who knew of Basil's rule through Rufinus' edition, recommended it to his monks. In fact, many of his own regulations reflect Rufinus' translation word for word, for example, Benedict c. 48 and Rufinus 192; Benedict c. 60 and Rufinus 9.

Basilian monasticism soon spread to Constantinople, which as the head of the empire, attracted all sorts of heresies both orthodox and heterodox. Most of the monasteries there followed Basil's rule with a few modifications. During the time of Abbot Isaac in the second half of the fourth century, monasticism was successfully established in and around Constantinople. There were hermit *monazontes* earlier and the Arians had made an abortive attempt to establish monasticism there. By 382 Isaac was surrounded by disciples whose numbers necessitated the erection of a monastery called Dalmate. Isaac wished to extend monasticism in the area and was encouraged by bishop John Chrysostom.

John Chrysostom, as Basil, had served his apprenticeship as a monk before his episcopal appointment. As a young man he had tried to become a monk, but his mother resisted. And when they attempted to make him a bishop, he fled to the solitude of the mountains, studying under an old Syrian monk for four years, then living two years in a cave. In 376 during the persecution of Valens he wrote three books *Against the Adversaries of the*

Monastic Life, showing the terrible persecutions the monks had had to endure. He chides both pagan and Christian parents for resisting their children's vocations, exhorting especially the latter to confide their children's education to the solitaries.

Monasteries would not be needed if the cities were properly Christian. But due to the recent Christianization of the empire, religion was largely a thin mask for paganism. Monasticism is the true philosophy which makes simple Christians more powerful than emperors with all of their authority, wealth and honor.

Chrysostom also praises monasticism in his homilies. For example, in Homily 68 on Matthew he contrasts monasticism with the theatre. The artificial riches and sex of the theatre make the viewer dissatisfied with his mediocre lot.

> But in the case of the monks there is no such result, but rather the contrary altogether. For when we shall see children of rich men and descendants of illustrious ancestors clothed in such garments as not even the lowest of the poor, and rejoicing in this, consider how great a consolation against poverty he will receive as he goes away. And should he be rich, he returns sobered, become a better man.... And his wife will receive her husband quiet and meek, freed from all unlawful lust, and will find him more gentle to her than before this (NPNF 10:419).

Since the church of the monks tended to operate outside of or at least independently of the church of the bishops, we find Chrysostom, as other bishops of the time, attempting to bring them into line. He was jealous of his authority, protecting and regulating the monks, repressing the wandering *monazontes,* corresponding with some monks, sending others as missionaries. Also he wanted them to respond willingly when he called them to orders. Chrysostom feared most the road-running *gyrovagi,* moving in from the country to the city, wandering around begging, ill-kempt, ill-mannered. Chrysostom was thrust from his see in 404. There were a number of counts against him, one of which was the protecting of Origenist monk fugitives from Egypt.

Monasticism in Constantinople continued to grow especially under the emperor Justinian (483-565). By the time of Basil of Macedonia (ninth century), there were hundreds of monasteries in and around Constantinople. Some had laurae or cells in which certain monks could live as recluses. Others had schools and hospices. They followed Basil's rule plus commentaries by the patriarchs such as John Chrysostom, John the Faster, and hegumens as Nil and Theodore the Studite. Novella 123 of Justinian formulated the principle monastic laws following Chalcedon. As Hannay writes,[2] "Basil conceived an ideal, Justinian enforced it from without, Theodore endeavored to realize it from within."

Yet as time passed some of Basil's ideals slipped from the Eastern monastic tradition. For example, cenobitism no longer dominated the Eastern scene, despite the favorable legislation of Justinian. Basil's alliance of the monks with the church of the bishops was more prominent since because of church and imperial legislation, bishops were to be recruited from among the monks, while the married parish priests are barred from highest office. Later Eastern monasticism did not preserve Basil's traditions of the education of the young and the care of the sick. This neglect of the practical in favor of the contemplative parallels the weakening of the cenobitic ideal.

C. Palestinian Monks

As elsewhere there were earlier ascetic trends in Palestine. We have already seen the Essenes and the early Christians. But the big impetus came from Egypt in the fourth century. Hilarion and Chariton were early leaders. Hilarion from near Gaza went to Egypt to drink in the ascetical spirit of Antony. Returning to Gaza, he built a hut in the marshes, but when crowds of the curious came, he fled to Cyprus (371), where he trained his famous disciple Epiphanius.

Chariton came from Iconium in Lycaonia going to Jerusalem

2. *The Spirit and Origin of Christian Monasticism*, London, Methuen, 1903, p. 199.

in the first quarter of the fourth century. Distributing his money to the poor and to some solitaries near the Dead Sea, he used the remainder to build a hermitage in a gorge near Jerusalem, using a small cavern for an oratory. Many Christians came to join him, settling in rocky niches nearby, coming down on Saturday and Sunday to assist at the mysteries at the oratory. As the numbers of his followers grew, Chariton built a large church consecrated by Macarius of Jerusalem in 330. This was the origin of the Laura of Pharon. Most Palestinian monasteries were built on this plan.

Besides the influence of Hilarion and Chariton and the many monks who fled persecutions in Egypt, there was also the Basilian trend of the Armenian Euthymius and the Roman invasion under the leadership of Melania the Elder and Jerome.

D. Rome and Palestine

Egyptian monasticism was brought to Rome by Athanasius and his monk companions. Friend and biographer of Antony, defender of Basil, Athanasius was chased into exile many times by unfriendly emperors. Exiled first in the Thebaid, then in Rome, he was a natural bridge between Egyptian monasticism and the Eternal City. Escaping from the Arians to seek the aid of Pope Julius in 341, he brought two monks with him, Ammonius and Isidore, whose simplicity and holiness impressed all. Athanasius' visits plus his *Life of Antony* were the catalysts of Roman monasticism, drawing Roman matrons to the deserts of Egypt and to the Holy Places. Even before the arrival of Athanasius, there had been some holy women living in the privacy of their own homes. Attracted by the enthusiasm of Athanasius, many wealthy women as Marcella sold their possessions and gave to the poor to live in poverty and charity in their palaces or villas.

As in Asia Minor and to some extent in Egypt, so in Rome the family monastery is common. Often a widow with her daughters and female slaves, living piously, would adapt a simple habit and ask for the guidance of a spiritual ascetic. Male monasteries developed similarly. Basically it was the Roman *familia*

with its *pater familias* ruling over the *filii familias* (*fratres*) or a
mater familias with her *filiae familias* (*sorores*). As members
of the family the *fratres* or *sorores* could not own property or
marry. Their common life included synaxes, good works and
sacred study.

After Athanasius, Jerome (347-420) was the most outstanding
spiritual guide of the Roman virgins, first in Rome and then in
Palestine. Educated in Rome, Jerome lived for a time as a monk
in the desert of Chalcis (375-379) where he studied Hebrew
and Chaldean to aid his investigations of Scriptures. There he
suffered the usual desert temptations of dancing girls (L 22).
Driven from the desert by calumnious accusations, he returned
to Antioch where he was ordained a presbyter by bishop Paulinus.
Then he went to Rome in 382 where pope Damasus asked him
to work on the bible and where he promoted the monastic way.

Many pious ladies were drawn to Jerome in spite of or perhaps because of his irascible ways. For example, Paula of the
great Aemilian family and her two daughters Blesilla and Eustochium, and Marcella who gathered her friends in her Aventine
palace for study and prayer. Jerome became their spiritual father
and Scripture professor, teaching them to chant the psalms in
Hebrew.

An example of Jerome's advice to the virgins is a letter (L 22)[3]
that he wrote to Eustochium in 384. He makes clear that in
lauding virginity, he is not condemning marriage, but comparing
a greater good with a lesser one. Not all men can receive the call
to virginity. "Some men may be eunuchs of necessity. I am one
by choice. 'There is a time to embrace, and a time to refrain
from embracing. There is a time to cast away stones, and a time
to gather stones together' (Eccl 3:5)" (19).

Jerome defends virginity as natural to man, while marriage
came after the fall. Marital wedlock produces virgin flesh a re-
version back to the pristine stock.

3. Loeb, **Selected Letters of S. Jerome**, New York, Putnam, 1933,
pp. 53-159.

I praise wedlock, I praise marriage; but it is because they produce me virgins. I gather the rose from the thorn, the gold from the earth, the pearl from the oyster. Shall the ploughman plow all day? Shall he not also enjoy the fruit of his labor? Wedlock is more honored when the fruit of wedlock is the more loved. Why, mother, grudge your daughter her virginity? She has been reared on your milk, she has come from your body, she has grown strong in your arms. Your watchful love has kept her safe. Are you vexed with her because she chooses to wed not a soldier, but a king? She has rendered you a high service: from today you are the mother by marriage of God. (20)

Then Jerome points out some of the advantages of virginity.

No soldier takes a wife with him when he is marching into battle. Even when a disciple was fain to go and bury his father, the Lord forbade him and said, "Foxes have holes and the birds of the air have nests, but the son of man has nowhere to lay his head" (Mt 8:20). So you must not complain if you are scantily lodged. "He that is unmarried cares for the things that belong to the Lord. But he that is married cares for the things of the world, how to please his wife. There is a difference also between a wife and a virgin. The unmarried woman cares for the things of the Lord, that she may be holy both in body and spirit. But she that is married cares for the things of the world, how she may please her husband" (1 Cor 7:32-34). (21)

Jerome points out the inconveniences of wedlock, which, however, can sometimes underline a selfish motive for virginity. Jerome feels that prayer and marriage are all but incompatible. And he compares the virgin to Mary the sister of Martha in the gospel story. The virgin is the bride of Christ.

Let the seclusion of your own chambers ever guard you; ever

let the bridegroom sport with you within. If you pray, you are speaking to your spouse; if you read, he is speaking to you. When sleep falls on you, he will come behind the wall and will touch your flesh and you will awake and rise up and cry: "I am sick with love" (Song of Solomon 5:8). And you will hear him answer: "A garden enclosed is my sister, my spouse, a spring shut up, a fountain sealed" (4:12). (25)

Do not roam about foolishly in search of the bridegroom, but within your chamber in secret. Do not be proud and vain in your calling, a danger to virgins. Do not be false as some women who masquerade as ascetics. Others go around dressed like men. Also stay clear of imitation monks with shaggy beards, long hair, black cloak, lugubrious manner and false fasts. These are a danger to virgins as also are the imposters among the clerics.

Jerome advocates poverty for many of the Roman virgins had retained their riches. Mary should be the supreme model of purity. When weary of the ascetical struggle, remember that the battle is short, while the victory is long.

When pope Damasus died (377), Jerome was left open to the attack of his enemies who spread false rumors about his relations with his Aventine friends. The sudden death of Blesilla, possibly due to too rigorous fasting and penances, crystalized hate against Jerome and monasticism in Rome (L 45). Jerome was also frustrated that he was not elected pope. At any rate, he left Rome with his brother Paulinian and some monks in 385. Paula and Eustochium followed and together they visited Egypt and Palestine, settling in Bethlehem in 386 where Paula built a double monastery, with Paula heading the convent, while Jerome ran the monastery. At first there were cordial relations with earlier Roman pilgrims, Melania the Elder and Rufinus in Jerusalem. But there was to be a falling off over the problem of Origenism.

While in Palestine, Jerome continued his Scriptural studies while writing a heavy correspondence and numerous ascetical works. He encouraged other Romans fleeing the barbarian invasions to join him (L 34). He wrote a number of works centering on monasticism. For example: *Life of Hilarion, Life of Malchus, Two Books against Jovinian in Defense of Virginity, The Illustrious Men,* and translations of Pachomius, Theodore, Orsisius, etc. He pointed out both the advantages and the faults of the monastic life. For example, the problem of dark melancholy and hypochondria following excessive asceticism (L 225:7; L 130: 8; L 125:16). Moreover, any serious attempt at a religious life can leave one open to the dangers of hypocrisy and pride (LL 15 & 18).

Penning to Rusticus a young monk of Toulouse in 411 (L 125) Jerome advises him against the anchorite life.

> But if for your part you desire to be a monk and not merely seem one, be more careful of your soul than of your property; for in adopting a religious profession you have renounced this once for all. Let your garments be squalid to show that your mind is white; and your tunic be course to prove that you despise the world. But give not way to pride lest your dress and language be found at variance. Baths stimulate the senses and must, therefore, be avoided; for to quench natural heat is the aim of chilling fasts. Yet even these must be moderate, for, if they are carried to excess, they weaken the stomach and by making more food necessary to it promote indigestion, that fruitful parent of unclean desires. A frugal and temperate diet is good for both body and soul. See your mother as often as you please, but not with other women, for their faces may dwell in your thoughts and so "A secret wound may fester in your breast" (Virgil, *Aeneid* 4:67) (7) (NPNF ser 2, 6:246-).

Jerome clarifies the dangers of the solitary life, namely, a lack of guidance and mutual support, temptations to pride, tendencies to laxness in discipline, violations of poverty, etc.

> Do I condemn a solitary life? By no means, in fact, I have often commended it. But I wish to see the monastic schools turn out soldiers who have no fear of the rough training of the

desert, who have exhibited the spectacle of a holy life for a
considerable time, who have made themselves last that they
might be first, who have not been overcome by hunger, or
satiety, whose joy is in poverty, who teach virtue by their
garb and mien, and who are too conscientious to invent —
as some silly men do — monstrous stories of struggles with
demons, designed to magnify their heroes in the eyes of the
crowd and before all to extort money from it. (9)

After outlining some of the scandals against poverty and the
dangers of sexual temptations in the solitary life, Jerome points
out the advantages of a good community life.

For there, while you will be under the control of one father,
you will have many companions. And these will teach you, one
humility, another patience, a third silence and a fourth meekness. You will do as others wish; you will eat what you are
told to eat; you will wear what clothes are given you; you will
perform the task allotted to you; you will obey one whom
you do not like; you will come to bed tired out; you will go
to sleep on your feet and you will be forced to rise before
you have had sufficient rest. When your turn comes, you will
recite the psalms, a task which requires not a well modulated
voice, but genuine emotion. . . . You will serve the brothers,
you will wash the guests' feet. If you suffer wrong, you will
bear it in silence. The superior of the community you will
fear as a master and love as a father. Whatever he may order
you to do you will believe to be wholesome for you. You will
not pass judgment upon those who are placed over you, for
your duty will be to obey them and to do what they are told,
according to the words spoken by Moses, 'Keep silence and
hearken, O Israel' (Dt 27:9). You will have so many tasks
to occupy you that you will have no time for (evil) thoughts;
and while you pass from one thing to another and fresh
work follows work done, you will only be able to think of
what you have in charge at the moment to do. (15)

Jerome is outspoken in his criticism of the false monks, whose renunciation of the world consists merely in a change of garments and empty words. But their former ways, including wealth, servants and table, remain the same. "Others, who though poor, think themselves discerning, and walk as solemnly as pageants through the streets and do nothing but snarl at every one whom they meet" (16). "Some, too, there are who from the dampness of their cells and from the severity of their fasts, from the weariness of solitude and from excessive study have a singing in their ears day and night and turn melancholy mad so as to need the poultices of Hippocrates more than exhortations from me" (16). Many keep their former trades and profit on tax exemptions, their Christianity a cloak of their fraud. But one who is a member of a community is preserved from these temptations, practicing good habits and striving for the good. Jerome's letter to Rusticus was to prove a reliable guide for future monastic founders as Columban (R. 10).

Although Melania the Elder and Rufinus had preceded him, Jerome soon became the self-styled leader of the Roman ascetics in Palestine. As Alaric approached the gates of Rome (409-410) wealthy Christian Romans fled to the Holy Places and some to Africa. We have already mentioned Paula and Eustochium who accompanied Jerome to Bethlehem, founding a double monastery there. Following the custom of Egypt, Paula divided the nuns into three sub-communities, each under a superioress. Although cenobites, the nuns work and eat separately, uniting for prayer and psalms at terce, sext, none, vespers and matins. They know the psalter by heart and also had to learn a passage of Scripture each day. On Sundays they meet in the Church of the Nativity for the liturgy after which they receive their weekly tasks.

Paula and Eustochium were joined by Paula's granddaughter, young Paula. Together they performed humble tasks around the monastery, sweeping, cooking, caring for the lamps. At the same time they kept up their Greek and Hebrew studies under Jerome, while serving as his secretaries. Jerome wrote his *Vulgate* to help them in their Scripture work. Paula's charity was known to all, using her money to erect a hospice for pilgrims and travelers. Jerome followed her example, selling his property in Dalmatia and giving to the poor. When Paula died in 404, Jerome wrote a eulogy to Eustochium (L 108) quoting the inscription on Paula's tomb:

Within this tomb a child of Scipio lies, a daughter of the far famed Pauline house, a scion of the Gracchi, of the stick of Agamemnon's self, illustrious; here rests the lady Paula, well-beloved of both her parents, with Eustochium for daughter; she the first of the Roman dames who hardship chose and Bethlehem for Christ.

Eustochium took over her mother's convent and when she died (417) there were fifty virgins there. Then young Paula took charge, aiding Jerome in his last days. By the time Jerome died (420) the number of nuns had dropped to twenty. The golden age of Roman monasticism in Palestine was drawing to a close. As family ties were broken by death and family fortunes were used up, and especially with the passing of their leader Jerome, there was less and less to hold the Bethlehem communities together. As so often in the history of monasticism, when the first generation passes away, the spirit and life passes away.

Let us move over to Jerusalem for a moment to take a better look at Melania the Elder, the dominant figure there for a period of twenty-seven years. She was a Spanish noble woman whose husband died when she was twenty-two. Placing her son in good hands, she left for Egypt in 372 with other illustrious women and accompanied by Rufinus. She traveled through Nitria and Scetis visiting the desert heroes: Pambo, Serapion, Paphnutius and others. When many of them were banished to Palestine by the Augustial prefect, she followed serving as their slave. But when they were allowed to return to Egypt, Melania stayed behind, building a monastery for fifty virgins in Jerusalem.

Rufinus dwelt in a nearby monastery, guiding Melania and her virgins, who spent much of their time helping pilgrims and serving as a calming influence in Jerusalem. We have seen how

Melania consoled Evagrius in his identity crisis. She also healed the Pauline schism, bringing four hundred monks back to the church. But Jerome turned against her in the bitter Origenist controversy in which she defended her friends Rufinus and Evagrius. Jerome retorted, "Her name testifies to her shady character" (L 133).

Melania returned to Rome (400), preaching the monastic way, persuading her granddaughter, Melania the Younger and her husband Pinian and her son's wife Albina to sell their goods and leave Rome for the calm and peace of Palestine. When members of the Senate objected to her tactics, she reminded them of the imminent barbarian invasions (410). "Little children, it was written over 400 years ago, it is the last hour, why are you fond of the vain things of life? Beware lest the days of the Anti-Christ overtake you and you not enjoy your wealth and your ancestral property" (Palladius, LH 54:5).

The barbarian invasions are not unconnected with the monastic movement. Many felt that they were a prelude to the eschaton, bringing home to them the finitude of earthly possessions and encouraging them to sell all and give to the poor to live eschatologically in a convent or monastery. Melania returned to Jerusalem to die (409) honored as "Thrice Blessed" and "The Female Man of God."

Inspired by her grandmother and fearing the invasion of Alaric, Melania the Younger and her husband Pinian began to live as brother and sister, leaving for Sicily with Rufinus (410), then to North Africa for seven years and on to Jerusalem (417) and Egypt (418). Attracted to the hermit life, Melania retired to a cell on the Mount of Olives when she returned to Jerusalem, living there for eleven years. Then she became interested in the cenobitic life, asking her husband to look around for virgins interested in the monastic life. She built a monastery for ninety, but refused to rule as abbess, preferring humble work and interfering only when the superior was too strict. She also erected a men's monastery.

Melania's monastery carried on the Roman liturgy in Jerusalem with prayer, chant and mass. There was a private oratory in the convent of virgins with mass on Friday and Sunday. She took a special interest in the Holy Relics, building shrines over their resting places and insuring the performance of the liturgy at the place of the Lord's ascension and the cave of his instruction to the apostles. Pinian and Melania took in the boy Gerontius whom they made a monk and had ordained a presbyter so that he could celebrate mass three times on Sundays: once each at the men's and women's monasteries and at the church of the Ascension, while celebrating daily in private for Melania according to the Roman custom. When Melania died (439) Gerontius remained as head of the double monastery, sharing with Elpidius the office of Archimandrite.

The Roman influence in Palestinian monasticism was relatively short but intense. Jerome was the dominant figure with his voluminous correspondence covering everything from widowhood to asceticism. Many Roman pilgrims came to the Holy Places, some staying on as monks. But as Jerome grew old, he saw a new generation of Greek monks rise up, led by men like Hesychius and Euthymius, whose popularity soon outshone his own.

E. The Rise of Greek Monasticism

As early as 405 Euthymius, a priest from Melitene in Armenia came to Chariton's laura at Pharon, bringing along the Melitan custom of retreating into the desert on the feast of the Baptism of Jesus and returning to Jerusalem on Palm Sunday. On one lenten retreat, Euthymius and his companion Theoctistus settled in large caves in the Wadi Mukellik, south of the Jerusalem-Jericho road. As the number of his disciples grew, a cenobium was built. But Euthymius soon withdrew to the solitude of Masada, then established a monastery east of Hebron before moving on again deeper into the wilderness, where a laura soon gathered around him.

Here was to be trained the next generation of monks including: Sabas, Theodosius, Cyriac and others. Many bishops and two patriarchs came from Euthymius' monastery, governing with his guidance. Other less influential abbots gathered around him such as Theoctistus, Gelasius, Elpidius, Gerontius, and Gerasimus. The Laura of Euthymius scattered its cells on the plateau of an isolated hill detached from the mountains of Pharan and Jericho.

Euthymius set the pattern for Judaean monasticism by having the lower monastery of Theoctistus serve as a novice house from which men would graduate to the semi-anchorite life of the laura. As Chitty comments: [4] "In the Euthymian system, canonized by Sabas in the next generation, the cenobium is ancillary to the laura, to which it normally forms an indispensable preliminary stage." Euthymius attracted disciples from Melitene, Cappadocia, Sinai and Palestine.

Each January 14th he left for his desert retreat with a few chosen disciples. For example, in 470 the group included Domitian, Martyrius, Elias, Sabas, Gerasimus and Cyriac. During the week they scattered in solitude, coming together on Sundays for the Eucharist celebrated by Euthymius. They returned to Jerusalem for Palm Sunday. Euthymius died in 473 to be succeeded by Elias.

Two of Euthymius' disciples, Theodosius and Sabas, both Cappadocians, were to become the chiefs of Palestinian monasticism, codifying the rules and liturgical traditions brought from Egypt and Syrian customs introduced by Euthymius and Theoctistus.

Theodosius built one of the largest monasteries in Judaea on a high hill to the east of Bethlehem. It was really a city including hundreds of monks, solitaries and cenobites. They had a hospice for the poor and travelers, sometimes serving a hundred tables a day. And they built hospitals for rich and poor strangers and a special monastery and chapel for monks who had become feebleminded due to a too rigorous asceticism, plus a home for the aged. There were 400 monks living in four separate houses with chapels, with many different choirs for the chanting of the office because of the diversity of language and rites. Though there also were churches for the Armenians and the Bessi, all

4. **The Desert a City,** p. 85. This section depends on Chitty.

united for mass in the Greek church. Theodosius was famous for his asceticism and hospitality with a strong emphasis on the divine office. He of all the Judaean abbots followed the Basilian ideal. Elsewhere Basil's influence seems to have been rather rare in Palestine.

As in Egypt the Palestinian monks were generally lay and tended to act independently of the bishops. Passarion (d. 428) an important figure in the Jerusalem church, was a liaison between the bishop and the monks. He founded an alms house outside the East Gate of Jerusalem and a large monastery on Mt. Sion. Stressing liturgy, cenobitism, and help of the poor, he also reflected the Basilian tradition. As archimandrite or supervisor of the monks of the Jerusalem diocese, Passarion visited the monasteries as a link between the bishop and the lay monks.

The Council of Chalcedon (451) illustrates a further attempt on the part of the bishops to control the monks. For example, canon four:

Those who lead a true and genuine monastic life shall receive due honor. As, however, some, assuming the monastic state only for a pretext, confuse the affairs of church and state, and go about the cities indiscriminately, and at the same time wish to found monasteries for themselves, the synod decrees that no one shall anywhere build or set up a monastery or a poor house without the consent of the bishop of the city; (further) that the monks of each neighborhood and city shall be subject to the bishop, that they love quiet, and give themselves only to fasting and prayer, stopping in the places to which they are assigned; that they do not encumber themselves with ecclesiastical and secular affairs, or take part in them, leaving their monasteries, except when, in case of necessity, they are required to do so by the bishop of the city; that no slave shall be received into the monasteries to become a monk without permission of his master. Whoever transgresses this our ordinance shall be excommunicated. That the name of God be not blasphemed, the bishop of the city ought to take careful oversight of the monasteries (*Hefele* 2: 389-390. (Also see canons 8, 23, 24.)

The emperor Marcian wanted the canon because of Eutychian and other monks who had withdrawn themselves from suspected Nestorian bishops. Also the council, adopting Leo's tome, condemned Monophysitism which had been espoused by many of the monks in Egypt and Palestine. Justinian's code incorporated many Chalcedonian regulations against the monks. Some would feel that this greatly hampered the free development of eastern monasticism by contrast with the large garden of monastic flowers in the West.

When Juvenal, patriarch of Jerusalem, went to Chalcedon with his bishops, he told his people to anathematize him if he signed Leo's tome. But when he signed it any way, Abbot Theodosius backed by Empress Eudocia — estranged from her husband and now living in Jerusalem — and most of the monks and even some bishops called it treason. On his return Juvenal met a large group of angry monks at Caesarea, forcing him to return to Constantinople. Theodosius was consecrated bishop of Jerusalem, filling the Palestinian sees with anti-Chalcedonians. Almost all the Palestinian monks joined Theodosius against Chalcedon, including the archimandrites Elpidius and Gerontius, a few such as Gelasius of Nicopolis and Euthymius holding back.

When in 453 Juvenal returned, supported by imperial troops, there ensued a slaughter of monks and Juvenal was restored as bishop of Jerusalem. Theodosius fled and the anti-Chalcedonian bishops were removed. Euthymius returned to his laura after a two year retreat at Rouba. But the Empress Eudocia with the majority of the monks remained firmly anti-Chalcedonian. But Eudocia had her doubts and sent the chorbishop Anastasius to consult with Simeon the Stylite who advised her to follow the Chalcedonian Euthymius.

In Egypt opposition to Chalcedon was led by Pope Dioscorus of Alexandria. And when he was forcibly deposed, his successor, Chalcedonian Pope Proterius, was promptly lynched (457). When

Basilicus seized power in 475 promulgating an encyclical ana-
thematizing Chalcedon, Pope Timothy the Cat, anti-Chalcedonian
patriarch of Alexandria, returned to the throne in 477. Other
anti-Chalcedonians returned to their sees, for example, Peter
the Fuller in Antioch and Peter the Iberian in Palestine. Anastasius, patriarch of Jerusalem, accepted the encyclical, but kept
in touch with both sides. He was succeeded by Martyrius.

The archimandrite Marcian of Bethlehem (d. 492) called
together all the monks, telling them to cast lots between the
church of the monks (anti-Chalcedonian) and the church of the
bishops (Chalcedonian). The lot fell for the bishops and there
was great rejoicing in Jerusalem over the second union, the first
having been the reconciliation of Eudocia and Elpidius with
Chalcedon. The patriarch Martyrius' subsequent pronounce-
ment was not so much an anathema on Chalcedon, but rather an
anathema on all who accept any doctrine other than that of
Nicaea.

In the middle of the fifth century the archimandrites Elpidius
and Gerontius were mediators between the Jerusalem church of
the bishops and the monks. Their successors in the 480's became
lax and worldly so that in 492 the monks came up from the
desert to ask for Sabas and Theodosius as archimandrites of
the anchorites and cell-dwellers and the cenobites respectively
with their aids in the desert, namely, the abbot of the Laura of
St. Gerasimus and the abbot of the cenobium of Martyrius. So the
episcopal supervision of the monks moved from the city to the
wilderness.

Sabas (439-532) was an important monastic founder of the
period. Since the early age of seven he had lived in a cenobium
in his native Cappadocia. As a boy of eighteen he migrated to
Palestine, first to the monastery of Elpidius, then to Euthymius
who refused to accept the beardless youth, sending him to
Theoctistus' cenobium for training. In 474 feeling the changing
times, Sabas retired from Wadi Mukellik for four years to the
desert of Coutila and Rouba towards the Dead Sea, where he
used to go with Euthymius during Lent. Near the mountain of
Eudocia's Tower an angel pointed out a cave to him in the

Cedron Gorge (478). The hospitable bedouins of the area brought him food. Slowly disciples came to join him, each settling in his own cave. On the summit of rock above the gorge Sabas built a tower and a little below a chapel where a visiting priest could say mass. In a large cave whose interior resembled a cross, Sabas made a church with an opening on the gorge. He called it Theoktistos, or the God-built church. On Saturdays and Sundays the monks came there for office. Faithful to his calling as a lay monk, Sabas put off consecration of the church which might require his ordination.

When Sabas' friend and former monk, patriarch Martyrius died (486), gripers arose among Sabas' monks. They went up to Jerusalem to ask the new patriarch Sallust for a new hegumen, complaining that Sabas was boorish and refused to allow any of the monks to be ordained. In reply Sallust (490) ordained Sabas before all the monks and consecrated the Theoktistos church. When some Armenians came in 491, Sabas gave them cells and the use of the first little chapel in which to sing the office on Saturdays and Sundays.

As his mentor Euthymius, Sabas used to go into the desert after the Epiphany. But first he kept the feast of St. Antony in his own laura and then went to Euthymius' monastery for his memorial on January 20, then to the desert till the eve of Palm Sunday. In his wanderings he fought off devils and beasts and found many good places for cenobia and laurae.

Sabas was a builder with three laurae, six monasteries, four hospices to his credit. His disciples founded three laurae and two monasteries. Using his own inheritance plus donations of pilgrims, he built a bakery, hospital and a great church of the Theotokos in his monastery. But the murmuring continued, forcing him to retreat to the area of Sythopolis and Gadara, founding cenobia. His enemies among the monks took the opportunity to run to the patriarch Elias with the story that Sabas had been eaten by lions near the Dead Sea. But Elias did not believe it and searched Sabas out, installing him once again as the head of his laura. Disgruntled, his enemies tore down his tower and escaped to the ruins of Romanus' monastery near Tekoa. But

Sabas followed them, building a bakery and a new church for them and calling the place the New Laura.

Besides serving as archimandrite, Sabas was an envoy to the imperial court in Constantinople in 511-512. Later he went to beg funds from Justinian to rebuild monasteries destroyed by the Samaritans in 529 and for other projects such as a hospital, the completion of the church of the Theotokos in Jerusalem and a fort against the marauding Arabs. In return he promised Justinian the reconquest of Africa, Rome, and the rest of Honorius' empire plus the suppression of Arianism, Nestorianism and Origenism.

When Sabas was dying in his tower, December 1, 532, he appointed as hegumen Melitas of Beirut, handing on to him the traditions of the laura. Although Sabas' *Life* implies that he left a rule, it did not survive except in the general customs of the monastery. As Chitty comments,[5] "Maybe it is more in keeping with the spirit of Eastern Christian monasticism that the written rule should not survive, while there remains the pattern of his living monastery, whose Typikon was continued through the centuries to take perhaps the first place among the Typika which regulate the liturgical order of the Eastern Orthodox Church." Sabas' laura was to mold the liturgy, dogma and hymnology of Eastern Orthodox monasticism besides contributing to the intellectual life through men like John of Damascus.

During the sixth century as the monasteries became more involved in controversies and ecclesiastical politics, the solitaries such as Cyriac and John the Hesychast became more popular. Meanwhile Origenism continued to dominate Jerusalem till it was condemned by the second council of Constantinople (553) and the Origenist monks expelled. The Saracen invasions of 609 drew to a close the golden age of Christian monasticism in Palestine.

As we have seen in this chapter, in the fifth century the focus of Christian monasticism moved from Egypt to Syria and Palestine. Whereas in Syria the *monazontes*, stylites and Basilians

5. The Desert a City, p. 117.

flourished, in Palestine the ascetics settled around the Holy Places, giving their foundations a certain stability. It has always been the monastic tradition to build on the relics of a hero. Here, of course, the hero is Jesus himself.

The laura was the monastic type of Palestine. Similar to the cells of Nitria, it was semi-hermitic, a step higher than the cenobium. The liturgy played an important part, reflecting both the Basilian and Roman influence with the cell-dwellers coming together in the central church for the mysteries. There was a strong cosmopolitan air in Palestinian monasticism because of the ceaseless pilgrimages from all over the empire. Roman, Greek, Syrian, Armenian monks lived separately but shared the Greek liturgy in the main church.

At the end of this era we find monasticism becoming institutionalized, really an institutional church similar to that which it initially fled with its own traditions, rules, and literature, integrated into the civil and ecclesiastical worlds, supervised by archimandrites and regulated by imperial law and church canons. And with it all came a certain loss of freedom of spirit which the first generations enjoyed.

6. How Good and Pleasant It Is When Brothers Dwell In Unity
(*Augustine*, EXPOSITION ON PS 132 [133])

A. *Augustine the Monk* (354-430)

gyptian monasticism had perhaps less influence in Western Africa than in most other places. Its impact on Palestine, Syria and Rome we have already seen and we will see it also in Gaul, Ireland and Italy. The pattern is similar: either Christian ascetics or ascetics-to-be tour the monasteries and anchorites of Egypt and the Holy Places or else they are familiar with Egyptian monastic literature such as the *Life of Antony*, Pachomius' Rules, etc. Augustine, called the father of African monasticism, never visited Egypt, but was inspired by the *Life of Antony* and the monks of Milan and Rome. Moreover, he was likely familiar with the ascetical traditions of northern Africa.

109

As early as the second century we find Montanist ascetics in Carthage, as Tertullian attests. Living at home rather than in community, the veiled virgins were honored with special places in the liturgy. Cyprian in the third century took special care of the Carthaginian virgins. Although bound as spouses of Christ, they did not practice communism and its correlative poverty. By the time of Augustine, African monasticism was still in its primitive stages with gypsy monks moving from place to place in dirty clothing and long hair. Often trouble-makers, the monk-like Donatist circumcellions hung around the martyrs' shrines, begging, selling relics, attacking the Catholics and, in general, defying civil authorities.

Augustine, one of the principal founders of African monasticism, was born in Thagaste in 354 of a pagan father, Patricius and a Christian mother, Monica. As a student and teacher of rhetoric in Carthage, he tried the Manichaean way. In Rome he was briefly attracted to the Academics, then on to Milan where Ambrose introduced him to the joys of Neo-Platonism while he continued his profession of rhetorician.

While living in Milan, Augustine's friend Alypius tried to persuade him not to become involved in a permanent marriage so that they could retire to a leisure life in pursuit of wisdom, as they had long planned. Alypius had had sex experiences as a youth and then turned away. But Augustine replied that many married men also sought wisdom. Besides, he felt that he never could tolerate celibacy, since for twelve years he had cohabitated with his common law wife by whom he had had a son, Adeodatus. Meanwhile Monica was preparing a good marriage for her son. But since the girl was too young, he would have to wait two years.

Yet the desire for a common life continued to grow among Augustine and his friends.

Many of us who were friends, detesting the tumultuous annoyances of human life, had by now, through thinking of the matter and joint discussion, almost decided to live in a quiet way removed from crowds. To secure this peaceful life, we planned to put together whatever possessions we had and set up one household out of all, so that as a result of true friendship, nothing would belong to one person rather than to another; instead, one fund would be made of all our possessions, and the whole thing would belong to each person singly, and everything to all (Conf 6, 14, 24). (FOC 21)

This was the prototype of the strict poverty of Augustine's religious community at Hippo. There were ten men in Augustine's Milan society, some of whom were wealthy as Romanianus, who no doubt would subsidize the plan. Two officers would be chosen to take care of all temporalities, holding office for one year, while the others would be left free for the leisurely life of philosophers as the Greek scholastics. However, Augustine and his friends soon abandoned their utopian dreams when it occurred to them that their girl friends (*mulierculae*) would not tolerate their bachelorhood.

One day later on when Ponticianus, a Roman court officer, visited Augustine, he was impressed by a copy of Paul's epistles lying on a table. When Augustine explained that he regularly read the Scriptures, Ponticianus told him the story of Antony the Egyptian hermit who was making such an impact on the West, especially since Athanasius' exile to Rome and Trier. Antony's humble life, miracles, teaching and asceticism excited Augustine and Alypius and proved a turning point in their lives.

When he saw that he had sparked their interest, Ponticianus told them more about the monks living in deserts or near cities. Actually there was a monastery outside the gates of Milan, but Augustine and his friends were unaware of it.

Next Ponticianus told them of two of his fellow officers who, while wandering through a garden in Trier came upon a house of the Lord's poor brethren in which they found a copy of the *Life of Antony*. These Trier ascetics may have dated from

Athanasius' visit there in 336. Leafing through the *Life of Antony,* one of the officers suddenly felt the call to be a monk. Turning to his companion, he cried:

> Tell me, I beg you, what goal do we hope to achieve with all these efforts of ours? What are we looking for? What reason do we have for engaging in public service? Could our aspiration at the court be anything greater than to become "Friends of Caesar?" And what is not unstable and full of dangers in that position? Through how many dangers must one go to reach a greater danger? And when will one reach it? Now, if I wish, I can be a friend of God immediately (Conf. 8, 6, 15).

One could see that he was going through the pangs of rebirth, turning away, stripping off his old worldly life, converting to the monastic way. "I have now broken away from our former hopes and have determined to serve God. From this very hour and in this very place I make my start. If it is too much for you to imitate me, do not oppose me" (Conf. 8, 6, 15). The two men joined together in building a tower, breaking off their engagements with their fiancees who dedicated themselves as virgins to Christ.

As Ponticianus told his story, Augustine looked into his own life.

> Thou, indeed, O Lord, didst twist me back upon myself, while his words were being uttered, taking me away from behind my own back, where I had placed myself because I was unwilling to look at myself, and thou didst set me right in front of my own face so that I might see how ugly I was, how deformed and vile, how defiled and covered with sores. I saw and was filled with horror, yet there was no place to flee from myself. If I attempted to turn my gaze away from myself, he kept on telling his story, and thou didst again place me before myself, thrusting me up before my eyes, so that I would discover my iniquity and detest it. I recognized it,

but pretended not to. I thrust it from my sight and out of my mind (Conf. 8, 7, 16).

The more Augustine admired these men who had given themselves to Christ, the more he hated himself, for he had always been searching for the truth. Even in his Manichaean days he had asked for the gift of continence, "but not yet" (Conf. 8, 7, 17). He gave himself the excuse that his delay in leaving off worldly pleasures was because he had not yet found anything certain on which to hang his hopes. Even now, although attracted to the monastic way, his old loves held him back.

Walking one day in the garden of his host, Augustine heard a child shouting, "Tolle, lege." At first he thought it was a game, then he remembered how Antony had been inspired by a gospel reading, "Go sell what you have, and give to the poor, and you shall have treasure in heaven, and come, follow me" (Mt 19:21) (Conf. 8, 12, 29). Running to Alypius, he picked up a volume of Paul which he had left near him. Opening it, his eye fell on a passage from Romans (13:13-14). "Let us conduct ourselves becomingly as in the day, not in reveling and drunkenness, not in debauchery and licentiousness, not in quarreling and jealousy, but put on the Lord Jesus Christ, and make no provision for the flesh to gratify its desires." Instantly Augustine felt a peace come over him and as light streamed into his heart, all dark shadows of doubt fled away (Conf. 8,12,29). The divine light drew Augustine as it had Antony and he responded with joy, telling first Alypius and then Monica.

The mystery of a vocation is often culminated in a dramatic moment. But its seeds are usually long planted. Many prayers, sermons, the example of Monica, Ambrose, Victorinus, Ponticianus and Antony and others had plowed, planted and watered. But it was at the reading of Paul's Epistle to the Romans that God gave the increase.

During the first week of August, 386, Augustine determined to give up his profession of rhetoric to devote his life to philosophy. Since he had been under a strain due to a heavy teaching schedule and his personal identity crisis, Augustine welcomed the use of his friend Verecundus' country place at Cassiciacum for rest and study, spending the fall and early winter there with his mother, Monica, his elder brother, Navigius, his son, Adeodatus, some cousins, his friends Alypius and Evodius and two young boys sent to him for instruction. Here they pursued in a family way the philosophical life they had planned earlier. Augustine began writing in dialogue form including: *Against the Academics, On the Happy Life, On Order,* and *Soliloquies.*

These scholastic days Augustine calls *"Christianae vitae otium"* (Retract. 1, 1), which was to be his way of life till his ordination in 391. And even when bishop, Augustine followed the intellectual way at Hippo. Although the life at Cassiciacum was not yet monasticism, it was a foreshadowing. The idea of monks as Christian philosophers was not foreign to Basil, Evagrius nor later to Dardanus, a retired prefect who would turn his village in the lower Alps into a theopolis for Christian philosophers.

While enjoying his philosophical leisure, Augustine planned that after a good marriage and perhaps a term as a civil magistrate, he might retire with honor and privilege to just such a country villa for the rest of his life. We know that at the time Monica was preparing a prosperous marriage for her son. When in preparation for this Augustine broke up his common law marriage, his consort left for Africa in sorrow, remaining faithful to him to the end.

But he soon abandoned all such plans, while continuing his soul-searching as his *Soliloquies* testify. Meditating and reading Scriptures, he formally resigned his post as civil rhetorician in Milan and along with Alypius and Adeodatus presented himself to Ambrose for Baptism during the Easter Vigil (387). Rising naked as a new-born baby from the cold baptismal waters Augustine felt entirely reborn, his past life dead. From now on he was to be a monk. Immediately he went to visit Ambrose's monastery outside the city gates.

Joined by Evodius, Augustine's group now resembled a monastic community more than the philosophers' study club of Cassiciacum. They intended to return as soon as possible to Thagaste to live a semi-monastic life on the family property there — a typical family monastery as found in Basil and Macrina's foundations, the palaces of Marcella and Paula in Rome and the home of Paulinus and Theresia in Nola.

During a delay at Ostia, Monica died, having seen her wishes fulfilled in her son's conversion. Grieving, Augustine went to Rome where he visited some of the local monasteries and continued his writings. By nature Augustine was a contemplative and a writer, by force he was to be also an ecclesiastical administrator. But his great impact on Western thought comes from his meditative writings and his monasticism.

While in Rome, he became angry with the Manichaeans who arrogantly considered themselves superior to ordinary Christians because of their continence and abstinence by which the elect could approach the uncontaminated light.

In his *Morals of the Catholic Church and the Morals of the Manichaeans* (388) Augustine employs the customary apologetic manner, namely, comparing the saintly Christian way of life with the corrupt way of the Manichees. Although he praises the frugal fathers of the desert, Augustine does not tarry here since some accuse them of abandoning their fellow men, while others feel they have gone too far in their ascetical rigors. Augustine goes on to praise the cenobites who are his inspiration.

> Who can but admire and commend those who, slighting and discarding the pleasures of this world, living together in a most chaste and holy society, unite in passing their time in prayers, in readings, in discussions, without any swelling of pride, or noise of contention, or sullenness of envy; but quiet, modest and peaceful, their life is one of perfect harmony and devotion to God, an offering most acceptable to him from whom the power to do these things is obtained? No one possesses anything of his own; no one is a burden to another. They work with their hands in such occupations as may feed their bodies without distracting their minds from God (*Morals*, c. 31, n. 61) (NPNF s. 1, v. 8).

They give the products of their work to the deans, who give

them in turn what they need for their sustenance. So without temporal worries, the monks are free to contemplate. The abbot, saintly and learned, rules with humility, instructing the monks daily before the main meal. Eating frugally, they avoid wine and meat which tickle the passions. And they distribute any excess to the poor.

There are also Christian nuns.

Who serve God assiduously and chastely, living apart and removed as far as propriety demands from the men, to whom they are united only in pious affection and in imitation of virtue. No young men are allowed access to them, nor even old men, however respectable and approved, except to the porch in order to furnish necessary supplies (*Morals,* c. 32, n. 68).

The nuns weave cloth which they give to the men in exchange for food.

Although Augustine claims that he is not eulogizing the Christian ascetics, he comes very close to this. Later he will be more realistic in his *On the Work of the Monks* (400) and in *Sermons* 355 and 356, where he chastises monastic abuses.

Later in his *Morals* Augustine describes other Christian ascetics who live in urban lodging houses, presided over by a presbyter, eminent in virtue and learning, charity, holy, free, ruling in a Pauline manner. Self-supporting, they fast rigorously, sometimes going three days without food or drink. There are also pious women, widows and virgins, spinning and weaving, presided over by a prudent and experienced woman, and usually guided by a male ascetic such as Jerome or Pelagius.

The law of charity governs these Christian ascetics.

There is charity in their choice of diet, charity in their speech, charity in their dress, charity in their looks. Charity is the point where they meet, and the plan in which they act. To transgress against charity is thought criminal, like transgressing against God. Whatever opposes this is attacked and expelled; whatever injures it is not allowed to continue for a single day. They know that it has also been enjoined by Christ and the apostles; that without it all things are empty, with it all are fulfilled (c. 33, n. 73).

In 388-390 Augustine and Alypius returned to Thagaste via Carthage as servants of God, that is, good pious Christian laymen living in the house of a pious churchman. Semi-monastic, they resembled the families of ascetics in Rome and Africa described above by Augustine. In their striving for perfection in community they were the predecessors of the monks. Augustine and Alypius moved into Augustine's family home in Thagaste, starting a small community of *servi Dei* there including Adeodatus, Evodius and a few others. Augustine sold most of the family property, giving the money to the poor. They spent their days praying, fasting, meditating and studying. When Augustine encouraged others to join (L 157), Severus came, but Nebridius died as he was preparing to be with them. As the little community grew in numbers, Augustine had to enlarge the house.

The servants of God appeared differently to different people. For example, Augustine described them to Nebridius "*deificari in otio*" and not just a philosophical study club as at Cassiciacum.

At Thagaste Augustine was faced with two real problems that were to affect his whole life, namely, the antagonism of the Manichees and the Donatists, and the fear that he would be drafted for a bishopric. Thus he was careful to avoid towns in which the episcopal chair was vacant.

When Adeodatus and Nebridius died, Augustine was shaken up and determined to organize the community beyond their present leisurely contemplation. Gradually the servants of God took on a monastic hue with Augustine as superior and a semblance of order.

When Augustine went to Hippo in 391 to talk to a friend about his vocation, the people drafted him for the presbyterial office so great was his reputation in learning and piety. Although he submitted humbly to the will of the people, Augustine always remained a monk at heart.

At Hippo with Bishop Valerius' permission, Augustine founded a monastery in the episcopal garden for his servants of God, living according to the rule established by the apostles with the main emphasis on poverty as the early Jerusalem Christians. This had been Augustine's ideal ever since his projected philosophical study club in Milan, which had been forestalled by the *mulierculae*. All things were to be held in common with no one having anything for himself, but only receiving what was needed from the one in charge. This had been their practice also at Thagaste.

One of the great attractions of religious communism for Augustine was the mutual support of the brethren in the hard road to chastity, for he knew himself and his weakness for the fairer sex. Since married priests and bishops were still quite common, Augustine and his friends could preserve their continence by the safeguard of the common life, with the brethren keeping an eye on each other, giving good example and encouragement.

Augustine was joined in his Hippo community by Alypius and Evodius from Thagaste, Possidius, his biographer, and others (L 158). Since Augustine always remained a professional educator, his monastery soon became a center of learning, training many of his followers to be presbyters and bishops in neighboring dioceses.

With the blessing of his bishop, Augustine preached, taught and catechized. For example, he impressed the assembled bishops at the council of Hippo (393) with his address on *Faith and the Creed*. His community not only received the full support of Valerius, but also of Aurelius, archbishop of Carthage and primate of Africa. Many intelligent government officials and well educated Romans joined in contrast to the simple local Donatist and Catholic clerics. Already was beginning the exodus of the intelligentsia from Rome to Africa in the face of the collapsing empire. Paulinus of Nola would see in Augustine's community, the kernel of a revolution in African church history as Augustine and his intellectual friends began to occupy the African sees.

Even after he was consecrated bishop in 395-396 Augustine continued to live with his community in the episcopal house which served as a center of contemplation, catechesis, a teaching seminary and parish hub. Always the rhetorician, Augustine had his clerical students learn secular authors, the Bible and church writers.

Augustine's community differed radically from the lay monasteries of the East. He and his servants of God by force of circumstances had become clerics, the predecessors of later clerical orders and canons, and in a sense the whole pattern of the Western clergy, celibate, reciting office, living in rectories for mutual support. Other contemporary Western bishops had fostered clerical communism, for example, Eusebius of Vercelli, Martin of Tours, Ambrose of Milan, Victricius of Ruen, Paulinus of Nola, Germain of Auxerre. Augustine also founded monasteries for lay men and lay women, his sister ruling over the latter with his guidance.

Augustine never lorded his authority over his community, but ruled by charity assisted by deacons in charge of the refectory, laundry, library and infirmary. He accepted all classes of applicants, rich and poor. While the rich should practice humility in their obedience, the poor should not use their new status to stimulate their pride. All should keep busy with physical or intellectual work to support themselves.

Clothing, food, etc. in Augustine's home was of modest proportions. Although his table was generally frugal, he served vegetables, meat and herbs for guests or the sick. And he always had wine, as Possidius writes, "Because he knew and taught, as the Apostle says, 'Every creature of God is good and nothing is to be rejected that is received with thanksgiving; for it is sanctified by the word of God and prayer'" (*Life of Augustine* c. 12). He also quoted Paul's advice to Timothy, namely, that a little wine is good for the stomach (1 Tim 5:23). Probably his life at Hippo did not differ greatly from that at Thagaste and Cassiciacum, except for an occasional splurge for visiting prelates.

Sometimes his sister would send over some goodies in thanks for the services of Augustine and his community.

At table Augustine the teacher preferred reading and discussion to idle chatter. He had a plaque placed over the table, forbidding gossip, "Whoever loves to rip the lives of absent brethren, let him know that this table is not for him" (*Life of Augustine* c. 22).[1] When one of his episcopal friends violated the rule, Augustine corrected him, saying that either the motto should be taken down or Augustine would leave the table.

Augustine's companions wore a black habit, with a cincture and a chasuble in bad weather. They shaved their heads and visited the public baths only to wash the sick and then in the presence of companions.

He assiduously kept all women from his house, for he knew his own weakness and, no doubt, remembered how the girls had broken his early plans in Milan. He did not even allow his widowed sister and his servant of God nieces to enter his house, although the canons allowed close relatives to live with clerics. Augustine agreed with the monks of the desert, namely, if you let one woman in, others will inevitably follow, for his sister and her daughters would require female servants. And not only would he and his clerical companions be tempted, but there would be a wagging of tongues. Augustine himself never even spoke to a woman without a clerical witness. Since the union of the sexes is a natural state, any attempt at separation must be surrounded by hedges of all sorts. Early western councils as Rome (386) c. 9; Turin (398) c. 8; Toledo (400) c. 1; Carthage (401) c. 4, were constantly concerned with clerical continence based at least partially on Jewish and pagan sacerdotal customs. Since clerical marriage was still in practice, probably many of Augustine's clerics were separated from their wives as Augustine himself separated from his consort.

Since he left the care of the church and house to capable

---

1. "Quisquis amat dictis absentum rodere vitam, hanc mensam indignam noverit esse sibi."

assistants, Augustine was free to devote his life to contemplation and intellectual pursuits according to his earliest dream in Milan.

Also following the Milan ideal, he insisted on community of goods according to the Acts of the Apostles (4:32): "Now the company of those who believed were of one heart and soul, and no one said that any of the things which he possessed was his own, but they had everything in common." And any violations were handled severely in the light of Peter's judgment of Ananias and Sapphira (Acts 5:1-11). In other words, in handing over one's property, nothing should be held back for a rainy day.

In sermons 355 and 356 Augustine outlines the rigors of his communism according to the apostolic norm (S. 355).

> The common life's exemplar is found among the first Christians. Augustine's monastery was first in the garden, then in the episcopal house. In a humble place safety is found, but in a high place, danger. Since the monastic life is in common, to hold anything as one's own is forbidden. I will not hold you long, since I am sitting, while you stand. All, or at least most of you know that we so live in the episcopal house as far as possible imitating the saints spoken of in the Acts of the Apostles (4:32) (c. 1, n. 2).

Augustine proceeds to give an apology of his monastic way.

> I who by the grace of God am your bishop, came as a young man to this city, as many of you know. I was looking for a place to start a monastery to live with my brothers, leaving every hope of the world and cutting off my options. I certainly did not seek to be what I am. "I would rather be a doorkeeper in the house of my God than dwell in the tents of wickedness" (Ps 84:10). Although I cut myself off from those who love the world, I did not make myself equal to the rulers of the people. Nor did I choose a higher place in the Lord's banquet, but a lower one. And it pleased him to say, rise up higher....

> I began to collect brothers of good intention, my equals,

having nothing as I had nothing. They imitated me. As I sold my small poverty and gave to the poor so did those who desired to be with me so that we could live in common. Together we possessed a large and productive estate, namely, God himself... (c.1, n.2).

See how we live. It is not permitted in our society for any one to have anything of his own. But perhaps some do have their own things, though this is not permitted. But if they have them, they act illicitly. I like my brothers and always believe well of them so I try to avoid any sort of inquisition, which would seem bad to me (c.2, n.2).

Although all the brothers knew of the agreement, some did not keep strict poverty. For example, Januarius, a presbyter, kept his property against the law of the monastery. He held back some money which he said was for his daughter who was in a convent. He actually made a will as he approached death, but Augustine would not accept the inheritance in the name of the church. Violaters of poverty were sent away from the monastery, but not deprived of their clerichood, for to simulate the agreement of sanctity is worse than to abandon it.

As all the Church Fathers, Augustine constantly quoted Scriptures on behalf of his decisions and in defense of his way of life. Besides the passage from the *Acts of the Apostles* (4:32) about having all things in common, Augustine found a favorite patristic theme in Psalm 132 (133) (c.f. Basil, LR 7).

Behold how good and pleasant it is when brothers dwell in unity. It is like precious oil upon the head, running down upon the beard, upon the beard of Aaron, running down the collar of his robes. It is like the dew of Hermon, which falls upon the mountains of Zion. For there the Lord has commanded the blessing, life for ever more.

Augustine applies the psalm to the monks:

These same words of the psalter, this sweet sound, that honeyed melody even beget the monasteries. By this sound were stirred up the brethren who longed to dwell together. This verse was their trumpet. It sounded through the whole earth, and they who had been divided were gathered together (On Psalm 132 [133], 5) (NPNF, sl, v8).

The early Christians answered the call, holding all things in common. Augustine continues:

Since the psalm says "Behold how good and pleasant it is when brothers dwell in unity" why then should we not call monks so? For *monos* is "one." Not one in any manner, for a man in a crowd is one, but though he can be called one along with others, he cannot be *monos*, that is, alone, as to make one man, so that they really possess what is written "One mind and one heart" (Acts 4:32), many bodies, but not many minds; many bodies, but not many hearts, they can rightly be called *monos*, that is, one alone (On Psalm 132 [133] 5).

The ointment of the Holy Spirit descended on the beard of Aaron, on the Christian apostles. So the dew of Christ makes a monk peaceable, quiet, submissive, prayerful and not murmuring like noisy cartwheels bearing their burden of straw. True, the murmurers dwell together, but only in body. Those who really dwell together are of one mind and heart towards God (Eccl 33:5). "Because there the Lord commanded blessing. Where did he command it? Among the brethren who dwell together. There he enjoined blessing, there they who dwell with one heart bless God, for you bless not God in division of heart" (On Psalm 132 [133]:9).

Unity is the very essence of monasticism as it is of the Church. Just as the early Fathers from Paul to Clement and Ignatius urged Church unity, so Augustine as monastic founders before and after counseled unity of the monks. And whenever he found a brother disrupting the community, he asked him to leave. For example, Boniface accused a younger monk, Spes, of making disgusting propositions, but when Spes turned the tables, Boniface resigned from the community to avoid a greater scandal, although Augustine kept his name on the diptychs. Nevertheless, a large scandal arose over this in Hippo.

African monasticism had its dissident elements. Some monk-like enthusiasts were the Donatist circumcellions, wandering from place to place without home or rule. They resemble the *gyrovagi*, the roadrunners of the East who may have been descendants of the earlier peripatetic prophet-apostles. Councils and Fathers cried out against the circumcellions who in their defense of Donatus, robbed, beat, and did violence under the pretext of religion. Augustine writes, "I see indeed marvelous works, the daily violences of the circumcellions (*circum cellas rusticorum ientes*), with the bishops and presbyters for their leaders, flying about in every direction, and calling their terrible clubs 'Israels' which men now living see and feel" (On Psalm 10 [11]:5) (Also On Psalm 54 [55]:25; On Psalm 132 [133]:3; *Life of Augustine* c.10). They spared no one, not even their own people, depriving them of their civil rights, robbing, injuring, torturing, throwing vinegar and lime into their eyes. They were especially vindictive towards Donatists who converted to the Catholic Church. Petilian, one of their leaders, calumniated the monasteries, accusing Augustine as the founder of African monasticism (*Against the Letters of Petilian* 3:48).

About the year 400 Aurelius, archbishop of Carthage, asked Augustine to write against a growing monastic problem in Carthage and perhaps elsewhere, namely, wandering monks, who seem to have been orthodox in contrast to the anarchistic circumcellions. Rejecting the established manner of life which included working for a living, they preferred to beg, relying on the Lord according to Matthew (6:26), "Look to the birds of the air. They neither sow nor reap nor gather into barns, and yet your heavenly father feeds them." Wandering from place to place, they sold relics, begging, with long hair and disheveled appearance. Many examples of shipwrecked lives joined their ranks.

Paul, writing to the Millenarian Thessalonians (2 Thes 3:10) said, "If any man will not work, let him not eat." But the lazy monks took this in a spiritual sense so that they could avoid physical work with impunity. But Augustine argues in his *On the Work of the Monks* that Paul's own example taught his followers to work for a living (2 Thes 3:7-12).

> For you yourselves know how you ought to imitate us. We were not idle when we were with you, we did not eat any one's bread without paying. But with toil and labor we worked night and day, that we might not burden any of you. It was not because we have not that right, but to give you in our conduct an example to imitate, for even when we were with you, we gave you this command: if any one will not work, let him not eat. For we hear that some of you are living in idleness, mere busybodies not doing any work. Now such persons we command and exhort in the Lord Jesus Christ to do their work in quietness and to earn their own living. Brethren, do not be weary of well-doing.

It seems that some of the Thessalonians, perhaps misinterpreting earlier directives of Paul, were sitting by idly awaiting the imminent eschaton.

Although Paul could have lived off the gospel as the other apostles did and as the Lord permitted, he rather chose to earn his own way as a tent-maker (*On the Work of the Monks* 12-13). The lazy monks claim that they need leisure for prayer, psalms, reading and preaching, but they can chant while working (17). Augustine is sympathetic with the wealthy monks who find it hard to work, but also those from peasant backgrounds seek excuses (21-22).

> In this Christian campaign for holiness, the rich are not humiliated so that the poor can be lifted up to haughtiness.

It is not at all fitting that, in a mode of life where senators become laborers, workmen should become men of leisure;
that peasants should be pampered in the monastery to which
those who were masters of estates have abandoned all their
goods (25) (FOC 16).

It seems that plebians were sometimes drawn towards the monastic life of ease and since monkhood was an honor, for them
it was a step up their social ladder. The monks, then, should
not tempt God by their indolence.

If through any infirmity or occupation we are not able to
work, God feeds and clothes us as he provides for the birds
and the lilies which perform no labor of this sort. But, when
we are able to work, we ought not to tempt our God, because
it is by his gift that we are able to do what we do, and
because, while we live on this earth, we live by his bounty,
since he has made our existence possible (27).

Augustine criticizes the hypocrites who go around in monks'
garb, wandering through the provinces without home or stable
existence. Some sell relics, either real or spurious. Others enlarge
their fringes or phylacteries as the Pharisees. Still others say
that they are searching for their parents or relatives whom they
have heard are living in distant places, begging rewards for their
destitution and pretended piety. When apprehended for their
evil ways, they discredit the whole family of monks.

Embarrassed at his own situation, Augustine apologizes that
he is too busy to do manual labor and sometimes feels too weak
physically.

So far as I am concerned, I would much prefer to do some
manual labor at certain hours each day as is the custom in
well-regulated monasteries and to have other hours free for
reading, prayer or for study of the sacred Scriptures than

to endure the very confusing perplexities of the problems of others in regard to worldly concerns which must be eliminated by our judgments or curtail our action (29).

Not only are the lazy monks tolerated, but are acclaimed as more righteous for their indolence. "So that monasteries established on wholesome principles are corrupted by a two-fold evil, the lazy license of leisure and the unmerited name of holiness" (30).

Many of these monks, so like the modern hippies, anti-social and lazy, also sported long flowing locks. And just as today, their Samson's manes drove some people wild. True, the Nazarites, the early Jewish predecessors of the monks, let their hair grow and, indeed, some of the Eastern Christian monks did likewise. But the custom was repugnant to clean-shaven Romans. Paul warned, "For a man to wear his hair long is degrading" (1 Cor 11:14). But the recalcitrant monks claimed that this did not apply to them since they were not men, but eunuchs for Christ. Though Paul was also a eunuch for Christ, he still advocated short hair. Augustine mourned that now even some of the good monks were adopting the new style, but they should stop lest they give scandal and cause contentions (33).

B. Augustine and the Virgins

Another and more serious problem in monasticism was the increasing attacks on virginity. For example, Jovinian, an ex-monk, preaching against the monastic life in the latter part of the fourth century, persuaded many monks and nuns to leave the cloister. He was condemned by Pope Siricius (389) and by the bishops assembled in Milan under Ambrose.

Jovinian claimed that those who advocated virginity were not saying anything different from the Manichees who condemned marriage. There is no doubt that there were parallels between heterodox dualism, disdaining the flesh and marriage and orthodox asceticism. In general, however, the orthodox looked upon man's passions not as evil in themselves, but rather in a weakened state due to man's sinful nature.

Since Jovinian felt that his accusations could only be answered by a condemnation of marriage, the wiley Augustine wrote first his *On the Good of Marriage* (401), then his *On Holy Virginity* (401). Because Jovinian had attacked Mary's virginity, claiming it was lost in the birth of Christ, Augustine started out in her defense, teaching that Mary was a vowed virgin who remained so throughout her entire life. She is the virgin mother of the Church, which is Christ's body. And the virginal Church is spiritually the mother of Christ in his members through Baptism. Likewise the consecrated virgin of the Church has a spiritual motherhood in union with Christ by bringing souls to eternal life in charity.

In the second part of his *On Holy Virginity* Augustine urges the Christian virgins to follow the Lamb wherever he goes (Apoc 14:2-4).

> Press on, then, saints of God, youths and maidens, men and women, celibates and virgins, press on unflaggingly toward the goal! Praise the Lord more sweetly, to whom your thoughts are more fully devoted! Hope in him more eagerly, whom you serve more eagerly! Love him more ardently whom you please more carefully, with loins girt, and lamps lit, await the Lord, when he returns from the wedding (c.27) (FOC 27).

Follow the virginal lamb away from the deceits of the world to far reaching and difficult pastures.

However, Augustine wisely warns, "Many things in him are proposed to all for imitation, but virginity of the flesh is not proposed to all for there is nothing they can do to become virgins whom it has befallen not to be virgins" (c.28). Although the multitude of the faithful will not be able to follow, they will rejoice with the virgins (c.29) in following the Lamb, not avoiding a forbidden marriage, but rising above a lawful one.

Yet the virgin must follow the humble Christ, for a trait of virginity is a tendency to pride (31).

Augustine chastises the false virgins who really want to marry, but do not out of fear of scandal or notoriety (34). Others dress in a worldly and immodest manner with unusual head-dresses and fancy hair-dos showing through thin veils and proud of their calling.

Christ is the model of virginal integrity and humility. It was not iniquity but charity that made him humble. A virgin should always live in humble fear lest she fall from her vocation. As today, numbers of virgins in Augustine's time left to marry. "Is it to be thought that God permits that many men and women who will fall away be included in the ranks of your profession for anything else than that by their fall your fear may be increased and by it pride may be crushed?" (40).

This brings up the important relationship of virginity and widowhood to marriage. Which is better? What about the virgin who leaves to marry? Is she not choosing the inferior way? Some even accused her of adultery. Augustine responds in his letter to Juliana, *On the Good of Widowhood* (414) (FOC 16).

> The marriages of such persons are not in themselves deserving of condemnation. What is condemned is the abandonment of purpose, the violation of the vow; not the choice of an inferior good, but the fall from a higher good. Finally such persons are condemned, not for having contracted marriage, but for having broken their first troth of continence (9).

But he would not accuse them of adultery.

> It is impossible for me to admit that women who marry after abandoning a more perfect state do not contract a valid marriage, but commit adultery. I do not hesitate to say plainly that the abandonment and the violation of a holier chastity pledged to the Lord is worse than adultery. If we must believe that it is an offense against Christ for one of his members to be unfaithful to her husband, how much more

grievous is the offense when faith is not kept with Him in
the observance of that chastity which he claims when it has
been offered, but which he did not require to be offered.
The iniquity of infidelity to the vow, which was made not
by force of a command, but by the invitation of a counsel,
is increased by the fact that there was no necessity in the
first place to make the vow that has been broken (11).

Let us return to Augustine's *On Holy Virginity* where he
continually exhorts the virgins to humility, "Let the first thought
of the virgin of God be to be filled with humility lest she think
that it comes to her from herself that she is such and not think
rather that this best gift comes from above" (41). Wisdom is
necessary to recognize continence as a gift of God. "Whoever
remains chaste from the beginning is ruled by him, and whoever
is made chaste from impurity is corrected by him, and whoever
is unchaste to the very end is abandoned by him" (42). All of this
he accomplishes by a mysterious judgment to increase fear on
our part and diminish our pride.

As the Roman Vestals, the Christian virgins were honored
in the liturgy and outside as well. But the virgin must humbly
acknowledge God's gift and not exalt herself over others. And
this is to be a real humility, for feigned humility is worse than
pride. Although virginity should be considered above marriage,
"Nevertheless let not this or that obedient and God-fearing virgin
presume to set herself above this or that obedient and God-
fearing wife. Otherwise she will not be humble, and God resists
the proud" (44). The virgin should be the chaste symbol of the
pure Church united to one spouse. Let the virgins follow the
Lamb in purity, truthfulness and humility (49), for he will exalt
those who follow him humbly (52).

There had been many letters and treatises on virginity by
John Chrysostom, Ambrose, Jerome and others, but Augustine's
tract seems so balanced, especially when taken along with his
On the Good of Marriage. Not a virgin himself, Augustine was
perhaps better able to evaluate virginity objectively as a gift

humbly received and not a Pelagian victory of the will over the sex appetites.

There were many convents of virgins in North Africa in Augustine's day. Since Roman women were not allowed in the professions, the convents were the logical gathering places for old maids, widows and virgins. Some young nuns were freed slave girls, while others were daughters of the rich.

Augustine's own widowed sister headed a convent in Hippo, another example of the brother and sister combinations which sparkle throughout the history of monasticism. When his sister retired as superioress, the new abbess encountered some opposition, evidently after ruling for some time. In 423 Augustine wrote a letter (L 211) to the community urging them not to remove their leader who had been in the community so long, who had trained many of them and loved them as a mother. Was their new spiritual director at fault? If so, he probably was a member of Augustine's own community.

The first part of the letter (1-4) is an *objurgatio* or reproof of the erring sisters. Since the earliest MSS follow this with "explicit," Augustine's Rule (5-16) which follows may have been a later addition to the letter. But it very likely was the rule obeyed by his community and, *mutatis mutandis,* also by his sister's convent. It is more of a mode of conduct than an organized rule.

Above all Augustine pleads for unity, having all things in common, with the superior distributing food and clothing according to need (Acts 4:32, 35). The rich nuns should give their goods to the common stock. Poorer members should fear lest they become puffed up, while the rich should not look down on the poorer sisters.

Prayer is essential to the religious life and it should be had at the proper time in the oratory, meditating on the verses of Scriptures. Fasting and abstinence are encouraged with due regard for health. Reading should be had at table so that soul and body can be nourished together.

But due care should be had for those who are used to delicate fare and a more luxurious way of life so they are allowed modifications in food, dress, bedding, etc. The more robust peasants should not be jealous of the weaker rich girls. This double standard may have led to the contentions mentioned above.

The clothing of the sisters should be modest with a net covering all their hair. When they go out they are to be accompanied by a companion. "If your eyes glance at any one, let them rest upon no one, for you are not forbidden to look at men when you go out, but to desire them or to wish to be desired by them." The unchaste eye is the messenger of the unchaste heart. Although she may escape the notice of men, the Observer from above sees all. The nun with wandering glance should be corrected fraternally.

Clothing should be especially cared for by those in charge. Religious should not be concerned about wearing some one else's clothing from the common stock. However, Augustine allowed for feminine desires, for if some one insisted on wearing the same dress she had before, at least it was to be kept in the common room when not in use. The common good must always precede the individual so any gifts from relatives or friends must be turned in for the use of all.

Clothes should be washed but not abstemiously so. Baths may be taken once a month, and for the sick more often. They should go to the public baths in threes according to the choice of the superior. Those put in charge of the storeroom, wardrobe and library should serve without complaint.

Quarrels should be avoided, but they are inevitable and should be quickly patched up. The sister who never asks pardon really has no place in the monastery. Mutual love should reign but without any carnal overtones.

The superior is to be obeyed as a mother and should not fail to correct the lapsed. In matters outside her jurisdiction she should consult the chaplain. "Let her esteem herself happy, not in having power to rule, but in having charity to serve. Let her be set over you in honor before men; before God let her be beneath your feet." She should reprimand the loud, encourage the feeble-minded and weak — above all patient — seeking rather to be loved than to be feared. The sisters should be obedient and considerate, realizing that the position of superior has a higher risk.

"May the Lord grant you to observe these regulations with love, as souls whose affections are set on spiritual beauty, whose good conduct is fragrant with the good order of Christ, not as a bondswoman under the law, but as a free woman established under grace." These rules should be read aloud to all once a week to keep them fresh in mind.

Several rules today carry the name of Augustine. Besides the *Regula Puellarum* (RP) of L 211, there is the *Regula Virorum* (RV), probably the original rule of Augustine's monastery in Hippo, the *Regula Consensoria* (C) from sixth to eighth century Spain, and the *Disciplina Monasterii* (DM) written by Augustine for the monks of Thagaste. Augustine's Rule (RV) is cited by Caesarius of Arles (sixth century), Benedict, Isidore of Seville, Benedict of Aniane and others. It was used by European canons from the eleventh century. Approved by the Fourth Lateran Council (1198-1216) it was adopted by Dominic Guzman and also the thirteenth century Augustinians. No less than one hundred fifty groups follow Augustine's rule today.

C. Augustine and Pelagius

Another problem that arose from the monk-like servants of God, stimulating Augustine's problem-centered theology, was the teachings of Pelagius. Probably from Britain, this peripatetic servant of God made his mark in Rome, Carthage and Jerusalem. His principle of self-discipline was the cornerstone of ascetical practice going back to the *apatheia* of the Stoics, Origen and Evagrius. In this struggle for perfection Pelagianism, asceticism and monasticism had something in common.

The history of asceticism seems equally balanced between the radicals and the orthodox. For example, the Encratists, Montanists, Euchites, Donatists, Pelagians were all seeking perfection and highly critical of contemporary church morals. As many of these, Pelagius exaggerated man's innate goodness and capabilities for perfection. Monasticism, of course, had similar origins and ambitions, but was kept within the bounds of reason by men like Antony, Athanasius, Pachomius, Basil, Jerome, Augustine, John Cassian, Benedict and others.

Pelagius came to Rome from Britain about the same time Augustine arrived there. He was highly virtuous, ascetic, well-educated, an excellent writer and esteemed by many around the Mediterranean area. Some such as Paulinus of Nola, Sulpicius Severus and Juliana thought of him as a saint. Later when Augustine and Jerome were attacking him, eighteen Italian bishops rose to the defense.

In the new ascetical movement of the times prominent and sometimes wealthy lay men and women put their palaces at the disposal of the great ascetics, for example, Jerome, Augustine and Pelagius. Pelagius joined his rich friends in studying Paul, writing letters to encourage their asceticism. There is evidence that there was a certain rivalry for the direction of the rich widows, just as there is today.

Pelagius' rigorous tenet was: if perfection is possible, it is obligatory. With no doubts about man's capabilities, he felt that by the use of his own free will and a certain Stoic asceticism one might reach a state where he would be beyond sinning. Since man's nature is a gift of God and basically good, he is free to choose between good and evil and so ultimately achieve his salvation. Pelagius is basically anti-Manichaean. This is why he uses Augustine's anti-Manichaean work *On Free Choice* in his own *On Nature* in which he wrote against the toleration of sin as human weakness.

Fleeing the sack of Alaric (410) Pelagius went to Africa briefly, then on to the Holy Land, while his disciple Coelestius remained behind to stir up Africa, challenging the heredity of Adam's sin and the necessity of infant Baptism and condemned by the bishops at Carthage (411).

Pelagius had a good number of followers who read and circulated his letters and works, forming Pelagian study groups in many places throughout the empire. With Rome decadent,

Christianity mediocre, and invasions imminent, the ground was well prepared for Pelagius' seeds. As Brown writes,[1a]

> While some might be driven into retirement by such catastrophes, the Pelagians seemed determined to turn outwards, to reform the whole Christian Church. This is the remarkable feature of their movement. The narrow stream of perfectionism that had driven the noble followers of Jerome to Bethlehem and had led Paulinus to Nola and Augustine from Milan to a life of poverty in Africa, is suddenly turned outwards in the Pelagian writings to embrace the whole Christian church.

In his ceaseless striving after perfection Pelagius wanted all Christians to be monks (*To Demetrias* 10). In this he resembled other Christian heterodoxies such as the Euchites.

Augustine saw in Pelagius' zeal for a perfect church a similarity to Donatism which claimed to be the true, pure and uncorrupted Christianity. Brown comments,[2] "The victory of Augustine over Pelagius was also a victory for the average good Catholic layman of the later empire over an austere, reforming ideal." Augustine preferred his ordinary believing Roman Christian who sometimes had intercourse with his wife purely for the pleasure, who was given to anger and quibbling over his property rights, to Pelagius' ascetic without faith (*Against Two Letters of the Pelagians* 3:14) (420).

Pelagius' disciples as Juliana, Melania the Younger and Pinian had broken with Roman society by sheer will power. They felt that the evils of the Roman world lay not within the natures of people which were good, but in external society in need of reform. Job was the hero of the Pelagians, asserting his rugged individuality against evil contemporary society. Pelagius tried to persuade his rich Roman friends to abandon their wealth, giving all to the poor. But when Melania and Pinian fled to Africa, Aur-

1a. **Augustine of Hippo,** University of California Press, Berkeley, 1967, p. 347.

2. **Ibid.,** p. 348.

elius, Augustine and Alypius persuaded them to endow monasteries rather than give all to the destitute.

Whereas Pelagius had put all his emphasis on man's responsibility for sin, Augustine was more realistic, reflecting his own experience, in stressing innate human weakness. Answering Pelagius' *On Nature*, Augustine wrote *On Nature and Grace* (415), asserting that man's nature, due to the fall of Adam, is weak and sinful and so in need of grace to reconcile him to God and lead him to righteousness. Moreover, this grace is not given because of any human right, but purely out of God's graciousness. Pelagius thought that it was possible for a man to live without sin, since his nature had not been weakened by sin. But Augustine accused him of replacing grace by nature. Man's nature, said Augustine, is weakened by sin and so necessitated to sin without the help of God's grace. Furthermore, by minimizing the necessity of grace and church, Pelagius had minimized the distinction between a good Christian and a good pagan.

It was the adverse influence of Pelagius that prompted Augustine to write his *On the Excellence of Widowhood* (414) to the widow Juliana of the great and influential family of the Anicii Probi. When her father-in-law, Probus, died, her mother-in-law Proba had consecrated her widowhood to God, founding a community of widows and virgins in Rome. She was known to both Augustine and Jerome and with Juliana defended the cause of John Chrysostom.

When Alaric invaded Rome (410), Proba, Juliana, and Juliana's daughter Demetrias fled to Carthage where they were promptly imprisoned by Count Heraclian and forced to pay a huge tax. Juliana joined her mother-in-law's community and when Demetrias also joined at the urging of Augustine (L 188), the Roman world was amazed. At the request of Juliana, Pelagius wrote to Demetrias to encourage her. Angry that Pelagius was invading his field of spiritual guidance to rich widows, Jerome implied that he was after their money (L 133).

Augustine in his *On the Excellence of Widowhood* warns Juliana against Pelagius without mentioning him by name. But she never lost her admiration for her mentor. "Your Priesthood knows that I and my little household are far removed from persons of that kind. All our family follow the Catholic faith so closely that we have never fallen into any heresy, nor even lapsed into any sect which seems to have even small errors, much less those which are outside the pale" (Quoted in Augustine's L 188) (418). Besides the advice on virginity and widowhood mentioned above, Augustine cautioned the little community that their decision to give themselves to Christ was not self-made due to their strength of will as Pelagius would have it, but rather a divine calling to a more blessed life, urging them to lead others by their good example and to read thoroughly his own work *On Holy Virginity.*

Although Pelagianism seemed to have been laid to rest by Augustine and Jerome, councils as Carthage (416) and Milevis (418) and popes such as Innocent I and Zozimus, we find the anti-Pelagian writings of Augustine causing consternation in the monasteries a decade or so later. As we have seen, Pelagianism had much in common with monasticism, especially the Origenist-Evagrian line in which the monk hopes to attain perfection by virtue of his austerities and spiritual exercises much as an athlete perfects himself for the games. Many monasteries around the Mediterranean such as Hadrumetum in Africa, Marseilles and Lérins in Gaul reflected these Eastern trends. Moreover, many of them in true monastic tradition were either ignorant of or opposed to the episcopal decisions and writings.

For example, two monks from Hadrumetum, Florus and Felix, on a visit to Uzala came upon a copy of Augustine's anti-Pelagian letter to Sixtus (L 194) (418), stressing the necessity of divine grace, human weakness and predestination. Since bishop Evodius of Uzala had been a disciple of Augustine, he undoubtedly had most of his works available in his library. Making a copy of the letter, the two monks brought it back to Hadrumetum, where the monks were horrified at Augustine's teaching on predestination for they felt that it destroyed man's free will.

Abbot Valentinus of Hadrumetum promptly wrote to Evodius and also to a presbyter Januarius seeking advice in the matter. Evodius replied affirming free will, but maintaining that it had been weakened by original sin. Man can freely choose God but only with his grace. Also Evodius recommended intellectual humility in these difficult matters.

Some of the monks of Hadrumetum went right to Augustine for advice. In reply he wrote letters 214 and 215 and also his *On Grace and Free Choice*, showing the monks that God's grace is perfectly compatible with man's free will. God works in man's heart to incline his will whichever way he wishes.

> The grace of God is always good and by it comes to pass that a man is of good will, though he was before of an evil one. By it also it comes to pass that the very good will which has now begun to be, is enlarged, and made so great that it is able to fulfill the divine commandments which it shall wish, when it shall once firmly and perfectly wish (31).

But one of the monks reacted, saying that if God controls man's will, there is no guilt in man when he sins. Rather than correcting him, we should pray that he receives the right grace. Augustine retorted with his *On Rebuke and Grace* (427). Since God's will is inscrutable, we cannot fathom his gifts. Because we do not know who is predestined and who is not, we should rebuke all who sin lest they perish or cause the ruin of others.

There also was a reaction to Augustine in southern Gaul which we will discuss more in detail in the next chapter. These monks rejected predestination and insisted that man could and should take the first steps towards his salvation. Certainly the Evagrian asceticism of St. Victor and the missionary zeal of the Gaulic monks based on the universal salvific will of God seemed at best incompatible with Augustine's predestination. But the Gaulic monks were just as firmly anti-Pelagian, strongly asserting the necessity of God's grace.

But as Brown comments,[3] Augustine never intended his predestination to lead to quietism.

A monk might waste his leisure worrying about his ultimate

3. **Augustine**, pp. 403-404.

identity. To Augustine, such an anxiety was misplaced. A doctrine of predestination divorced from action, was inconceivable to him. He had never written to deny freedom, merely to make it more effective in the harsh environment of a fallen world.

As Augustine wrote his final treatises on the matter, *Predestination of the Saints* and *The Gift of Perseverance* (428-429), his eschaton approached as did that of Africa with the Vandal invasions. Although his doctrine of predestination had, indeed, shaken up the monks, to his dying day Augustine looked upon it as a message of confidence and assurance that God alone is man's salvation.

In conclusion, we have seen that Augustine as many of his intellectual contemporaries was inclined to a common life of leisure contemplating the truth. He had planned it at Milan and come close to it at Cassiciacum. After his conversion he became sold on monasticism, inspired by the *Life of Antony* and the monks of Milan and Rome. He and his fellow servants of God led a semi-monastic existence in the family home at Thagaste. When he went to Hippo to found a monastery, he was reluctantly ordained first presbyter and then bishop. Remaining a monk in spirit, he turned his bishop's house into a clerical-seminary-monastery. He did much to defend and correct African monasticism and also fathered along with some of his contemporary bishops a type of clerical monasticism the results of which can still be seen in the Western clergy. If he and his friend Jerome objected to any type of monasticism, it was the Origenist-Evagrian-Pelagian type which seemed to put the burden on man's own efforts toward salvation, at least in the beginning of his spiritual life to achieve a certain Stoic *apatheia*. Augustine rightly challenged: how does this differ from pagan asceticism? Perhaps as some of these ascetics over-played the part of man, Augustine in his anti-Pelagian works seemed to over-play the part of God in salvation. John Cassian's Conference thirteen seems to strike a balance as we will see in the following chapter.

7. Be Pleased, O God, To Deliver Me: O Lord, Make Haste To Help Me

(*John Cassian, Psalm* 69 [70] *in Conference* 10:10)

A. Early Gaulic Monks

In the last chapter we saw Augustine's differences with some of the African and Gaulic monks. Although at the time of his conversion Augustine was attracted to Egyptian monasticism, praising the Italian monks against the corrupt Manichees, his later anti-Pelagian works, placing all the emphasis on God, seemed to weaken, at least implicitly, the importance of ascetical practices.

In this chapter we hope to take a closer look at some of the Egyptian and Syrian influenced Gaulic monks who rejected Augustine as an innovator whose exaggeration of man's fallen state and whose teaching on predestination were undermining the

141

monastic spirit. By the end of the fourth century monasteries of
both sexes flourished in Italy and southern Gaul especially at
Marseilles and in the islands. Also there were some peripatetic
Sarabaites who caused trouble wherever they went.

Martin (316-399) is generally considered the father of Gaulic
monasticism. He was born in Sabaria, now in Hungary, where
his father was a commander of a cohort of the Roman army.
When his family moved to Pavia in northern Italy, Martin became
a catechumen at the age of ten and felt drawn towards the life
of the local ascetics. To get him away from these foolish ideas,
his father enrolled him in the army. While he was serving at
Amiens in Gaul occurred the famous legend in which he parted
his cloak for a naked beggar. When Jesus appeared to him that
night clothed in his half-cloak, Martin hastened to Baptism,
wishing to retire from the world to begin a new life. Although
he would fulfill his military term, he explained his wishes to
Caesar, "Hitherto I have served you as a soldier. Allow me now
to become a soldier of God. Let the man who is to serve thee
receive thy donative. Since I am a soldier of Christ, it is not
lawful for me to fight" (*Life of Martin* 4). When his courage was
questioned, Martin offered to go into battle unarmed, protected
only by Jesus Christ.

At last released from service, Martin went to Hilary, bishop
of Poitiers, who conferred minor orders on the reluctant candidate.
Then he returned to convert his parents. But growing Arian
power soon forced both Hilary and his friend Martin into exile.
Martin escaped first to a monastery in Milan, then to the semi-
desert island of Gallinaria near Genoa.

When Hilary returned to Poitiers in 360, Martin followed,
founding the monastery of Ligugé outside the city gates, traditionally considered the oldest in Gaul. From here he was drawn
unwillingly to be made bishop of Tours.

Although he fought against pagan Druids and Christian
Arians, he was opposed to the violent treatment of heretics. Amid
the cares of ruling a diocese, and still longing for the ascetical
life, Martin founded a monastery at Marmoutier (either *Martini
monasterium*, or *majus monasterium*). There he lived in a simple

cell made of branches, with his companions dwelling as semi-hermits in the nearby rocks. They followed no definite rules, but led austere lives, confined to their cells except for common prayer and meals, reminiscent of the eastern laurae. Their rough clothing included a black cloak (*pallium*) and a camel's hair cassock as the eastern monks. The younger monks transcribed manuscripts, while the older ones spent more time in prayer and contemplation. Because of the great need for secular clergy, some were pressed into this service.

With the aid of his friend Sulpicius Severus, Martin's fame soon spread far and wide. Sulpicius' *Life of Martin* soon rivaled Athanasius' *Life of Antony* as a gospel of monasticism. Pilgrims, renunciants and ascetics flocked to Martin's grave; churches and towns were named after him. Most monastic founders dedicated their first chapel to him. Martin's diminutive cape (*capella*) was especially honored by the Merovingian kings who carried it into battle as a national standard. The place where it was kept was called *capella* and the attending clerics *capellani*, terminology which soon spread to all Christian oratories.

Sulpicius Severus (363-423), Martin's biographer, was honored by men like Jerome, Augustine, and Paulinus of Nola and he is listed by Gennadius in his *Book of Illustrious Men*. When his wife died, Sulpicius, following the advice of Martin, sold all to become a presbyter and monk first at Elusa, near the Pyrenees, then at Primuliacum, where with a number of clerics and monks he led a semi-monastic life, praying, working, and writing. Although Gennadius says that Sulpicius was led astray by the Pelagians, he probably is referring to the anti-Augustinian movement in southern Gaul at the time.

Sulpicius was quite a writer, producing his *Life of Martin* (397), which he revised (400), *Chronicle*, a sacred history (400-403), *Dialogues* (404), besides a large correspondence. As we have seen, he was the chief public relations man for Martin whom he knew intimately 391-397, and whose praises he sung not only in his *Life*, but also in the latter part of his *Chronicle*, the *Dialogues* and many letters. Modeling his life on his mentor, he kept his picture in a prominent spot in his church at Primuliacum. According to the literary customs of the times, he embroidered Martin's life with many miracle stories, using figures from classical mythology. Athanasius' *Life of Antony* may well have served as his model, stressing the humility, simplicity and miraculous powers of the saint, an edifying portrait around a historical nucleus.

Martin was not at all times popular with his fellow bishops and Sulpicius points out the reason why as Norah Chadwick comments,[1] "Sulpicius' *Dialogues* are so strongly colored by the author's representation of Martin's hatred of the episcopal party that one is tempted at times to suspect that the main object of Sulpicius in writing of Martin was to 'show them up.' " Also in his *Chronicle* Sulpicius exposes the ill-will of the bishops of Aquitaine against the monks. Here we find in another form the basic opposition of the church of the monks and the church of the bishops. "As we read the last chapters of the *Chronicle* we hardly feel any doubt that the struggle of the rising monastic movement in Gaul against the opposition of the established episcopal party was the most serious concern of Sulpicius' intellectual endeavors."[2]

In the *Dialogues*, Martin, equal or even better than the ascetics of Egypt, appears as a national Gaulic hero-saint. Constantly he is contrasted with the worldly bishops. For example, while Martin walks or humbly rides on a donkey, the clerics have fine horses (*Dialogues* 1 [2], 3). Though Martin abides in a humble cell, the clerics have elaborate homes (*Dialogues* 1, 21). Martin sits on a low stool, while the secular bishops occupy high thrones (*Dialogues* 1 [2], 4). It seems that the bishops of Gaul were generally from the upper classes and so kept their former high standards of living, whereas monastic democracy tended to attract the lower classes.

Martin also objected to the governmental alliance with the episcopals in religious matters, specifically the Priscillianist affair.

---

1. **Poetry and Letters in Early Christian Gaul,** London, Bowes and Bowes, 1955, p. 105. This section owes much to Mrs. Chadwick's book.

2. **Ibid.,** p. 108.

Either over this or some other matter Martin did not attend episcopal synods during the latter part of his life (*Dialogue* 2 [3], 13).

It might be well here to mention something of Paulinus of Nola (353-431), a mutual friend of Martin and Sulpicius, for he and his wife Theresia represent a popular type of religious life of the time. Originally from Bordeaux, Paulinus studied under the famous Ausonius. He was a friend of Martin, Sulpicius, Ambrose and Jerome who advised him to renounce his wealth for a life of seclusion (L 58).

Paulinus and Theresia were attracted to the shrine of St. Felix at Nola in Campagnia, where they built a hospice for the sick and the poor (387) and also had a basilica to S. Felix surrounded by a nice garden and orchard. There they lived as brother and sister with a few friends and relatives. At one time the group included ten persons, among them several married couples, some with children.

Paulinus and Theresia's little retreat was known to all the greats of the time. Besides those mentioned above, Rufinus, Melania and Augustine either wrote or visited them. This was no formal monastery, but just a little group of friends and relatives withdrawn from society, living at peace, pooling their wealth for the service of God and man. Paulinus' letters to Sulpicius describe the daily life of the community with prayer, work for the sick and poor, hospitality to travelers, building and decorating the basilica (LL 1,5,11,17).

On one occasion when Sulpicius had requested a picture of Paulinus to place next to that of Martin in his baptistry, Paulinus also sent along some verses.

All you who wash your souls and bodies in this font should behold the paths set before you for good deeds. Martin is here so that you may see a model of perfect life, whereas Paulinus schools you in how to merit forgiveness. Martin should catch the eye of the blessed, Paulinus of sinners. So Martin must be the example for the saintly, Paulinus for the guilty (L 32:3) (ACW 36).

Paulinus and Theresia with their relatives and friends had a family community so typical of many of the early ascetics such as Augustine and his friends at Thagaste, Marcella and Paula in Rome, Melania and Pinian, and many others.

Although there were many examples of recluses, solitaries and small monastic establishments as Martin's, Sulpicius' and Paulinus' in Gaul and Italy, larger monasteries soon flowered especially in southern Provence near the mouth of the Rhone and on the islands along the coast. Besides safety from the barbarians, the islands offered a delightful climate which still attracts tourists today.

Honoratus, the founder of a monastery on the Lérins islands in the Bay of Cannes (400-410), hailed from Gallia Belgica. With his brother he set out to study under an anchorite Caprasius. They went to Greece for a while, perhaps to visit the monasteries there. At any rate, when his brother died, they returned. Going to Lérins, Honoratus was soon surrounded by disciples who turned the island into a garden. Lérins was to become a school of bishops, saints, missionaries and scholars.

The great literary and intellectual heritage of Lérins may perhaps be traced to the Greek traditions of nearby Marseilles. For one hundred years the principal bishops and the most distinguished thinkers of Gaul were educated at Lérins; for example, Hilary of Arles, Eucherius of Lyons, Lupus of Troyes, Faustus of Riez, Vincent of Lérins, Caesarius of Arles. Lérinsian missionaries went through Gaul and into Britain, and there are records of British monks and abbots at Lérins.

The barbarian invasions of the fifth century helped increase the population of Lérins as the educated and aristocrats fled to the islands. When abbot Honoratus was consecrated bishop of Arles, he was succeeded by his disciple and relative, Hilary, who when he succeeded to the see of Arles acted in a forthright manner against the secular bishops until halted by Pope Leo I, underlining again some of the differences between the monk-bishops and their rival episcopals.

B. *John Cassian the Monk* (369-435)

The monastery of S. Victor near Marseilles farther West along the Provence coast was another early Gaulic monastic center. It was founded over the tomb of the third century Roman martyr-soldier by John Cassian.

In this section we owe much to Owen Chadwick's excellent study *John Cassian* (Cambridge, 1950). Cassian's birthplace is uncertain. Some say Sythia, although there is evidence of a Western origin. At any rate, following the custom of the time, he made a pilgrimage to Bethlehem with his friend Germain, entering a monastery there. Anxious to visit the desert heroes of Egypt, Cassian and Germain set out from Bethlehem, but not without promising their brethren to make a speedy return. In Egypt they met the famous anchorite Archebius, who introduced them to fathers such as Chaeremon, Moses, Paphnutius, Daniel, etc., whose discourses on perfection, chastity, spiritual knowledge, accidie, etc. are recorded in Cassian's *Conferences.*

While in Egypt they met their old friend Pinufius, head of a monastery near Panephysis. They had known him earlier in Bethlehem whither he had fled from his abbotship. Taken in as a novice, he had been assigned as a cell mate to John Cassian. But when his own monks finally searched him out, they brought him back to Egypt in triumph. While at Pinufius' monastery, Cassian and Germain witnessed the admission of a novice and heard Pinufius discourse on penance and satisfaction (Conf. 20). They also met abbot Piamun who spoke to them of the three kinds of monks: cenobites, anchorites and Sarabaites (Conf. 18), exciting in them a desire for the anchorite life which would never leave them. At the monastery of abbot Paul they met the famous abbot John, who had given up the anchorite life for the cenobite in order to practice humility and obedience (Conf. 19). After seven years of moving from monastery to monastery and dialoging with the fathers, Cassian and Germain returned to Bethlehem as they had promised, but promptly obtained permission to return to Egypt to visit the monks of Scetis. There at Calamus they met abbot Moses who spoke to them of the goal of a monk and on discretion (Conf 1 & 2). Then Paphnutius, nicknamed "The Buffalo" because of his love of solitude, spoke on renunciation (Conf 3). Then his disciple Daniel, who although a presbyter never functioned as such before his lay mentor, discussed the lust of the flesh and spirit (Conf 4). Next they traveled to the Cells where Theodore consoled them over the slaughter of the Palestinian monks by the Saracens (Conf 6). Serenus and Isaac dialoged on inconstancy, evil spirits and prayer (Conf 8,9,10).

But are Cassian's *Conferences* with the desert fathers historical or rather imaginative recollections twenty-five years later (425)? Certainly there is a historical nucleus to the *Conferences*. First of all, John Cassian and his friend Germain really interviewed the desert giants and accurately describe life in Egypt. Moreover, some of his anecdotes are repeated in the *Apophthegmata Patrum*. It is true that Cassian looks at Egyptian monasticism through Origenist or Evagrian eyes and adapts his conferences to his western audience by translating Origenist terms into more acceptable Latin words. The *Conferences,* as Owen Chadwick comments (33), reflect the ideal of the Greek ascetics of lower Egypt tempered by Cassian's association with John Chrysostom and his experiences in the western world, for example, the contemporary problem of grace and free will.

Did John Cassian have conferences with the Origenist Evagrius while visiting the Cells? Although there is a heavy Origenist flavor in Cassian's works, he never mentions Evagrius' name. Most modern scholars presume that he had contact with Evagrius. He may have eliminated Evagrius' name from his writings because of the anti-Origenist and anti-Pelagian tenor of the time.

While Cassian and Germain were visiting in the Cells, pope Theophilus of Alexandria issued his famous festal letters (399) against the anthropomorphist Coptic monks who believed firmly that they could see God in his corporeal visible form. Although Cassian claims victory for the Origenists (Conf 10), the anthropomorphists, under the leadership of Shenoute of Atripe forced

Theophilus to change his position and to drive the Origenists out. Many fled to Palestine and some to Constantinople seeking the aid of John Chrysostom.

John Cassian and Germain probably joined this exodus, for we next find them at Constantinople where John Chrysostom ordained Cassian a deacon and together with Germain he was put in charge of the diocesan treasury. The appointing of foreigners to lucrative posts, his favoring of the Origenists, plus his forthright criticism of the empress and erring bishops soon earned Chrysostom an exile (403-404). But his friends sent Cassian and Germain to Rome to appeal to Pope Innocent I on his behalf, at the same time taking the cathedral treasury there for safe keeping.

Probably Innocent ordained Cassian a presbyter, after which the pair proceeded to Gaul. By this time Gaulic monasticism was pretty well established at Ligugé, Marmoutier and Lérins. The barbarian invasions gave the age an apocalyptic aura, encouraging flight from the crumbling secular world into eschatological enclaves.

At the tomb of S. Victor near Marseilles John Cassian fulfilled his ambition of continuing his monastic life under the Origenist traditions of lower Egypt, founding two monasteries there, one for men named for SS Peter and Victor and one for women, S. Savior. Cassian was a turning point for Gaulic monasticism, bringing his educated background to bear on his Palestinian and Egyptian training, his *Institutes* and *Conferences* becoming landmarks in the history of western monasticism.

He wrote his *Institutes* between 419-426 for bishop Castor of Apta Julia forty miles north of Marseilles, who wanted to start a monastery there. Basically the work is for beginners in the monastic life. Books 1-4 cover exterior rules for dress and worship, while books 5-12 concern faults to be removed from the monk's life. Cassian shows a great respect for the Christian ascetical tradition going back to the Jerusalem community founded by the apostles. Whereas the *Institutes* counseled the perfection of the outer man, the *Conferences* were more for the inner man of contemplation.

John Cassian is noted for his moderation. His works are free of bigotry, superstition, and minimize the marvelous. In tempering the sometimes severe customs of the Egyptian fellahin for the milder Gaulic temperament, he made use of Basil's rules. Although Cassian founded a cenobium at S. Victor, he always had a predilection for the semi-hermitic life of Nitria and Scetis where the cenobium served as a preparatory stage for the anchorite life. But he never admired the solitary completely removed from civilization, for the true hermit associates with other hermits and is subject to the traditions of the elders.

Although Cassian was encouraged by Honoratus of Lérins and helped in the direction of Castor's monastery at Apta Julia, he did not want his monks to follow Lérins which had become more like a center of learning or seminary, sending presbyters and bishops throughout Gaul. Though John Cassian was himself a cleric, he fought to keep the original lay spirit of Egyptian monasticism.

> Wherefore this is an old maxim of the fathers that is still current — though I cannot produce it without shame on my part, since I could not avoid my own sister, nor escape the hands of the bishop — namely, that a monk ought by all means to fly from women and bishops, for neither of them will allow him who has been joined in close intercourse any longer to care for the quiet of his cell or to continue with pure eyes in divine contemplation through his insight into holy things (Inst 11:18).[3]

In spite of Cassian's good intentions, S. Victor as Lérins was to supply presbyters and bishops to the churches of Gaul.

John Cassian was realistic in realizing that most of the Gauls were unfit by temperament for the highly individualistic life of the desert hermits. So his foundation was cenobitic from the beginning. He always saw himself as only a beginner in spite

3. Cassian's quotes are from NPNF series 2, vol. 11.

of his long and varied training in asceticism and so not yet ready for the solitary life. In Conference 19 the abbot John describes the advantages of the cenobitic life, namely, obedience, humility and less time spent on trivialities, for the hermit is constantly piddling to maintain himself.

Cassian imitated Pachomius in requiring the renunciant to wait outside the monastery door while the brethren attempted to despise him as insincere. If the newcomer lasted through this he was allowed to enter, stripped himself of his possessions including his clothes and putting on the monastic garb, though his old clothes were saved in case he proved unsuitable. The novice lived in the guest house for a year of probation while he was instructed by an elder and waited on guests (Inst 4:6-7). Cassian seems to have innovated this novitiate which was only required by the Egyptian and Syrian abbots for those who had led evil lives. His probation over, the novice was admitted to the community and with nine other juniors placed under the care of a senior (Inst 4:7).

In John Cassian's monastery the beginner did not specifically promise the three counsels of poverty, chastity and obedience which did not come into the admission formula as such till medieval times. Among the desert fathers, the evangelical counsels stood out among many virtues to be practiced by the monks. As Owen Chadwick points out (53) they became distinguished from other virtues because they more easily lent themselves to regulation. Nevertheless, these three virtues are essential to any true communism, whether that of the Roman *familia* or that of the monks. There is little doubt that the wandering monks of Cassian's day as well as our own, were escaping the obedience and the discipline of the monastery for the independence of the vagabond or hermit life.

In general, Cassian treated the counsels as virtues rather than special vows. Since the monastic life necessitated the separation of the sexes, an unnatural condition, all sorts of safeguards had to be ordered to keep them apart. As when fasting the appetite for food grows stronger, so the desert celibates often found themselves surrounded by dancing girls. And it was a constant struggle to remove these images to arrive at the purity of heart necessary for contemplation.

Cassian taught the three-fold renunciation of the desert tradition based on Genesis 12:1, "Go from your country and your kindred and your father's house to the land that I will show you" (Conf 3:6). Having abandoned one's property, crushing sin and the desire of attachments, then rise up to God. Poverty is an essential part of *apatheia* and necessary for purity of heart. Stripping himself of his worldly possessions, the monk is invested by the abbot in the robe of the monastery (Inst 4:4-5).

Obedience, which is the very foundation of the cenobitic life is to be so perfect that the writer will not finish the letter when the knock summons him to prayer (Inst 4:12). Junior monks should humbly submit to the will of the elders seeing in it God's will (Inst 4:10), even when they are ordered to do the impossible, for example, to water a dry stick (Inst 4:24) and even when commanded to do something seemingly sinful, as when abbot Patermucius was ordered to throw his son in the river, but the superior hid monks nearby to prevent it (Inst 4:27).

Cassian's system of government is not as well organized as Basil's or Benedict's. He speaks of a superior (Inst 4:10), abbot (Inst 4:16) and obedience to the elders (Inst 4:9). It seems he had no formal vows, allowing his monks to leave for the hermit's life when they were ready for it. As Owen Chadwick remarks (58), the Egyptian tradition tended to frown on vows fearing they might lead either to pride or perjury.

Confession of the juniors to their elders was another eastern monastic tradition adopted by Cassian (Inst 4:9) for he was convinced that unceasing repentance helped to perfection and revelation of interior thoughts helped psychologically in the struggle against temptations and aided towards purity of heart and contemplation.

Although the lay monastic tradition had always emphasized the liturgy of the Word, the monks generally attended the Eucharist in the town church on Saturdays and Sundays. Because some monks were reluctant to receive the mysteries often due to their unworthiness, Cassian writes:

> It is much better to receive them every Sunday for the healing of our infirmities with that humility of heart, whereby we believe and confess that we can never touch those holy mysteries worthily, than to be puffed up by a foolish persuasion of heart, and believe that at year's end we are worthy to receive them (Conf 23:21).

There seems some evidence of a daily reception of the Eucharistic medicine against the sickness of the soul. For example, Cassian quotes abbot Serenus:

> For in this way we have lately seen abbot Andronicus and many others cured. For the enemy will more and more abuse the man who is possessed, if he sees him cut off from the heavenly medicine, and will tempt him more often and more fearfully, as he sees him removed further from this spiritual remedy (Conf 7:30).

Cassian's divine offices, said at set hours, were a mixture of Palestinian and Egyptian customs with services at terce, sext, none, vespers and nocturns.

He mitigated rigorous Egyptian austerities for the Gaulic temperament, for he felt that fasting for its own sake was not a virtue, and could even lead to pride. "If we hold fasting to be included in that list of virtues so that abstinence from food is placed among those things which are good in themselves, then certainly the partaking of food will be bad and wrong" (Conf 21:13). In itself fasting is indifferent and can be used well or not used at all. Although it can be used as an aid to virtue, if over done so as to harm the body it is wrong (Conf 21:13-18). Cassian felt that all mortification should be adjusted to fit the needs of the individual and should be done humbly in secret as Jesus recommended in contrast to some of the ascetical contests of some of the Eastern monks (Conf 2).

In Cassian's monastery both sleep and eats were moderate. All days were fast days except for Saturdays, Sundays and feasts with station fasts on Wednesdays and Fridays when the midday meal is postponed till three P.M. On Saturdays and Sundays a voluntary supper is served in the evening. The daily order was more relaxed between Easter and Pentecost (Conf 21). A half-starved monk has no more advantage than a glutton when it comes to praying.

> There is one aim and object of continence in the case of all these, namely, that no one may be over-burdened beyond the measure of his appetite by gluttony. For it is not only the quality, but also the quantity of food taken which dulls the keenness of the mind, and when the soul as well as the flesh is surfeited, kindles the baneful and fiery incentive to vice (Inst 5:5).

Although Cassian's *Institutes* are well balanced, they lack the attention to detail which later rules sometimes over-specified. Indeed, Cassian may have left them intentionally vague to allow for freedom of action and interpretation. They were primarily for beginners, whereas the *Conferences* were for the more advanced in the spiritual life.

C. The Influence of Evagrius

The basic themes in both the *Institutes* and the *Conferences* are Evagrian although the teachings of Origen, Jerome, Basil and John Chrysostom can also be detected. As Owen Chadwick comments (86), Evagrius stood at the watershed of Eastern and Western spirituality, swaying the West through John Cassian and the East by Simeon the New Theologian. Evagrian parallels can be found throughout both the *Institutes* and the *Conferences,* for example: the emphasis on the practical and contemplative lives; virtues and vices; apathy and agape; pure prayer and the *gnōsis* of God. Cassian's Latin equivalents of apathy, *gnōsis* and *theōria* lost some but not all of their Stoic, Platonic and Gnostic flavor.

Cassian, as his friend Evagrius, divided the monks into two classes, namely, the beginners of the active life (*bios praktikos*) and the proficient contemplatives (*bios theōrētikos*). But he was realistic enough to see that few would attain the latter ideal state; he himself never seems to have reached it. The active life, largely defined in the *Institutes*, was a purging of vices and the practice of virtues, paving the way for contemplation through purity of heart, Cassian's parallel to Evagrius' apathy.

Egyptian dualism is visible in Cassian's war of the flesh against the spirit. But this is not a Manichaean or Gnostic dualism equating the flesh with the body. Commenting on Paul's "The flesh lusts against the spirit and the spirit against the flesh" (Gal 5:17) he writes:

> Wherefore in this passage we ought to take "flesh" as meaning not man, that is, his material substance, but the carnal will and evil desires, just as "spirit" does not mean anything material, but the good and spiritual desire of the soul.... And since the two, that is, the desires of the flesh and of the spirit coexist in one and the same man, there arises an internal warfare daily carried on within us, while the lust of the flesh which rushes blindly towards sin, revels in those delights which are corrected with present ease (Conf 4:11).

Without mortification and vigilance the spirit of lust cannot be kept in check. However, man's carnal motions are not evil in themselves. "These impulses were implanted in us by the Creator and he will not on that account seem blameworthy, if we choose wrongly to abuse them, and to pervert them to harmful purposes..." (Inst 7:4).

By the purgative way of the active life the monk aims for purity of heart, Origen's and Evagrius' apathy. Freed from the desires of lust, the mind can contemplate God in an angelic manner (Conf 9:20). Yet Cassian did not buy the Stoic concept of apathy for he believed that sinlessness is impossible amid the ceaseless temptations of this life. Conscious of the basic weakness of human nature, the monks should not mercilessly condemn the faults of others, lest they fall into the very same sins themselves (Conf 11:10). Although it is possible for a man to be free from grosser sins, this does not mean he will not be tempted.

As Evagrius so Cassian lists the principal sins to be eliminated in order to attain purity of heart, namely, gluttony, fornication, avarice, anger, accidie, vainglory, pride. The practical life is a ceaseless struggle against vice, purging the soul and leaving it open to God. For both Cassian and Evagrius, God is more the goal of the spiritual life, than the means to the goal, although Cassian always taught that man cannot effect his purgation alone "through the grace of God, instilled like dew by his spirit in our hearts, the heats of fleshy lusts can be altogether deadened" (Conf 5:14).

One of the vices most troublesome to monks is accidie, which combines feelings of loneliness, ennui, low periods, dejection and discouragement. The hermits, but to some extent also the cenobites, lived an unnatural existence, apart from normal family affection of wife and children, compounded by rigorous fasting and a tough regimen of prayer, leading sometimes to a psychological and spiritual imbalance. We have already seen the dangers of hallucinations among the solitaries.

"Accidie," says Cassian, "is especially disturbing to a monk about the sixth hour like some fever which seizes him at stated times, bringing the burning heat of its attacks on a sick man at usual and regular hours" (Inst 10:1). Some have likened it to the noonday devil of Psalm 90 [91]. At noon the monk is weary and hungry and dejected. On week days he has not eaten in almost 24 hours. With a minimum of sleep and maximum of hard work he is fatigued, run-down, an ideal candidate for accidie.

When this has taken possession of some unhappy soul, it produces dislike of the place, disgust with the cell, and disdain and contempt of the brethren who dwell with him or

at a little distance, as if they were careless or unspiritual. . . .
It does not suffer him to stay in his cell, or to take any pains
about reading, and he often groans because he can do no
good while he stays there, and complains and sighs because
he can bear no spiritual fruit so long as he is joined to that
society. And he complains that he is cut off from spiritual
gain, and is of no use in the place, as if he were one who,
though he could govern others and be useful to a great
number of people, yet was edifying none, nor profiting any
by his teaching and doctrine. He cries up distant monasteries
and those which are a long way off, and describes such
places as more profitable and better suited for salvation; and
desiring this, he paints the intercourse with the brethren there
as sweet and full of spiritual life. On the other hand, he says
that everything about him is rough, and not only that there
is nothing edifying among the brethren who are stopping
there, but also that even food for the body cannot be procured without great difficulty (Inst 10:2).

He is sure that he will never be well again as long as he stays
here especially as weariness and pangs of hunger increase in the
fifth and sixth hour.

He looks about anxiously this way and that, and sighs that
none of the brethren come to see him and often goes in and
out of his cell, and frequently gazes up at the sun, as if it
was too slow in setting. And so a kind of unreasonable confusion of mind takes possession of him like some foul darkness
and makes him idle and useless for every spiritual work,
so that he imagines that no cure for so terrible an attack can
be found in anything except visiting some one of the brethren
or in the solace of sleep alone (Inst 10:2).

The monk suffering from accidie feels that he should visit the
sick and brethren near and far, or go to see his family, or pious
and understanding women. All of these seem more worthwhile
than staying uselessly in his cell.

So eloquent is John Cassian on this disease that he must have suffered from it himself. Maybe it spurred him and Germain on their far-reaching tours. Accidie either makes a monk dull and listless or else it drives him out of the monastery. He is constantly restless, going in and out of his cell, visiting the cells of other monks, searching for refreshments, looking for kindred souls either men or women and immersing himself in their affairs (Inst 10:5-6). Undoubtedly in Cassian's day as well as our own, accidie was the most frequent cause of defections from the monastic life.

The routine of the abbey, the sameness of the daily order, prayer and work brings boredom, gloom, gruffness, griping, pessimism, straying of the mind after forbidden pleasures, talkativeness, a flagging of the voice, finally despondent renunciation of vocation. Accidie is especially deadly for those in the noon day of life who have lost the energy of youth's morning and the road ahead leads downhill to death. Of course, as the other vices, accidie is by no means limited to monks. It is probably just as common today among layfolk, seeking relief from boredom by any means whatsoever. Cassian with the Apostle (2 Thes 3:12) recommends hard work to eliminate the idleness which is not only the root of accidie but of all other vices as well (Inst 10:14).

John Cassian as some of the other church Fathers was not above appealing to selfish motives for the ascetical life, exaggerating the problems of married life and eulogizing the happiness of the monks (Conf 24:26), quoting abbot Abraham who had been married before his call to the monastic life. For example, family love is short-lived and easily broken, while monastic love is enduring. Continence is one hundred times more pleasing than fleeting sexual ecstasy. The one hundred fold of the gospel promise (Mark 10:29-30) is his theme. Whereas the married man has one wife, one house, one field, the monk owns all things that belong to the Father. But the highest motive for the monk should be his love of virtue and his pursuit of undistracted divine contemplation.

Cassian was one of the first demythologizers, leaving out the legends and miracles of the desert Fathers from his instructions, "to supply our readers merely with necessary instruction for the perfect life, and not with matter for idle and useless admiration without any correction of their faults" (Conf 18:1). Perhaps in contrast to Sulpicius Severus' brilliant miracle stories, Cassian plays down the marvelous. For example, whereas the watered stick blossoms in Sulpicius' account (*Dialogues* 1:19) Cassian's stick rotted (Inst 4:24). For Cassian the greatest miracle is virtue itself, the expulsion of evil from the soul (Conf 13).

Cassian, as Evagrius, looked upon virtue as sinlessness. For example, chastity is the absence of fornication, humility is lack of pride, etc. As Evagrius had related apathy to agape so Cassian taught that purity of heart is the obverse of charity, which includes all the other virtues. Since it is the love of God, charity transforms the soul into the image and likeness of God. As most other religious founders, Cassian stresses humility which includes a spirit of mortification, openness, docility, obedience, kindness, patience, loyalty to the rule, low self-esteem, taciturnity, slowness to laugh (Inst 4:39).

Cassian saw the interrelationship of the virtues and vices, so that if you conquer one sinful habit, you are on the way to vanquishing others. Morality is rather a means to charity than a fruit of it.

He was cautious about engaging in the active apostolate, converting others to the neglect of one's own life. This is the great temptation of monasticism and one of the reasons it tried to avoid the distracting and often worldly clerichood. Cassian writes, "It results that while they fancy that they can make larger profits by the instruction of others, they are actually deprived of their improvement" (Conf 24:13).

Who when ministering support to the poor, or when receiving with benevolent kindness the crowds that come to him, can at the very moment when he is with anxious mind perplexed for the wants of his brethren, contemplate the vastness of the bliss on high? And while he is shaken by the troubles

and cares of the present life look forward to the state of the
world to come with heart raised above the stains of earth?
(Conf 23:5).

The ideal of contemplating God apart from the problems of men
had been one of the chief accusations against monasticism as it is
today.

But this individual contemplation of God by no means ex-
cludes love of the brethren. In Conference 16 on friendship abbot
Joseph identifies love of the brethren as true love between those
who love God. But he also carefully distinguishes between love
of all and affection which by its very nature is shown to the few
who are united to us by kindred dispositions and mutual goodness, although it has degrees and differences (Conf 16:14).

As for Evagrius, so for John Cassian the goal of the spiritual
life, including the elimination of vices and the cultivation of the
virtues, is purity of heart, leading to contemplation of God.
Although absolute sinlessness is impossible, nevertheless, the
mind should strive to control its thoughts, eliminating the de-
scending and concentrating on the ascending (Conf 7:4). This
mental stripping leads to a state of pure prayer in which the
monk is not even conscious of himself (Conf 9 & 10). All the
faculties of the mind are silenced, leaving only a simple longing
for God together with feelings of spiritual delight. This can arise
at many opportunities. For example, the hearing of a psalm sung,
the death of a monk, etc. (Conf 9:26). This state of pure prayer
Cassian identifies with contemplation, which is an indirect per-
ception of God (Conf 10:11) leading to union with the indwell-
ing Christ and Holy Spirit. Yet Cassian's contemplation is not
just a philosophical exercise or a type of natural mysticism, for
a prayerful meditation on sacred scriptures can give a spiritual
knowledge (*gnōsis*) leading to it. Prayer must progress from
a more complex and diversified thought to a simplified style.
For example, Cassian offered this small formula of recollection:
"Be pleased, O God, to deliver me; O Lord make haste to help
me" (Psalm 69 [70] in Conf 10:10). Introducing the divine

offices, this was to become the shibboleth of Western monasticism.

D. *Conference* 13 *On the Protection of God*

Augustine's doctrine on original sin and predestination was not greeted with joy by the monks as we have seen. When a copy of his *On Rebuke and Grace* (427), written originally for the monks of Hadrumetum, arrived in Gaul it was spurned as an innovation by the Massilians, especially those from Lérins and S. Victor. These monks were not Pelagians or even semi-Pelagians for they rejected Pelagius as much as Augustine. More correctly they have been called anti-Augustinians, rejecting his novel teaching of predestination as against Christian tradition and undermining man's efforts towards salvation. They looked upon predestination as a case of over-kill, but admitted that all men are somehow involved in Adam's sin and no man can save himself. Moreover, they accepted divine foreknowledge, but asserted that God's grace is given according to human merits and not independent of them.

Prosper of Aquitaine, a learned lay Christian of southern Gaul, along with Hilary took an active part in the controversy, writing to Augustine, (LL 225, 226), that the Massilians objected to his *On Rebuke and Grace* and his earlier *Books vs Julianus*. The Massilian position was based on a long monastic and ascetical tradition, probably Egyptian and Evagrian in origin. Both Hilary and Prosper asked Augustine to answer the Massilians, who although fundamentally good men, had been misinformed.

One of the leaders of the Massilians was Cassian who probably wrote his Conference 13 in reply to Augustine's *On Rebuke and Grace*. In his earlier writings Cassian followed the Eastern monastic line in which man's efforts prepared the way for God. Yet man should always realize his essential dependence on God (Inst 5:21; 6:18; 8:12). "When we say that human efforts cannot of themselves secure it (perfection) without the aid of God, we thus insist that God's mercy and grace are bestowed only upon those who labor and exert themselves, and are granted (to use the Apostle's expressions) to them that 'will' and 'run'..." (Inst 12:14). Ask and you shall receive, seek and you shall find, knock and it shall be opened to you (Mt 7:7).

Although his *Institutes* placed more emphasis on man's struggle for perfection, Cassian's *Conferences* balanced God and man. For example, in Conference 3:11 Germain asks Paphnutius how man can do anything at all worthy of praise since God begins and ends all his salutary acts.

But how about the middle, responds Paphnutius? Although God gives man the opportunities for good acts, it is up to him to make good use of them.

> But it is well for us to be sure that although we practise every virtue with unceasing efforts, yet with all our exertions and zeal we can never arrive at perfection. Nor is mere human diligence and toil of itself sufficient to deserve to reach the splendid reward of bliss, unless we have secured it by means of the cooperation of the Lord, and his directing our heart to what is right.... None of the righteous are sufficient of themselves to acquire righteousness, unless every moment when they stumble and fall the divine mercy supports them with his hands, that they may not utterly collapse and perish, when they have been cast down through the weakness of free will (Conf 3:11).

> We have no wish to do away with man's free will by what we have said, but only to establish the fact that the assistance and grace of God are necessary to it every day and hour (Conf 3:22).

In Conference 13 Cassian quotes Chaeremon on the necessity of God's grace for the monk.

> Who I ask, could, however fervent he might be in spirit, relying on his own strength with no praise from men, endure the squalor of the desert, and I will not say the daily lack,

but the daily supply of dry bread? Who without the Lord's consolation could put up with the continual thirst for water, or deprive his human eyes of that sweet and delicious morning sleep and regularly compress his whole time of rest and repose into the limits of four hours? Who would be sufficient without God's grace to give continued attendance to reading and constant earnestness in work, receiving no advantage of present gain? (Conf 13:6).

But sometimes Cassian taught of man as capable of that first turning towards God. "And when he sees in us some beginnings of a good will, he at once enlightens it and strengthens it on towards salvation, increasing that which he himself implanted or which he sees to have risen from our own efforts" (Conf 13:8). Although free will and grace appear as contraries, they really agree. Man's will is weakened by sin, but it is far from dead (Conf 13:12). As many of the Gaulic monks, Cassian stressed God's universal salvific will against Augustine's predestination. It is true that some souls are lost, but against God's wishes (Conf 13:7).

Augustine responded to the Massilians with a treatise now divided into two books, *Predestination of the Saints* and *The Gift of Perseverance* (428-429). Soon after Augustine's death (430) the Massilians continued the attack with *Objections of the Gaulic Liars,* to which Prosper promptly responded (431). Prosper and Hilary even went to Rome to enlist the aid of Pope Celestine in the struggle against the Massilians. Celestine wrote a letter to the Gaulic bishops, defending Prosper and Augustine and warning against novelties. Finally Prosper answered Cassian's Conference 13 with his *On Grace and Free Will, Against the Contributor.*

In general, however, the anti-Augustinian school of Marseilles continued through the fifth century with Vincent of Lérins, Faustus of Riez, and Gennadius. The matter was not settled till the second council of Orange (529) under the leadership of Caesarius of Arles, strongly reasserting prevenient grace.

The resistance of the Gaulic monks to Augustine was based

largely on the fear that predestination weakened the whole ascetical scheme. Why be an athlete in the games of salvation when the victory is predetermined and when our nature is so corrupt that we are helpless in the struggle?

John Cassian died in 433, three years after Augustine. But his *Institutes* and *Conferences* continued to influence southern Gaul and were to be required reading for future generations of monks. Cassian's prestige was limited by his rather prosaic life and a lack of spectacular miracles or shrines to attract pilgrims. Moreover, he had no public relations man of the caliber of Athanasius or Sulpicius Severus. Cassian's strength was more as a reporter or adapter of Egyptian asceticism than as an original thinker. His demythologized works made less interesting reading than the lives of Antony and Martin. Furthermore, the Augustinians probably hindered the spread of his teachings.

In Italy Benedict and Cassiodorus used Cassian and recommended that their followers read him. There are many hints of Cassian in Benedict's rule. For example, the degrees of humility, strict obedience, renunciation of the will, spiritual direction, acceptance of novices and the use of Psalm 69 [70] "Be pleased, O God, to deliver me." Indeed, Benedict's monks helped spread Cassian's teachings. Many great religious founders quoted John Cassian including Dominic Guzman, Ignatius of Loyola and Francis DeSales.

While Cassian was an ascetic, Benedict was more of an organizer. And whereas Cassian held up the anchorite life as the ideal for which the cenobitic is a preparation, Benedict followed Pachomius and Basil for whom communism was supreme. As Cassian placed broad general principles, Benedict wrote more in detail.

As we have seen, Cassian favors the lower Egyptian predilection for the contemplative, the desire for the semi-anchorite life, the search for God which is more individual than corporate, with the Eucharist and the divine offices aiding the monk on his road to contemplation.

John Cassian is the first Western doctor of the science of the spiritual life including mental prayer, but he also gave an impetus to the liturgy and the office. His was a moderate spirituality better adapted to the Western temperament. Owen Chadwick writes (186):

> Cassian bequeathed to Latin Christianity the idea that the spiritual life was a science in which prayer reigned: that it is possible to analyze temptation and the nature of sin: that methods of prayer and mortification are neither haphazard nor individual, but ordered according to established experience. All the guides to spirituality in which Western Europe later abounded are his direct descendants.

By the end of the fifth century monasticism had spread throughout the Roman empire. Fired by apocalyptic barbarian attacks it was to serve as a catalyst among the invaders themselves to form the Christian matrix of medieval Europe. Far from striving to turn the whole world into a cloister, the monks only wanted to create islands of peace and refuge in the midst of a stormy existence. They ennobled manual labor, formerly only for slaves and when Roman education disintegrated, the monks preserved it. Although fighting to preserve their lay status, as elite Christians they were often called upon to fill bishoprics. Most of the Fathers and Doctors of the fourth and fifth century were either monks or trained in the monastic way.

The monks resembled four phenomena of the ancient world: the Roman *familia* under the *pater familias* in their communism; slaves in their dedication to manual labor and their lack of rights; soldiers in their celibacy, mobility and obedience, and martyrs by their ascetical lives. As yet we have no religious orders for each monastery is independent and the wandering monks still are the bane of the Church. In a sense the golden age of monasticism lasted only 100-150 years for by the end of the fifth century it was paling in the East and also in the West after the passing of Jerome, Augustine, Pelagius, John Cassian. But the British and Irish monks inspired by the Gauls and Benedict's disciples were to be the glories of sixth and seventh century Europe.

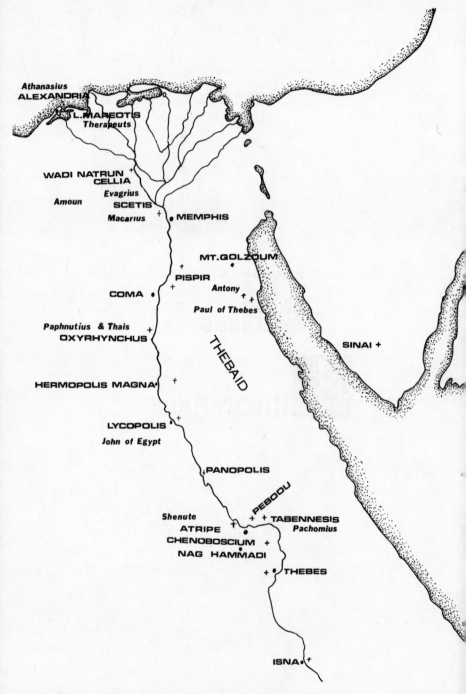

1. Monastic Egypt, Fourth and Fifth Centuries.

2. Asia Minor, Fourth and Fifth Centuries.

3. Judaean Monasteries, Fourth to Sixth Century.

4. North Africa and Gaul, Fourth — Fifth Century.

Comgal.
Columban.
BANGOR

DERRY
IONA
Columba

LINDISFARNE
Aidan
Colman

Patrick
ARMAGH

YORK

Columba
DURROW

ARAN
KELLS

Ciaran
CLONMACNOIS
KILDARE -------- Brigit
CLONARD ------ Finnian
Brendan
CLONFERT
GLENDALOUGH

INNISFALLEN
LISMORE

GLASTONBURY

Columban
LUXEUIL
BREG
LURE
ST. GAL

BOBBIO
Columban

5. Principal Irish Monastic Centers, Fifth to Seventh Century.

LOMBARD
KINGDOM
OF
PAVIA

MILAN
• PAVIA
+ • BOBBIO
Columban

POMPOSA

RAVENNA
EXARCHATE
OF
RAVENNA

LOMBARD DUCHY
OF
SPOLETO

SPOLETO •

SUBIACO
+
MONTE CASSINO •
ROME •
+Benedict
+
Gregory

LOMBARD DUCHY
OF
BENEVENTO

BENEVENTO •

SALERNO •

BYZANTINE
POSSESSIONS

• VIVARIUM
Cassiodorus

6. Italy, Sixth to Eighth Century.

1. Qumran Monastery, Series of Rooms.

2. Simeon Stylites' Pillar and Basilica at Qal' at Sim'an, Syria.

3. Bethlehem, Statue of Jerome. Justinian's Basilica of the Nativity in the background with tombs of Paula, Eustochium and Jerome nearby.

4. Theveste, North Africa, Fifth Century "motel" Caravansary for pilgrims

5. Hippo Regius, North Africa, Augustine's Basilica with Monastery to the right.

7. Monte Cassino Abbey, Italy, (Today).

8. Jarrow, England, Ruins of old Abbey Church and Tower where Bede

8. The Sons and Daughters of the Kings of the Irish are Seen To Be the Monks and Virgins of Christ

(*Confessions of S. Patrick,* 41)

reland had never been incorporated into the Roman empire and so had never been under "official" Christianity. Consisting mainly of tough shepherds and agricultural peoples, the Celts had always given the Romans a hard time. The raid that captured Patrick was probably one of many over the centuries. Since there were no large towns in Ireland as in Britain or Gaul, the political and later the ecclesiastical unit was the clan under its leader or king.

The Celtic clans were natural extensions of the family circle, including all patrilineal descendants, giving mutual support and protection to the weak, prohibiting intramarriage, etc. The clans were more enduring than single families and guaranteed a continued succession in both civil and monastic lines. When territorially united, the clans lasted a long time in comparison to the scattered sub-groups. For example, the Celtic clans of Scotland were not destroyed till 1746 and even then their fallen stalwarts were united in common clan graves.

Two other Irish social phenomena which would affect Christian beginnings were the druids and the bards. The druids, known throughout Europe and the islands, were magicians and prophets who formed a separate priesthood in charge of sacrifices, sorcery, magic. They believed in an after life of gods and fairies. They are supposed to have foretold the coming of the Christian missionaries and challenged their power. Their prestige seems to have been succeeded by the wandering bards or balladeers, singing of war and love. Basically poets, they were sometimes princes and warriors who possessed the principal educational, musical and sometimes even political influence among the Irish. By the sixth century they seem to have had a corporate form appearing as poetic assemblies under the chief or king. As a powerful national organization of poets, musicians and historians, they were honored for their learning and as trusted keepers of the annals. Since they had charge of property lines, they wielded a great political influence. The Irish kings employed the bards as their chief public relations men, eulogizing their chiefs in song and annal. When Christian monasticism was established in Ireland, each monastery had its own bard as poet-historian. Later the bard-monk Columba was to be the protector and patron of the bards against the persecuting chiefs.

Britain seems to have been proselytized in the fourth and fifth centuries by Gaulic missionaries, some of whom stemmed from Lérins. Victricius of Ruen, Germain of Auxerre and Lupus of Troyes helped introduce monasticism to Britain whence it flowed to Ireland. The British and Irish churches were to develop certain peculiarities, especially when cut off from the continent by the Anglo-Saxon invasions.

A. *Patrick* (385-461)

Patrick, founding father of Irish Christianity, was born at Daventry in Britain, the son of a deacon and grandson of a presbyter. Captured by Irish pirates during one of their coastal raids, he was sold as a slave to a druid who put him to work keeping the pigs. During his long solitary watches, he felt remorse over his ill-spent youth. Hearing the call of God to a life of mortification and prayer, he escaped back to Britain (407), firmly convinced that he was called to convert the Irish to Christianity.

Modern scholars such as Hanson [1] feel that Patrick remained in Britain from his return from captivity to his consecration as bishop of Ireland. However, since there was a common interchange of clergy and monks between Britain and Gaul and Patrick later expressed a desire to make a pilgrimage there (Conf 43), it is not at all impossible that he may have lived in Gaul, perhaps at Auxerre or Lérins. Hanson [2] feels that Patrick probably was a monk or at least a servant of God during this period. This would be logical for it was normal for a person to seek this life after his conversion as Augustine, Basil, Martin and many others had done. Moreover, certain references have a monastic flavor such as the elders (Confession 26, 37), and the brethren and saints of Gaul (43). Finally Patrick's encouragement of ascetics and virgins in Ireland shows a predilection in this direction.

What is Patrick's relationship to Palladius the missionary sent by Pope Celestine I to the Irish about 432? Hanson conjectures:

Palladius arrived first, and began his mission somewhere in the south of Ireland. Patrick arrived later, sent by different people, by the British church instead of by the Pope, under different auspices, as an Irish-speaking Briton with previous experience of Ireland, to spread the Christianity of the British church, instead of as a representative of a Roman mission to spread Roman or Gallic Christianity, to the north of Ireland. [3]

1. **S. Patrick**, Oxford, 1968, pp. 128ff.

2. **Ibid.**, pp. 157-158.

3. **Ibid.**, p. 193.

Although Palladius died early leaving Patrick in charge over all Ireland, two traditions continued, namely the Palladian Roman and the Patrician British.

Patrick's missionary labors are described in his *Confession* and in the canons drawn up with his auxiliaries, Auxilius and Iserninus. Later documents are largely embroidered. As most early missionaries, Patrick concentrated on the conversion of the northern Irish chiefs, organizing his churches around the small states (*tuatha*) with his clergy living in semi-monastic chapters like those of Gaul and Africa. Patrick converted thousands, baptizing, confirming, ordaining and appointing bishops. Some churches were entrusted to presbyters or occasionally to a deacon or a consecrated virgin.

Patrick's church was primarily episcopal and clerical, but with a growing interest in the non-clerical ascetical life. As primate of Ireland Patrick resided at Armagh which, according to Ryan,[4] was probably the chief church in the territory of Dáire, a petty chieftain, whose state (*tuatha*) was Patrick's *paruchia*, or diocese. Because of the special position of Dáire in Ireland at the time, Armagh became the chief see. The exact extent of Patrick's jurisdiction is not certain for even in the more advanced church of Gaul the limits of dioceses were often uncertain. Patrick seems to have consecrated many bishops, for it was customary to have bishops over all but the smallest churches, although the delegation of authority to presbyters was increasing. Many of Patrick's bishops were from Britain or from Gaul. The episcopal candidate should be "A man of good birth without defect or blemish, and of moderate wealth, a man of one wife into whom has been born but one child" (*Book of Armagh* Add. 35b).

Patrick's foundation or *civitas* at Armagh was surrounded by a high wall of earth about one hundred forty feet in diameter.

4. **Irish Monasticism**, Dublin, Talbot, 1931, p. 84, referred to henceforth as "Ryan."

Within were three large buildings, a house for the clerics, a church, and a kitchen and refectory. The term *civitas* was borrowed from the ecclesiastical seats in other countries. Since Ireland did not have urban centers, *civitas* was applied to monasteries and places of assembly. Distinct from the cities were the smaller churches under one or two clerics.

Patrick and his clerical assistants probably led a regular life similar to that of Ambrose, Augustine and Germain of Auxerre in their episcopal houses, giving mutual support in poverty, continence and piety. When Patrick consecrated Fiall in Leinster, he gave him seven clerics to form the nucleus of his new community. Although Patrick encouraged ascetics and virgins, there were not yet the fully developed monasteries of the next generations. "Hence how did it come to pass in Ireland that those who never had a knowledge of God, but until now always worshipped idols and things impure, have now been made a people of the Lord, and are called sons of God, that the sons and daughters of the kings of the Irish are seen to be monks and virgins of Christ?" (Conf. 41)(ACW 17:34). Vocations are increasing despite parental objections (Conf. 42). The early consecrated virgins either lived at home or else in small groups, assisting the local clergy.

This is the First Order of Irish Saints described in the *Catalogue of Irish Saints* (8c).

The first order of catholic saints was in the time of Patrick, and then there were bishops, distinguished and holy, and full of the Holy Ghost, 350 in number, founders of churches. They had one mass, one liturgy, one tonsure from ear to ear. They celebrated one Easter on the fourteenth moon after the vernal equinox. And what was excommunicated by one church, all excommunicated. They did not reject the service and society of women, because founded on the rock of Christ, they feared not the blast of temptation. This order of saints lasted for four reigns, those namely of Loiguire, of Ailill Moct, of Lugaid, son of Loiguire, and of Tuathal. All these bishops were sprung from the Romans and Franks and Britons and Scots.[5]

Here we see a foreign episcopal church structure. If we can accept the large number of bishops, there must have been one for almost every church, although we know that the smaller chapels had lesser clergy in charge. In general, the ecclesiastical structure resembled that of the continent but less organized. The peculiar druid tonsure and the ancient Easter practice were to be defended with their lives by the Irish monks of future generations.

It would seem that clerical marriage was still the custom in Britain and Ireland as elsewhere in the church. Patrick himself was the son and grandson of clerics and he required his bishops to be devoted to their wives. As with Augustine, those clerics living in the episcopal community were separated from their wives. Were any of the pious virgins aiding the clerics *subintroductae* or spiritual wives?

The canons of the Synod of 439 approved by Patrick, Auxilius and Iserninus, reflect the clerical situation of the times. For example, they legislate against vagabond clerics (3, 34). The cleric should wear the Roman tonsure with the entire crown bald (6), and his wife should be veiled (6). Clerics should be present in the church for matins and vespers (7). Excommunicated clerics are not to be received by others (11), nor are they to be allowed to pray with the community, offer, or consecrate (28). Newcomers in the community are not to baptize, offer, etc., without the bishop's permission (24, 27, 33). Lower clerics should not take for themselves gifts offered to the bishops (26). Bishops should not ordain outside their own parishes without permission and should make arrangements to offer on the Lord's day (30).

Some canons dealt with the problems of the early monks and virgins. They should take care not to have too close association

5. Haddan and Stubbs, **Councils and Ecclesiastical Documents Relating to Great Britain and Ireland**, vol. 2, Oxford, 1869-1878, p. 292.

in order to avoid scandal (9). "A virgin who has made a vow to God to remain chaste and afterwards has taken a spouse in the flesh, shall be excommunicated until she changes her ways. If she converts and dismisses the adulterer, she shall do penance; and afterwards they shall not live in the same house or on the same farm" (17). Other canons concerned marriage, theft and penitentials for crimes. For example, sinners had to do penance for one year for murder, adultery, and swearing before druids (14).

Most of the clerics in Patrick's church seem to have been foreigners, with the natives drawn more to the ascetical way. Soon the foreign clerics were replaced by British monk-missionaries so that the Irish church became largely monastic in scope.

Patrick himself was not only the founding father of the Irish church, but also the first witness we have of the early British church with its bible text, church Latin, doctrine, worship, discipline and customs. As bishop, Patrick had a high sense of the authority of his office, baptizing, confirming, ordaining, presiding at the Eucharist, encouraging ascetics, fighting paganism and idolatry. He was an eschatological evangelical missionary, coming in the "last days" of the fifth century, spreading the good news of Christ. His simple forthright *Confession* is a welcome change from the later mythologized versions of his life.

When Patrick died (461) his name was kept on the diptychs of the church at Armagh and although there may have been a local devotion to him, there is little mention of him during the next two hundred years. For example, his name does not come up in the lives of Brigit, Columba, Columban, or in Bede's history. By the seventh century Cogitosus and Cuimíne, clerics of the Patrician churches, began to assemble records and legends about Patrick. But it was principally the honor and interests of the Patrician churches that contributed to the mythological Patrick. As James Kenney writes [6] the *paruchia Patricii*, the league of monastic churches which regarded Patrick as their patron and

6. **Sources for the Early History of Ireland** I, New York, Columbia University Press, 1929, p. 326.

founder, and especially the church of Armagh, found the Patrick
legend an aid to their prestige and finances. So Patrick's life was
enmeshed with popular folklore.

Kenney feels that many of the early churches may have felt
threatened by the newer and stronger monastic foundations.

> The early stages of the development of the Patrick legend
> were in part the product of a movement to unite all the older
> churches under the leadership of Armagh into a *paruchia*
> such as that of Columcille, on the basis of an assumption,
> largely fictitious, that they owed their foundation to Patrick,
> first apostle and greatest of the saints of Ireland.[7]

After Patrick, the Irish church was largely monastic. Some
Welsh, British and Gaulic monks may have come to help Patrick
(their fellow monk?). The missionary zeal of the Western monks
spurred them on. The invasions, particularly the Saxon attacks
on Britain, brought an apocalyptic and even millenarian aura to
the age, driving the British and Welsh monks to the shores of
Ireland and Armorica to convert, teach, and spread the British
church customs and the monastic way.

The question is frequently asked: how early was monasticism
established in Britain? It may date from the visit of Victricius
of Ruen, great patron of monasticism in 396. Also the life and
miracles of Martin may well have been known in Britain by 400.
An early British mission center was established at Galloway in
northern Britain by Ninian a generation before Patrick. Ninian
seems to have been trained in Rome and consecrated bishop,
establishing his see at Whithorn on the West shore of Solway
"*ad candidam casam*," dedicated to Martin. He may have had
a loose form of monasticism there. At any rate, a century or so
later "*candida casa*" turns up as a monastic training center. As
was mentioned earlier, British monasticism was related to that
of Gaul especially that of Lérins.

Illtud (450-525) an Armorican disciple of Germain of Auxerre

7. Sources, p. 329.

built a monastic settlement on the island of Ynys Pyr (later C'aldey), off the coast of Wales, reaching its peak in the sixth century. In the Lérinsian tradition, the presbyter-abbot taught his disciples both spirituality and the liberal arts. Called the first great abbot of the British church, he sent forth his disciples to spread the monastic way, for example: Samson of Dol, Paul of Aurelianus, Cadoc, Gildas, and perhaps David.

Finnian (d. 549), an Irishman, studied in Leinster, Ireland, visited the monks of Wales and corresponded with Cadoc on matters of monastic and liturgical discipline. His foundation at Clonard was one of the first Irish monasteries. As founder of the second order of Irish saints, Finnian reflected the popular Lérinsian tradition of learning, and particularly of sacred science. One reason for the popularity of the British and Welsh monk missionaries in Ireland was their learning, the Irish transferring their honor from the educated bards to the knowledgeable monks. Finnian of Clonard had a large number of disciples including the twelve apostles of Ireland, e.g., Ciaran of Saigher, Ciaran of Clonmacnois, Columba of Iona, Brendan of Clonfert, Brendan of Birr, etc.

After Patrick died, episcopal succession was at best haphazard with the monks filling in the ecclesiastical vacuum. Monasteries built along clan lines tended to become ecclesiastical centers. Although some monks were ordained presbyters and bishops in order to administer the sacraments, they continued to live in the monastery and follow the rule.

Though Patrick had spoken of monks, but not of monasteries and his disciple Assicus is called abbot, as was Cormac of Armagh, the great wave of Irish monasticism in the sixth century flowed over from Wales. Besides Clonard founded by Finnian before 515, we find Ciaran establishing Clonmacnois on the Shannon (545) and Comgall building Bangor on the south shore of Belfast Loch (555-559), Brendan instituting Clonfert in Connacht (558 or 564) and Columba erecting Durrow, Derry and Iona also in the sixth century. Along with Armagh, Kildare and Aran, these monastic foundations were to become the intellectual and spiritual centers of Ireland. Some such as Bangor were to become missionary centers, sending monks to found other houses in other lands.

So by the middle of the seventh century the Irish churches were largely monastic, each with a little walled city in which the monks or nuns of the clan lived according to the monastic discipline and ministered to the spiritual needs of their people. There were also smaller chapels of ease administered from the main monastery. The head of the clan church was the abbot, a blood relative of the founder, inheriting his power, prestige and property. The central monastery with its satellites formed a clan *paruchia* under the abbot, a *familia,* not necessarily territorially united. One reason for the success of monasticism in Ireland was the natural bent that the Irish had for the life. It also may have provided a haven for non-inheriting sons, old maids and widows of the clan.

The monastic buildings, enclosed in a circular wall, included a church, refectory, school, guest house, and cells for two or three monks. Although we have no written rules for the period, no doubt later models imitated earlier ones such as at Bangor. In general, the life was based on the counsels, asceticism, prayer and liturgy, taciturnity, mortification, fasting, celtic tonsure, work, study, calligraphy. There seems to have been a custom of clan families donating a son as a tithe to the monastery. Private confession to the monks began to replace the repugnant public penance and Irish penitentials were formed to aid the confessors.

Although Patrick had spoken of virgins, they probably either lived at home or were attached to a particular church. But with the advent of the male monasteries came also those for the ladies. Brigit (c. 460-528) was an early legendary foundress. Born of a noble father and a slave girl, but well-educated, she vowed her virginity before bishop Maccaille who gave her a white dress and veil. Then she went to live in an oak forest, formerly dedicated to a pagan god or goddess, founding a female monastery there called Kildare (Cell-dara, Cell of the Oak), in the valley of Liffey.

This was a double monastery, a rarity in Ireland, although more common in the East where it eventually was legislated out of existence due to abuses. Brigit's double monastery had houses or cells for monks and nuns not far apart so that they could come together in the central church and follow the same rule. The men dispensed the sacraments, gave spiritual direction, did the heavy work and afforded protection, while the women sewed, cooked, etc. In their synaxes in the church they were separated by a high partition with special entrances for the monks and nuns. Although the men were under abbot Conlaed, Brigit probably dominated the whole setup.

In the middle of the seventh century the community of Kildare asked Cogitosus to write Brigit's life. Since he knew little of her history, he embroidered the story with popular legends and myths so that she resembled the popular pagan goddess of fire.

Brigit was born at sunrise neither within nor without a house, was bathed in milk, her breath revives the dead. A house in which she is staying flames up to heaven. Low cow-dung blazes before her, oil is poured on her head. She is fed from the milk of a white red-eared cow. A fiery pillar rises over her head. Sun rays support her wet cloak. She remains a virgin and she was one of the two mothers of Christ the anointed. She has, according to Giraldus Cambrensis, a perpetual ashless fire watched by twenty nuns, of whom herself was one, blown by fans or bellows only and surrounded by a hedge within which no male could enter.[8]

Brigit's feast, February 1, corresponds to that of the pagan Imbolc. Actually Brigit was the name of a popular Celtic goddess and, indeed, seemed to be a common name for all the Celtic goddesses. Brigit took over the attributes of the pagan goddess, namely, patroness of poets, healing and smith-work. Cell-dara may well have been a pagan shrine before Brigit took it over. The sacred oaks and the perpetual fire complete the picture. A college of priestesses may have been in attendance to keep the sacred fire, honoring the fire-goddess Brigit. Moreover the

8. W. Stokes, Preface to **Three Middle Irish Homilies**.

head of the college may have been looked upon as the reincarnation of the goddess. Perhaps on conversion to Christianity she brought her virgins with her. This is the theory of R.A.S. Macalister,[9] trying to explain the mix of pagan myth with Christian tradition.

In Irish folklore Brigit is inferior only to Patrick, a prophetess of Christ, queen of the South, Mary of the Gael, missionary to all of Ire. It seems that the Patrician *paruchia* looked with favor on Brigit and her community, dedicating a church to her at Armagh. Together with Patrick and Columba she is patroness of Ireland.

Another famous Irish monastic foundation was that of Ciaran at Clonmacnois (545), ranking after Armagh as a great Irish church, although not as well organized as Patrick's or Columba's *paruchiae*. But by the seventh century its *paruchia* covered one half of Ireland including some of the Patrician churches. The monastery helped conserve the Gaelic and Latin learning through the Viking raids to become the national annals, including the *Chronicon Scotorum* and *Annals of Tigernach*. Present day ruins embrace two towers, eight churches, three Irish crosses, a castle and two hundred grave stones. In the tenth century Clonmacnois became a diocese under the abbot bishop.

Another celebrated Irish monastic tradition is Brendan of Clonfert (d. 577 or 583) in County Galway. His close association with the west Irish coast and the Scottish isles may have given substance to his maritime legends mixed with secular stories. The Irish monks Brendan, Columba and Columban, urged on by monastic wanderlust and the desire for the idyllic desert isle, set out across the seas. By the seventh and eighth centuries the Irish monks were to be found on the most remote islands along the Scottish and Irish coasts, the Hebrides, Orkneys, Faroes and even Iceland. Some say they reached Greenland and Vinland. Brendan, as many of his confreres, sought the far distant island paradise where he and his monks would find the solitude away from the world to pursue their monastic way in peace and union

9. RIA 34 C (1919), pp. 340-341.

with God. His legend passed through Britain and Brittany in the ninth century and into European literature.

B. *Columba of Iona* (c. 521-597)

The name Columba or dove (Hebrew, Jonas) was a common one in Irish monastic history. There are twenty others in the Irish calendar of saints. Columba, also called Columcille or Dove of the Cell, belonged to the royal family of Nialls (or O'Donnells, Clan-Domnaill) who ruled in the northwestern part of Ireland, covering Hibernia and also Caledonia, including the two shores of the Scottish Sea by the sixth century. Right up to the twelfth century the O'Donnell kings held the primacy of Ireland, the two chief branches, the O'Neills and the O'Donnells often at war, and even after Reformation times they resisted the Tudors and the Stuarts.

Columba's father descended from one of the eight sons of the great King Niall (379-403) and Columba himself could well have been a king of Ireland. Born at Gartan, Donegal, in 521 he was at an early age given in fosterage to a presbyter who baptized him and gave him an elementary education. Later he went to Clonard for further studies under Finnian.

After a pilgrimage to the tomb of Martin, Columba founded a number of monasteries including Durrow, Kells, and Derry, supervising their discipline, study and works. A learned man and a bard in his own right, he authored poems in both Latin and Gaelic. As his bard friends, he was a great lover of manuscripts and books. In fact, there is a legend about his dispute with Finnian over a manuscript which led to a clan war and Columba's subsequent exile.

At the synod of Teilte (562) Columba was excommunicated for having been the occasion of the shedding of Christian blood in the war. But when he was defended by Brendan of Birr, the excommunication was withdrawn, but Columba was ordered to win pagans to Christ to replace the brethren lost in battle. Smitten with remorse, he went from monastery to monastery, seeking what to do to obtain God's pardon. The monk Abban consoled him with the thought that the deceased enjoyed eternal life. Another monk Molaise advised him to go into exile away from Ireland.

So at the age of forty-two, accompanied by twelve disciples in a large boat of osier branches covered with hide, he rowed and sailed to the island of Io off the coast of Caledonia (563). Afterwards it was known as Iona. It is a small isle, two by three miles, low, flat and rocky, overshadowed by the height of Mull Island. Choosing the eastern shore away from the prevailing western winds, Columba and his brethren built huts of branches. Since it was necessary to have a tomb over which to build the monastery and so claim permanent possession, he asked the monk Odran to oblige. So he quickly died and was buried there.

Columba's irascible temper was mellowing. But he still longed for his native land. Although he kept jurisdiction over his Irish foundations, Iona was to remain his headquarters. He worked hard physically and intellectually, keeping his love of manuscripts, making over three hundred copies of the gospels alone. His life was austere even to sleeping on the floor with a rock for a pillow. New satellites spread from Iona to neighboring isles and into Caledonia. All told, Columba built over three hundred monasteries and churches in Caledonia and Hibernia, fifty-three in what is now modern Scotland (thirty-two in the western lands and the country of the Irish-Scots, twenty-one in the land of the Picts).

Besides the warlike Picts who had terrorized the Romans, fighting naked with painted bodies, Columba found some of his own race settled to the west and southwest of the Picts. These were the Irish-Scots who were to become the masters of Caledonia, eventually giving their name to the country, Scotland. These were the Scottish Dal Reti who in 500-503 had crossed the sea to settle on the islands and on the west coast of Caledonia between the Picts on the north and the Britons on the south, their chiefs becoming the root stock of the Stuarts. They also had an alliance with the Niall princes, which was a great help to Columba in obtaining Iona as a gift from the king of the Dal Reti. These migrating Scots were only nominally Christian. Columba not only worked with them but also with the northern Picts. Struggling with the local druids, he converted the Pict king Brude.

Columba returned to Druimm Cete, Ireland (575) to mediate a dispute between the native Irish and the independent Scots of Caledonia. He also spoke in favor of the powerful bards who were under fire due to jealousy and opposition to their influential positions. It was the bard-monk Columba who saved the bards although not without some restrictions to their powers. Despite abuses, Columba recognized the cultural value of the bardic profession. In gratitude they sang his praises in hymn and poem. No longer would there be opposition between the Christian religion and the Irish bards, whose music and poetry were to prove strong allies of church and country. To this day the bardic harp has remained the emblem of the Irish, reflecting their fierce independence and spirit of song. And the vagabond harper, vestigial descendant of the once powerful and glorious bards, can be found playing at the liturgy, singing of the troubles and the longings. Not only in Ireland, but wherever the Irish migrated, Caledonia, Gaul, the Celtic muse was in hot pursuit.

Living on an island, Columba and his monks had to be skilled seamen, sailing and rowing back and forth to Ireland, Caledonia and other islands in their osier boats covered with buffalo hides. The monastic longing for solitude lured the brethren to distant and deserted isles. Cormac, abbot of Durrow, one of Columba's monasteries, was a noted sailor, floating far up into the icey northern oceans in search of his wilderness paradise. Columba himself often went on voyages with his monks, founding monasteries along the way, praying for good weather, helping with the rowing. Still today he is the patron of winds and sailors in distress.

When Columba died in 597, his body was taken to Down where it was buried with Patrick and Brigit, his co-patrons. Both his royal lineage and his primacy of Ireland and Caledonia contributed to his stature. The monastic church had replaced the haphazard episcopal system of Patrick. Although there had been bishops from the beginning, from the end of the sixth century they were monks living in the monastery. Yet the presbyter-abbot Columba was careful lest he celebrate mass in a bishop's presence or usurp his power to ordain.

Did Columba write a rule? Bede (HE 3:25) has Wilfrid of York speaking of it at the synod of Whitby (664). But he could have meant the monastic tradition of Columba's family. Following a probationary period, the monks took vows to live a life of celibacy, poverty, obedience, fasting, prayer and study of Scripture. They practiced auricular confession and received the Eucharist at solemn mass on Sundays. Even if Columba did not write a rule, his family tradition lasted for several centuries to be eclipsed by the continental Benedictines. As a clan monastery most of the monks were related, for example, of the first eleven abbots after Columba ten are of the race of Tyrconnel, descendants of the same son of King Niall. The abbatial succession of Iona was uninterrupted till the invasion of the Danes in the ninth century, then leadership of Columba's family was transferred to Kells for three centuries.

Columba was the central figure in the golden age of the Irish monastic church lasting till the ninth century. In this era Ireland was the religious and intellectual center of Europe. Leaders in education, preaching, missions, poetry, classics, calligraphy, the writing of annals, the monks founded monasteries in Scotland, Britain, Armorica, Gaul, Alsatia, Bavaria, Helvitia, Allemania and Italy. Untroubled by Barbarian invasions, Irish monastic schools attracted English students especially from the seventh to the eleventh centuries to learn classics, poetry, music, scripture.

Although the monks were holy and studious, they were not above engaging in an occasional bloody clan war. We have already seen the clash over the copied manuscript of Finnian. Two centuries after Columba we find two hundred of his monks killed in a battle with the monks of Clonmacnois.

By the seventh century a decline of discipline was evident in the great monastic cities of Kildare, Bangor, and Clonmacnois. As earlier in monastic history, by the third generation the ideals of the founder grew dim. By their work and tithing vast estates had accrued. The people of the *paruchia* had to pay a regular tithe called the *lex* of the founder, who went around in the person of his relics just as the king used to visit subject territories to collect taxes. Another source of wealth was the pilgrim offerings, and the lives of the saints were written in legendary form to attract more tourists. Eventually lay abbots were to arise, passing along the rich properties from father to son.

C. *Columban* (c. 543-615)

Columban was another of the many doves of Irish monasticism. Born of a noble family of Leinster, he was well read and knowledgeable in the arts and Latin authors. A handsome lad, he felt strong urges of sensuality. In a conversation with a woman hermit, he realized his vocation. And although his mother objected strenuously to his call, he walked out of the house over her prostrate body, traveling to Cluain Inis where he studied scriptures and sacred doctrine under Sinell a disciple of Finnian of Clonard and at Bangor he was trained under Comgall's rigorous rule, acquiring a reputation as a teacher.

In 591 Columban set out with the customary twelve apostles for the Gaulic missions via Britain and Armorica. There he found the Christian religion weak due to the plundering of the Franks and the immorality of the clergy. There were a few monks and hermits, but the countryside was filled with superstition. When the Merovingian king Childebert invited him to stay in Burgundy, he settled first at Annegray in Vosges where amid the desert, solitude, rocks and forests he wrote little books of sentences for the natives. When the number of monks grew, he moved to Luxeuil to a strong castle. Columban built three monasteries in succession: Annegray, Luxeuil and Fontaines, stressing perpetual praise of God, agriculture and severity of discipline.

Used to the Irish church where the monks ran everything, Columban ignored the local clergy. And here began a long clash between the vagabond, free-wheeling Irish monks and the Gaulic hierarchy, which was not finally settled till Benedict's rule supplanted Columban's in Gaul. First of all, Columban did not bother to ask the local bishop's permission to settle in his diocese according to the canons of Chalcedon and sixth century Gaulic councils. Moreover, he acted as a prophet when dealing with those in authority, either bishops or civil authorities. Also his Irish customs, tonsure and Easter caused consternation.

Under fire, Columban wrote to the bishops and appealed to Pope Gregory the Great (600). Although maintaining his firm loyalty to the holy see, he defends the Irish customs as true ancient Catholic tradition. Gregory, always sympathetic to the monks, placed Columban's foundations under the protection of abbot Conon of Lérins.

When summoned to defend himself before the synod of Châlon (603), Columban wrote:

> I am not the author of this difference. I have come to these parts a poor stranger, for the cause of the Christ savior, our common God and Lord. I ask of your holiness but a single grace: that you will permit me to live in silence in the depth of the forests, near the bones of seventeen brethren whom I have already seen die. I shall pray for you with those who remain to me, as I ought, and as I have always done for twelve years. . . .
>
> But before you throw me overboard, it is your duty to follow the example of sailors, and to try first to come to land. Perhaps it might not be excess of presumption to suggest to you that many men follow the broad way, and that when there are a few who direct themselves to the narrow gate that leads to life, it would be better for you to encourage than to hinder them. . . . Regard us not as strangers to you; for all of us whether Gauls or Britons, Spaniards or others, are members of the same body (L 2).[10]

One of the main bones of contention was the celebration of the Irish Easter on a different date from the rest of Gaul which

10. Quoted by DeMontalembert in **The Monks of the West** II, Boston, Noonan, 1860, pp. 555-556.

followed the Roman custom. Early Christians had commemorated the Resurrection of Jesus on the Passover, the fourteenth of Nisan, the first full moon after the vernal equinox. Then on the Sunday after or on the Passover as instituted by Pope Demetrius of Alexandria (189-232) and approved by the council of Nicaea (325). The old Jewish cycle of eighty-four years for determining the date of Passover and Easter was followed by the British and Celts from their earliest missionary days. Cut off from Rome by the Saxon invasions of the sixth century, they were unaware of the change in Rome in 527 in favor of the Alexandrian cycle of nineteen years. In Gaul Columban's little band soon became painfully aware of the discrepancy. Besides the Irish Easter, their druidic tonsure and different Baptismal customs irritated the Gauls.

At the time Queen Brunhild was regent of Burgundy in the name of her grandson, Theuderich II, preferring to see him surrounded by a harem, rather than take a young queen who would deprive her of her power. When Columban preached prophetically against the king's conduct, refusing to bless his bastards, Brunhild forbade him and his monks to leave their monastery. Then when Columban refused Brunhild's courtiers entrance into the monastic cloister, she angrily ordered his exile.

While waiting at Nantes for passage back to Ireland, a storm came up delaying the passage. Columban turned back, taking care to avoid Theuderich's territory by way of Paris, Metz, Coblenz, Mainz, following the Rhine to Lake Constance. He remained at Bregenz two or three years before moving on to avoid Theuderich. When his companion Gall begged to stay behind due to illness, Columban angrily forbade him to say mass until after Columban's death. Gall set up a hermitage there which would develop into the famous monastery of S. Gall.

Meanwhile Columban traveled south into Italy, crossing the Po River and stopping beyond Pavia at the foot of Mt. Penici at the junction of the Bobbio and Trebia Rivers, where a church was located. Columban received the right to the place from King Agilulf. Columban maintained his allegiance with Rome, writing to Pope Boniface IV (612-613) to encourage him to stand firm

against the Three Chapters which had condemned the alleged
errors of Theodoret along with those of Nestorius. Columban was
not above twitting the pope about one of his lax predecessors
"Vigilius non bene vigilavit." And once again he defends his
Irish orthodoxy.

> We Irish have never included heretics, Jews or schismatics. . . .
> Ever since Christ, the supreme Lord of chariots came to us,
> borne by the sea gales on the backs of dolphins, Rome became
> for us noble and famous above others. If you are held in
> high honor through the honor of your see, you should beware
> of losing such honor by any lapse whatsoever. Your power
> will last as long as your discernment, for the heavenly porter
> is he who opens the gates to the worthy and closes them to
> the unworthy. . . . If he act otherwise he will be unable either
> to open or to close them (L 5).[11]

Columban died in 615, leaving a long string of foundations
all over Europe. Besides the most notable, Luxeuil, Bobbio and
S. Gall, there were Rebais, Jumièges, Fontaines, Chelles, Fare-
moutiers, Corbie, S. Omer, S. Bertin, Remiremont, etc. His monks
did missionary work among the Allemani, Bavarians, Thuringians
across the Rhine, the Germanic tribes preferring the Irish to
their natural enemies the Franks.

Celtic monasticism was not to be of a very long duration
in Europe for several reasons. First, the idea of foreign extra-
episcopal foundations was not compatible with the episcopal
framework of the Gaulic church of the time. Secondly, the Irish
monks were wanderers, moving from place to place, seeking
a peaceful paradise. Also their peculiar Irish customs were repugnant to the natives. Finally, the harsh Irish rule did not appeal
to the Gauls or Italians. Just as Cassian had mitigated Egyptian
monastic rigors for the Gaulic monks, so Benedict's rule would
become a modifying force in Celtic monasticism.

Columban's rule (PL 80: 209-216) is the only surviving Irish

11. Quoted from J. DeCarreaux, **Monks and Civilization,** pp. 201-202.

monastic rule and its rigor may well reflect the traditions of
Bangor. Rather than a set of specific regulations, it is a general
mirror of perfection as Cassian's *Institutes*. He starts out with
fundamental obedience, for example, rising immediately at the
call of the senior. Throughout the rule he cautions against the
proud and the murmurers. He recommends silence and moderation in food and drink (1-3). Cupidity and vanity should be
crushed (4-5). The monk's virginity should be of both body
and mind (6). The synaxes should be recited in the canonical
manner varying with the seasons (8).

Mortification is important but must be done under the guidance of the elders. It is difficult to lean on the advice of others.

> Though this training seem hard to the hardhearted, namely,
> that a man should always hang upon the lips of another, yet
> by those who are fixed in their fear of God it will be found
> pleasant and safe, if it is kept wholly and not in part, since
> nothing is pleasanter than safety of conscience, and nothing
> safer than exoneration of the soul, which none can provide
> for himself by his own efforts, since it properly belongs to
> the judgment of others (9).[12]

"*Nemo sui casu iudex*" is the basis of monastic conferences and
confession to the elders and ultimately auricular confession of
the laity which grew out of it. Monastic mortification should be
sought in three ways, namely: not to argue or disagree, not to
speak whatever one wishes, not to have complete freedom to
come and go (9). The last section of Columban's rule (10) is
taken from Jerome's letter to the Gaulic monk Rusticus (L 125).

Columban's Common Rule (PL 80:216-223) is more specific,
delineating stiff penalties for violations of the rules. These consisted generally of blows on the hand with a stick. For example,
if some one ate without waiting for grace, six blows; talking at
table, six blows; calling anything his own, six blows; cutting the

12. Columban's rules quoted from L. Bieler, **Ireland, Harbinger of the
Middle Ages,** Oxford, 1963, pp. 32-39.

table with a knife, ten blows. The refectory was a problem area. Many of the monks, no doubt, were rude peasants, who, hungry from fasting and hard work, attacked the food voraciously, spilling, elbowing, knocking, etc.

> If it is much that is spilt, according to the measures of beer or portions of whatever things he has lost in spilling through the occurrence of neglect, let him supply for an equal number of days what he had been accustomed to receive lawfully for his own use, and know that he has lost them to his cost,— for example, that he drink water in place of beer. For what is spilt on the table and runs off it, we say that it suffices to seek pardon from one's seat.

Prayer was another area of lax discipline. For example, one who left the house without prostrating himself before the abbot to ask a prayer and after receiving his blessing not blessing himself and not approaching the cross, twelve blows; forgetting to pray before and after work, twelve blows. Coughing during the synax, twelve blows; smiling, six blows; but laughing out loud punished with a special fast. However, allowance was made for pardonable laughter in case of a humorous lapse by one of the reciting monks. Heavier penalties: fifty blows (twenty-five at a time) for unrepentant talebearing; fasting is prescribed for slander, abuse, and not asking pardon when corrected.

Those doing penance should only wash their heads on the Lord's day. Monks who experienced wet dreams should chant a few extra psalms. Following the custom of John Cassian, Psalm 69 (70) "Be pleased, O God, to deliver me; O Lord, make haste to help me" is recited at the end of the synax.

As his rule, so Columban's penitential (PL 80:223-230) is based on earlier Irish monastic legislation with many passages corresponding with the penitential of Finnian of Clonard. The purpose of the Irish penitentials was to aid the monk confessors, an institution which Columban introduced into the Gaulic church.

As we have seen, for a short period the influence of Columban was great in Europe with numerous foundations overshadowing the few Italian monasteries of Benedict. But it seems that the Gaulic monks in general found Columban's rule too severe, eventually preferring the more moderate rule of Benedict. Also, of course, imperial, papal and episcopal approval would, in time, favor Benedict's. Besides prestigious Bobbio, Gall's monastery not far from Lake Constance was to be the intellectual beacon of the Germanic world and Luxeuil was the monastic capital of Gaul. Other monasteries followed its lead, even the great Lérins whence monks had originally set forth for the conversion of Britain and Ireland and whose influence had come full circle in Columban. Luxeuil became a nursery for bishops and abbots, preachers and reformers in Gaul, Burgundy and Austrasia and a monastic school established there according to Irish tradition became one of the most illustrious in Christendom. Luxeuil produced many saints including Columban, Gall, Lua, Valery, Waldolenus, Hermenfried.

At the council of Mâcon (624) the peculiarities of the Irish monks were again a matter of concern. And although the bishops defended Luxeuil and its abbot Eustace, from this time on we find a mitigating of the Irish monastic rule in Gaul, with Columban's rule often accompanied by Benedict's In 641 Pope John IV of Rome exempted Luxeuil from episcopal authority, placing it directly under himself, following the precedent of Gregory the Great. The alliance of the monks and the papacy was to prosper both.

In conclusion, Columban's missionary endeavors gave the impetus to the growth of Gaulic monasticism. His rule and penitentials made an initial impact, although soon mitigated by Benedictine influence. Most of his Irish customs were lost as the first generation passed away. The fierce independence of Columban's monks from the local bishops underlines once again the basic dichotomy between the church of the monks and the church of the bishops. Eventually, under the protection of the popes, they would be exempt from episcopal jurisdiction. This along with the penitentials and dedication to the intellectual life were lasting contributions of the Irish monks to European monasticism.

D. Description and Influence of Irish Monasticism

A fine discussion of the Irish monks and their customs may be found in John Ryan's *Irish Monasticism* (Dublin, 1931). The Irish monk, as Basil's, was a soldier of Christ in a war against the devil and the world. He is the successor to the soldier-martyrs who fell in persecution.

Young Irish lads attracted to the monastic way were generally drawn by the example of the monks under whom they studied. The Irish had always honored learning, first in the druids and bards, then in the monks. Usually an Irish boy would begin his studies under the fosterage of a local cleric, but some went directly to the monastery for training.

When a youth who had studied under a cleric asked for permission to enter a monastery, he was lodged in the guest house where he was questioned by the abbot. If approved, he was admitted with a habit, Irish tonsure and perhaps a new name. In these days there was no novice master; rather the newcomer followed the monks by imitation under the guidance of the seniors. Jerome's letter (L 125) to Rusticus was used as a guide to monastic conduct. The young monks confessed regularly to the seniors. Columban followed Cassian and the desert fathers in training the young men by opposing their wills, for example, if talkative — silence; active — restraint; gluttonous — fasting; lazy — vigils. Traditional monastic heroes as Martin and Brigit were placed as examples.

Both Columba and Columban insisted on mutual love as the basis for community peace. They must guard their tongue for detraction and murmuring are the bane of monastic peace.

Although there is little evidence of a formal probation period in Irish monasticism, there undoubtedly was some training after coming in from the world. When the proper time arrived (age twenty for the younger ones) the aspirant made his vow of obedience on his knees before the abbot and all the monks. Following monastic tradition the great emphasis was on obedi-

ence even sometimes unreasonably as when Columban ordered
the sick to work (Jonas, *Life of Columban* 1:12), or when the
cellarer who was called while filling a jug of beer, went away
leaving the spigot running (*Ibid.* 1:16). Another story told in
the *Lives of the Irish Saints*: when some monks were working
alongside a stream, the senior in charge yelled "Colman get into
the water." Immediately twelve Colmans jumped in. The brother
who left the letter unfinished to answer the call of obedience is
found in all monastic literature.

In the Irish monasteries everything was held in common with
no one having his own property under heavy penalties. Of course
the monastery could own property and the eventual accumulation
of wealth by industry, tithing and gifts brought the very worldli-
ness that the monks had initially sought to escape. In every case
riches spelled the downfall of monastic institution and a falling
away from pristine fervor.

It seems that the Irish monastic vow was permanent so that
to leave without permission was classed with fornication, murder
and theft in Columban's penitential. However, a monk could leave
the monastery for the higher hermit's life. As we have seen Irish
monastic wanderlust drove them to far distant shores in search
of paradise.

As frequently found in monastic history, Irish monasticism
was based on the family, here in the broader sense of the clan,
with the abbot frequently a clan leader as Columba. The clan
monasteries dominated the Irish church with cleric monks
to ordain and dispense the sacraments. The clan *paruchiae*
were wide spread, sometimes covering a large section of the
country with rival clans often disputing territory.

In general, the Irish monks maintained a good rapport with
Rome. While their leaders respected the primacy of the See of
Peter, Rome, in return, served as a court of higher appeal when
the Irish monks were persecuted by local bishops.

The Irish monks served the laity wherever they went. And
often the pious laymen who worked the monastery fields were

difficult to distinguish from the monks themselves. Irish law describes the mutual relationship between the monks and their tenants.

> The social connection which subsists between the Church and its tenants of ecclesiastical lands is that of 'preaching and offering and requiem for souls which is due from the Church to its tenants of ecclesiastical lands, and the receiving of every son for instruction, and of every such tenant to right repentance.' Tithes and first-fruits and alms are due of them to her, and full honor price when they are in strong health and one-third honor price at the time of death. And the church has the power of pronouncing judgment and proof and witness upon its tenants of ecclesiastical lands.[13]

The divine office was the principal prayer of the Irish monks as in the whole of monastic tradition. By the eighth century the *Cursus Scottorum* had developed fully alongside the other *Cursus* of the church. With seven hours, Columban imitated John Cassian's division of the psalms. At the chanting of the office, the abbot with his assistants sat in the middle of the oratory, with the monks ranged on the right and on the left. Silence, reverence and punctuality were insisted upon. They stood during the chanting, bowing at the end of the psalms and kneeling during the collects, followed by the *"Deus in adjutorium meum intende"* (Ps 69 [70] three times in silence. Then all arose to leave. The Irish office bore resemblances to the Egyptian through Lérins and Britain, although further developed. Ryan (345) comments on the Irish devotion to the divine office.

> Perhaps because they were less capable of contemplation than the Easterns, the Irish monks showed an exceptional zeal in reciting the psalms and other vocal prayers. This trait remained with them through the centuries. Remarkable later

13. From S. Bryant, **Liberty, Order and Law under Native Irish Rule**, London, Harding & More, 1923, C.5, N.2, pp. 75-76.

is the devotion to the long psalm 118, apparently because of its unusual length. Genuflections and prostrations in phenomenal number during prayer are likewise a mark of later Irish asceticism.

Mass was celebrated on Sundays and feasts such as Easter, Christmas, S. Martin, Peter and Paul, and the feast of the founder. The fifty days of Easter-tide were looked upon as Sundays. Mass was usually at an early hour preceded by a confession of sins, then litany of the saints, two prayers, wine and water poured into the chalice. Then after various prayers, epistle and gospel, creed, offertory, the canon of Pope Gelasius, reception of the Eucharist under both species, communion and post-communion prayers.

A monk-bishop presided at the Eucharist and no monk-presbyter could celebrate in his presence without his permission. And when several presbyters were present, only one celebrated, although he could ask another to help break bread. The monks received the Eucharist each Sunday and feast with an emphasis on its medicinal value. They agreed with Cassian that the Eucharist is for sinners and they should not keep themselves from it under pretext of sin. But capital sins and sins of the flesh are to be avoided, even sins of thought before communion. The monks carried the blessed sacrament with them in small chrismals when on journeys or while working in the fields, taking care not to desecrate it.

We have already mentioned the Irish monastic confession. The early Egyptian conferences were basically spiritual dialogues with an elder. Columban (Common Rules) suggests confessing twice a day before dinner and before bed. The penitentials grade the punishment according to the offense. Irish confession was also extended to the laity and made a great contribution to the development of the sacrament of Penance.

As we have seen, the Irish monks made an outstanding contribution to the intellectual life of Europe. Removed from the main stream of the barbarian invasions, Ireland was able to preserve the classical heritage brought by the British monks.

By the fifth century the Roman educational system of grammar and rhetoric was common throughout the empire with the emphasis on the classical authors. Christianity and Roman culture did not always mix well with some such as Tertullian and Sulpicius Severus against the use of the pagan classics, while others as Augustine and Jerome saw them useful although not without qualification. Lérins combined a serious study of the sacred Scriptures with a lesser use of the classics. The Lérinsian tradition spread to Britain in the monastic schools of Illtud, Finnian and Gildas thence flowing to Ireland.

The Christian Latin education of Lérins dominated the sixth and seventh century Irish monasticism with the holy Scriptures as the main stay, but the Fathers were read also. And profane Latin literature was studied to help gain a mastery of the Latin tongue. Although native Irish traditions were often looked upon as superstitious and pagan, the gulf began to close between the two cultures as the monks developed the native Irish tongue into a written language using the Celtic sounds with the Latin language as a model.

On the frontiers of the church, the Irish monks were in a strong position as go-betweens of the Roman church and the Celtic culture.

> Having accepted, assimilated and fostered the national culture, their influence in Ireland was immense. Having assimilated classical culture which the church saved for Europe, they were able to return to the continent and play no mean part in repairing the intellectual losses caused by the barbarian invasions (Ryan 377).

With a good basic knowledge of Latin, the monks concentrated on theology including dogma, moral, canons, liturgy, but especially the Latin bible. Most study was based on reading (*lectio*). At least in the beginning, the monk-teachers and the books, too, were from Britain. But the transcription of manuscripts, many of which were beautifully illuminated became a chief vocation of the Irish monks. Thus excellent monastic libraries were built up. Although holy Scriptures were the chief works transcribed, sacred and some profane authors were also copied.

The monks not only taught their own, but secular students as well, with many coming from Britain especially during the seventh century. Usually they went to the cells of the monks for private tutoring, although there seem to have been school houses attached to some monasteries. The monk-educators were distant ancestors of the tutorial system of the medieval universities which took over when the monasteries abandoned education in the twelfth century. Their grand tradition as religious teachers dating back to Basil, the Irish monks swelled the intellectual tide on the islands and the continent in manuscripts, libraries and schools.[14]

And so Irish monasticism adds its synthesis to the long ascetical inheritance beginning in Egypt. Brought to the West by men like Athanasius, Jerome and Cassian, the monk's life was mitigated for the western temperament. Although obedience, asceticism and office are essentially the same, more emphasis is placed on liturgy and office. And more stress on intellectual pursuits as the Lérins model passed to Britain and Ireland.

By the sixth century monasticism is firmly established in Ireland, austere, learned and zealous for souls. Many of the monks were clerics as the Lérinsian missionaries. But they were not clerics following the monastic way as in many episcopal centers of the time. No, they are monks who for the necessity of the apostolate and the lack of secular clergy became clerics. But even the monk-bishops were just as the other monks, taking precedence only in the administration of the sacraments.

Although basically cenobites, the Irish monks always dreamed of the lonely paradise where, free from the distractions of the

14. D. Knowles in his introduction to Workman's **Evolution of the Monastic Ideal** (Boston, Beacon, 1962, pp. xii-xiii) writes that perhaps too much emphasis has been attached by some to the monastic schools of the early Middle Ages. These schools were usually of a short duration and did not handle large numbers of students. The monks mostly educated their own and local clerics and provided first rate manuscripts and libraries.

world, they could find peace with God. Their multifarious pere-grinations were often coupled with missionary zeal. Needless to say, their search for paradise was frustrated, but as they trudged and sailed their way to such distant lands as Gaul and Italy they brought along the Irish tradition of love of Christ and learning to the rude barbarians of the continent, forming the matrix for the Christian Middle Ages.

9. Nothing That Is Harsh, Nothing Rigorous
(Prologue of the Rule of S. Benedict)

he rule of St. Benedict marks a turning point in the history of Christian monasticism. Although the Christian monks achieved a reasonable, though sometimes short term success in Egypt, Asia Minor, Palestine, Africa, Gaul and Ireland, it was for Benedict to organize earlier traditions into a workable rule adapted to the European soul and with the help of papal patronage to spread the Benedictine family throughout Europe.

What was the condition of Europe at the end of the fifth century when Benedict came on the scene? Confusion! Barbarian invasions had reduced Europe to a shambles. Monasticism which had enjoyed a brief success earlier, was on the wane. Italy, already pillaged by Alaric and Attila, now enjoyed a relative peace under Theodoric.

The barbarians had founded new states and kingdoms throughout the empire. Germany was pagan. In Britain the young faith was throttled by the invading Angles and Saxons. Gaul was plundered on the north by the heathen Franks and on the south by the Arian Burgundians, while Spain was ruined by the Visigoths, Sueves, Alans and Vandals, the latter going on to lay waste Africa. Many of these countries in which Christianity was still in its infancy, were ground down by the advancing hordes, mostly Arians. The morals of the empire were at a new low. In Italy there remained a Catholic substratum of the old Roman population, all but smothered by many settlements of the Arian Teutons. And underneath it all still survived layers of paganism.

Rome in the fifth century was the capital of popes, but no longer the head of the empire. The clergy were split into factions, some serving the Arian king Theodoric, while others looked to Byzantium. A schism arose dividing the church of Rome from Byzantium (484-518) with Pope Symmachus who opposed Byzantium faced by a rival pope Laurentius. But Symmachus was restored to power by Theodoric. When Justinian acted against the Arians (520), Theodoric ordered Pope John to Constantinople to defend the Arian cause. Later Pope Vigilius, who owed his job to Justinian, compromised in the Three Chapters incident (544-), prompting Columban's famous remark about his lack of vigilance (L 5).

Monasticism had had a popular run in the fourth and fifth century Italy, with foundations at Milan, Rome, and elsewhere. The visits of Athanasius plus his *Life of Antony* had whetted Roman interest. Roman ladies as Marcella and Paula lived as nuns in their palaces under the guidance of ascetics like Jerome and Pelagius. With the last days at hand, they escaped the impending invasions into Africa and the Holy Places to found convents there. Although the rules of Basil and Pachomius were known, Italian monasticism was rather unorganized. Fifth century Roman asceticism was eclectic with borrowings from Pachomius, Basil and the traditions of the desert fathers. Basically it was Egyptian cenobitical, yet with a love of solitude. But laxity had crept in by the time of Benedict.

A. *Benedict of Nursia* (480-543)

Benedict was born in 480 in Nursia, a municipal town and episcopal seat on the slopes of the Sabine Apennines, thirty miles east of Spoleto. As a youth he was sent to Rome to study law and rhetoric. But tempted by women and a spirit of pride, he fled to Nero's abandoned villa, Sublaqueum (Subiaco) on three lakes on the Anio River, twelve miles from Tivoli and thirty miles from Rome. There he found a hermit Romanus, who became his spiritual father. Benedict lived in a cave there for three years, while Romanus supplied him with food. Although the local shepherds at first feared him, he soon won them over by his austere life and example.

Some monks of a neighboring monastery, hearing of his virtue, asked Benedict to be their abbot. But when he tried to reform their lax ways, they attempted to poison him. Chagrined, Benedict returned to his cave, where his disciples continued to increase until he had to erect twelve new houses, each for twelve monks on nearby hills. Clerics, laity, Romans and Goths came to help him till the soil and follow the ascetical way.

A local priest, Florentius by name, was jealous of Benedict's success, and tried to defame, poison him, finally employing seven nude nubile young maidens. This was too much. Appointing superiors for the twelve houses, Benedict fled to Monte Cassino (529), a 1,700 feet high hill overlooking the Liris River near its head. At the foot of the hill is an ancient amphitheater in the ruins of the town of Cassinum. When he found the local people practicing paganism in a temple of Apollo in a sacred grove, Benedict persuaded them to cut down the woods and tear down the temple. On the ruins he built two oratories, one to John the Baptist and the other to Martin.

Benedict lived at Monte Cassino fourteen years (529-543), building up the monastery, cultivating the sides of the mountain, preaching to the local people. Parts of the earliest monastery may date from this period, for example, the low entrance gate and the lower portion of the square tower which may have been the residence of Benedict and his companions. Over the centuries Monte Cassino was destroyed and rebuilt many times from the Lombards (sixth century) to the Americans (twentieth century). At its height in the fourteenth century the abbot of Monte Cassino was the first baron of the Kingdom of Naples and head of a spiritual diocese.

Benedict attracted many followers from all classes, rich and poor, Goths and Italians. He had a great zeal for the welfare of his neighbors, preaching, healing, giving alms and provisions in time of need. For example, in the famine of 539 he gave away all the monastery's bread until only five loaves were left. But the next day two hundred bushels of flour were found at the monastery gate.

Benedict insisted on the family spirit in his monastery based on the Roman *familia,* with the abbot as *pater familias.* His sister Scholastica joined him in a nunnery down the valley. Both died in 543 and are buried at Monte Cassino. Although he left only three foundations, namely, Subiaco, Monte Cassino, and Terracino, Benedict's Rule was to become more widespread under Pope Gregory the Great.

Benedict's rule was written at Monte Cassino near the end of his life. According to tradition, he is the author of the *Rule of Monks,* but he may have used the anonymous *Master's Rule,* for many important passages in the two rules are identical. Although different hypotheses are entertained concerning the interrelationship of the two rules, most hold that Benedict was the teacher if not the author of the *Rule of Monks.* Workman notes [1] that Benedict's rule coincides with the promulgation of Justinian's code (529) and the closing of the schools of philosophers in Athens.

There was a need of an organized rule for the Western monks, for up to this time there had been an amalgam of customs,

1. **The Evolution of the Monastic Ideal,** p. 142.

some monks following Basil's rule, others trying to adapt Egyptian customs. From his early experiences Benedict saw the need of a moderate rule, avoiding both harshness and laxity. He studied the earlier traditions of Cassian, Basil and Pachomius. Whereas earlier rules were more general guides including spiritual wisdom sayings and discourses, Benedict built monastic tradition into a true legislation. He knew the lives of the fathers including Antony and Pachomius, Rufinus' *History of the Monks* and the *Apophthegmata Patrum,* plus Latin translations of the rules of Pachomius, Basil, Macarius and the rules of Augustine and Caesarius of Arles in the west. He also was familiar with the writings of Cyprian, Jerome, Leo, Sulpicius, and, of course, Holy Scripture.

Benedict's genius is not so much in originating, but in organizing, editing and adapting to the Italian temperament, eliminating things that are harsh and burdensome. He had no preconceived plan, but just seems to have written as the ideas came to him. Reflecting little educational background, his rules show a moderate talent in rhetorical composition.

Benedict's rule is for those starting out in the spiritual life. "We have, therefore, to establish a school of the Lord's service, in the institution of which we hope to order nothing that is harsh or rigorous" (*Prol.*).[2] Those who are beginners in spirituality must go to a spiritual school where they will learn the way of the Lord. This training for the Lord's army is not as violent and rigorous as Egyptian asceticism, yet, on the other hand, it is not an easy road, but a long struggle against sin, taking many years. "So that never departing from His guidance, but persevering in His teaching in the monastery until death, we may by patience share in the sufferings of Christ, that we may deserve to be partaking of His kingdom" (*Prol.*).

Having experienced various types of asceticism, Benedict felt that the anchorite life was not what was needed at the time.

2. Benedict's rules are taken from P. DeLatte, **The Rule of S. Benedict,** Latrobe, Penn., S. Vincent Archabbey, 1950.

Moreover, the solitary life never made the impact in the West that it had in the East. Neither did Benedict prefer small groups of hut-dwellers or the vast Pachomian institutions. Rather he wanted a moderate sized monastic family. Monastic life has always adapted to the ways of living of the times and places where it has thrived throughout history. In fact, it is a prime example of the inexorable law "Adapt or die." Benedict felt that the family style cenobium under an abbot was best suited to his times. In a sense it is a military family, with the monks serving (*militantes*) in the battle against Satan. The monks as soldiers of Christ had been a common teaching of the Fathers from the beginning.

Although theoretically Benedict, as John Cassian, may have seen the advantages of the hermit's life, he was practical enough to see it as unattainable for most. It is the wandering Sarabaites and Road-runners that Benedict wishes to counteract in particular. The tendency of the monks to wander, seeking greener pastures in far distant places, has always been a plague to monasticism. The Egyptian fathers and John Cassian blamed it on accidie and Benedict struck a blow against it with his vow of stability. "Leaving these (hermits, Sarabaites, etc.) alone, let us set out to work, by the help of God, to lay down a rule for the cenobites —that is, the strongest race of monks" (1).

The abbot is the key man in the Benedictine family (2, 64).[3] He is the counterpart of the father bishop of the episcopal church. Both of these are families of Christ, namely the church of the bishops and the church of the monks, whose leaders take the title of Father in lieu of Christ himself.[4] As father and shepherd,

3. See C. Butler, **Benedictine Monachism**, London, Longmans, 1919, pp. 184 -.

4. In general, the qualities of the abbot parallel those of the bishop, except for the power of orders and, of course, the presidency of the Eucharist, if the abbot is a layman. But, increasingly we find a cleric as abbot especially in Gaul and Ireland. And in the medieval period it was not unusual for abbots to ordain with papal permission.

the abbot should have concern for all, and as Christ's vicar and steward, he is responsible to the Master for all of those who are under him. He is a wise physician, applying the proper medicine to heal spiritual sickness, even amputating a diseased member for the good of the whole family (28). He should be wise and learned in order to teach by word and example, chaste, sober, merciful, not turbulent or anxious, not overdoing things, but prudent and considerate (64). Besides the natural virtues such as chastity and sobriety, the abbot should be of a conservative bent leaning to prudence and circumspection rather than zeal. Although slow and conservative church leaders both in the monastery and out have been a drag on progress, they are probably preferable in the long run to wild-eyed liberals.

Though the abbot should consult the community in matters of great importance and the seniors in lesser matters, the ultimate decision is his and the community must obey. So the family life of the monastery hinges on the abbot's judgment, command and permission. Any one who attempts anything without his approval is to be punished (67). As a father he has the care of the monk's souls; he must be just and prudent, fearing God and giving all that is necessary to avoid sadness and murmuring (41), having special concern for the weak (48, 64). The abbot is really the servant of the characters and temperaments of the monks, urging the obedient on to greater heights and reproving the negligent (2). But he should be careful not to overdo correction, ruling rather by love than by fear.

Quis custodiat custodes? Who keeps check on the abbot, if his power is absolute? First of all, great care should be had in his selection (64). But it could happen and did happen frequently in the history of monasticism that a decadent community elected an abbot who would allow them to continue in their laxness. Then the local bishop, neighboring abbots, or the laity should act to depose him (64). "Let him that has been appointed abbot always bear in mind what a burden he has undertaken, and to whom he will have to give an account of his stewardship. And let him know that it behoves him rather to profit his brethren than preside over them" (64). His conscience is the ultimate guarantee of the abbot's moral conduct. God alone will be his judge.

The good Christian family with all of the problems and advantages of sibling life, is the model of Benedict's monastery. Reflecting early church practice, emphasizing the local *ekklēsia,* each monastery is an independent family. Although Pachomius and the Irish monks had loose federations under an abbot general, it was not till after the more centralized church of the West under a powerful papacy, that we find the rise of the large ecumenical orders centered in Rome.

So the Benedictine family is the local community under its abbot. And love should be its governing principle, the love of the abbot for the monks and the monks for the abbot, and the love of the monks for each other (63). Cliques destroy family unity so one should not defend another nor take him under his protection (69). The young should honor their elders, who, in turn, should show love for the young. Moreover, in family differences, which are bound to rise, the young should show deference to the old (71).

As there is a zeal of bitterness which separates from God and leads to hell, so there is a good zeal, which separates from vices and leads to God and to life everlasting. Let monks, therefore, practice this zeal with fervent love, that is, in honor preventing one another. Let them most patiently endure one another's infirmities, whether of body or character. Let them obey one another with rivalry. Let no one follow what he judges good for himself, but rather what seems good for another. Let them tender the charity of brotherhood with chaste love, let them fear God, and love their abbot with sincere and humble affection. Let them prefer nothing whatever to Christ, and may he bring us all alike to life everlasting. Amen (72).

Benedict describes the ideal Christian family. But he is realistic enough to know that the monks would be jealous, envious, with personal likes and dislikes, lazy, gluttonous. The sleepy heads are to be encouraged to roll out of bed at the sound of the bell. "Let not the younger brethren have their beds by themselves, but among those of the seniors, and when they rise for the work of God, let them gently encourage one another, because of the excuses of the drowsy" (22). During the time assigned for reading, the elders go around to make sure that indolent monks are not sitting around gossiping and wasting time (48).

Although the abbot rules absolutely, he is not a disembodied head and so consults with his family as occasion demands. Moreover, he has assistants or deans in charge of ten or twenty monks (65) and other auxiliaries such as the cellarer with delegated authority. The idea of the perpetual abbot, based on the Roman *pater familias,* gives a certain stability to the monastic family.

Admissions are to be handled with caution (58). This is in accord with monastic tradition for the prospect of free meals, no responsibility and a secluded life drew all sorts of misfits: runaway slaves, escaped convicts, draft-dodgers, the lazy, not to say neurotics and psychotics just as it does today. Pachomius and Cassian had tested rigorously the sincerity of their candidates. So does Benedict, making them stay outside the monastery gate to endure the abuse of the brethren for four or five days before being admitted to the guest house.

The monastic life was looked upon as a conversion, a *metanoia*.[4a] So when the postulant is accepted, he begins a new life. In the early days of monasticism this change of life was a natural consequence of Baptism. The old life of sin is dead, replaced by the new life of grace. After his initial testing, Benedict's neophyte receives his novice habit, joining the other novices under the guidance of an elder. After two months the rule is read to him. "Behold the law under which you desire to fight: if you

4a. Although originally **conversi** were public penitents who had consecrated themselves to a life of celibacy and asceticism, by the sixth century the term is also applied to those who entered the monastery as adults. Monastic life as a conversion had been taught as far back as the Buddhist Samgha and the Qumran Covenant.

can keep it, enter; if you cannot, freely depart" (58). The challenge is repeated again after six months and once again after four more months. If the novice promises obedience to the rule he is to be admitted into the community on a permanent basis. Kneeling in the oratory before the abbot and all the monks, he promises stability, conversation (conversion) of morals, and obedience in the presence of God and his saints. Writing his petition in his own hand, he places it on the altar, or, if he is unable to write, he signs it. Then he recites "*Suscipe me, domine, secundum eloquium tuum et vivam; et non confundas me ab expectatione mea.*" The whole community answers three times, adding the *Gloria Patri*. "Then let the brother novice cast himself at the feet of all, that they may pray for him, and from that day let him be counted as one of the community" (58). Having given his property to the poor or to the monastery, stripped of his clothes, he puts on the monastic garb. But his old clothes are kept in the clothes room in case he leaves the monastery.

Although Shenoute of Atripe had a signed formula, it seems that Benedict is the first in the West to advocate it. Stability, conversion of morals and obedience are vowed, while poverty and chastity are included under obedience to the rule.

Stability was of prime importance in Benedict's monasticism, since the monks had a built-in wanderlust and once they got away from the strict monastic discipline, they tended to end up as bums as the Sarabaites, road-runners and the monk-like circumcellions. The tools of the spiritual life are best used within the cloister of the monastery and the stability of the community (4). The novices are to be tested thoroughly to see if they give promise of stability (58, 60, 61). Stability for Benedict means more than merely perseverance as a monk and observance of the rule, but rather an irrevocable life in the family in which he has been trained and recited his profession.

The monk should rarely leave the enclosure and then only when necessary and with the abbot's permission (60, 67). When a group of monks left the monastery to form a new house or mission, they took their stability with them. Although stability served well in the Benedictine centuries, it was to give way to the peripatetic Friars in the later Middle Ages when more mobility was needed for preaching and missionary work.

"*Conversatio morum suorum*" is the second vow. Some texts have "*conversio.*" In the Latin translation of Evagrius' *Sentences to Monks* we find, "*Conversationem monachi custodit scientia*" (63). The purification of morals aids towards and is guarded by the gnosis. Cassian has a similar message in Conference 14, 1. This seems to be the same "*conversatio*" or "*conversio*" that Benedict is talking about and which is a necessary prelude for any progress towards contemplation. Conversion of manners or morals is really what the religious life is all about. It is a new life, a stripping off of the old ways of sin. Of course, this is not achieved over night, but is a lifetime battle.

Obedience is a foundation stone of all cenobitic life and the humility and submission required makes religious communism superior to the independent and proud solitary. Actually obedience to the rule implies all the rest including poverty and chastity. The monk should see in the command of the abbot the will of God: "He who hears you, hears me," and act with all speed. This is the first degree of humility (5). Obedience should be spontaneous and be interior as well as exterior, choosing in a cheerful manner the way that leads to life. "For if the disciple obey with ill-will and not merely murmur with his lips but even in his heart, although he fulfill the command, yet he will not be accepted by God, who regards the heart of the murmurer" (5). If commanded something too difficult or impossible, the monk should represent the case. But if the superior insists, he should try to do the best he can (68). Obedience is not something reserved only towards the abbot and superiors, but also the monk must be obedient to the needs and requests of his fellow monks, especially the young towards the old (71).

Monastic tradition demanded poverty and chastity, for the family life precludes individual ownership of private property and marriage. As a *filius familias* the monk has no property of his own nor can he marry without the permission of the *pater familias* and when he does he leaves to found his own *familia* (*Code of Justinian* 2:22; 4:13; 10:62). For all practical purposes the monk is legally a child. This has been an objection to monasticism, namely, that it fosters immaturity. Perhaps an answer can be found in the Lord's words, "Unless you become as little children, you shall not enter the kingdom of heaven" (Mt 18:1ff; 9:33ff; Lk 9:46ff).

In entering his new family, the monk must dispose of all his personal property giving it either to the poor or to the monastery. Then he will receive all that he needs: food, clothing, shelter, etc. from the *bonus et diligens pater familias* who should give freely all that is necessary to avoid having the monks seeking things without permission (55). Benedict insists that his monks be dressed properly and not disreputable as the road-runners, for there is no virtue in wearing worn out clothing (55). Probably the monk's dress did not vary greatly from that of the minor ecclesiastics and the laity of the time. Nevertheless, in either food or clothing, *parcitas* or frugality is the norm (39).

Since all property now belongs to the family, corporate riches could accrue over the years, with lands, slaves, tithes, farm produce, tax exemptions. This was to spell the eventual downfall of many monasteries.

Benedict makes little mention of chastity, perhaps because it was taken for granted that to remain a *filius familias* precluded marriage. Certainly the vow of stability removed many if not most of the occasions of meeting with the opposite sex. In rule four Benedict lists among the instruments of good works (63) "*castitatem amare.*"

Manual work played a strong role in Benedict's monastery. Idleness was a basic cause of many monastic troubles as Augustine's *On the Work of the Monks* and Cassian's *On the Spirit of Accidie* (*Institutes*, Bk. 10) attest. From Easter to the Calends of October the monks worked from the first to the fourth hours and from the eighth hour to Vespers. The hours varied with the seasons of the year. "They are truly monks when they live by the labor of their hands, as our Fathers and the Apostles did, but let all things be done in moderation for the sake of the faint hearted" (48).

The principal work of the monks is the *Opus Dei*. The recitation of the divine office had always had a place in Christian tradition from the very beginning, based ultimately on the Jewish synaxes. Benedict takes up this inheritance and places it in the forefront. The monastery is the palace of Christ the King and the office is homage to him. So important is the office to Benedict that he devotes chapters 8 to 20 to regulations concerning the hours and psalms according to the season. The hours of Benedict's office are: Lauds, Prime, Terce, Sext, None, Vespers, Compline and Nocturns.

> We believe that the divine presence is everywhere and that the eyes of the Lord behold the good and the evil in every place. Especially do we believe this, without any doubt, when we are assisting at the Work of the Lord. . . . Therefore, let us consider how we ought to have ourselves in the presence of God and of his angels, and so assist at the Divine Office that mind and voice be in harmony (19).

All should lay aside their work immediately when the signal for office is sounded, so that nothing should be placed before the Work of God (43). Those who come after the 94th psalm in the night office should stand in the last place. However, Benedict mercifully recommends that the 94th psalm be recited slowly to give the sleepy heads a chance. But he was stricter on day time late-comers.

On Sundays and feasts there is a conventual Mass and Holy Communion (35 & 38). But following the lay tradition of monasticism, greater emphasis is on the liturgy of the Word. Benedict admitted clerics reluctantly into his family for as the Egyptian founders, he felt that the ecclesiastics destroyed the family spirit by dividing the brethren into clerical monks and lay monks. If a priest is accepted, he is to be treated as the lay brothers. Nevertheless, his priesthood is honored, for he stands after the abbot, giving a blessing and saying Mass with the abbot's permission (60). Priest monks were under the abbot even though he be a lay man or a deacon. Benedict himself probably never advanced beyond the deaconate.

Not only in public worship and the liturgy but in his whole life the son of Benedict should make his sacrifice to God, a *conversatio morum* in self-discipline and prayer. Minimizing the severities of the East, Benedict had no hairshirts, chains, scourges and prescribed the proper amount of food, sleep, clothing, etc. (39, 40, 17, 55). The lack of meat except for the sick probably reflected the Italian peasant diet. From mid-September to Lent there was one meal a day at 2:30 P.M.; during Lent it was in the late afternoon; from Easter to mid-Sepetember there were two meals at noon and in the evening. So although the food is sufficient, it was by no means a soft life.

Benedict's main asceticism came in the denial of self-will. The *filii familias* are required to bend their wills to that of the *pater familias* in lieu of Christ and the Father. It is not easy for an adult to play a child's role "Living not by their own desires and pleasures, but walking according to the judgment and commands of another, they live in community, and desire to have an abbot over them" (5). They must imitate Christ who came not to do his own will, but that of his Father who sent him.

Basic to obedience and self-denial are Benedict's twelve degrees of humility (7), for the proud, independent man cannot bring himself to bend his will to that of another. Degrees 4-11 are from John Cassian, but 1-3 and 12 are Benedict's own. The first degree is required of all Christians and in it a man should live in fear of the Lord, obey the commandments, avoiding sin. It is the fundamental realization of our dependence on God. In the second and third degrees a man denies his own will, submitting to the will of the superior. The next four degrees are harder — even difficult assignments should be embraced. Completely open to the abbot, the monk must be willing to accept the worst things in the house, considering himself lower than all others. The last five degrees describe the effect of humility on the monk's whole life. Following the rule, taciturn and moderate, he shows his humility by interior and exterior manner. "Having, therefore, ascended all these degrees of humility, the monk will presently arrive at that love of God which being perfect, casts out fear" (7).

The humble man prays not only at the public Opus Dei, but privately as well. Besides the common mental prayer at the end of the office, Benedict encourages private prayer of personal devotion during the day (52, 20). The monk's prayers should be short, but frequent, following John Cassian and Egyptian practice. Many of Benedict's ideas on prayer came from Cassian's *Conferences* Nine and Ten.

Lectio Divina was had at fixed hours, for example, from Easter to October from the fourth to the sixth hour (48). At the time reading and meditating seem to have been analogous. J. DeCarreaux writes: [5]

> Meditation was not a matter of reflection, examination or mental analysis, but the repetition of what had been read. Spoken aloud and retained by ear, such repetition which was really a form of memorization, was a form of mental training and preparing the will to go into action. . . . To read and meditate on a book was, literally to chew on it, digest it, and assimilate it as one might in the case of actual nourishment.

Lectio Divina was an important part of the monk's day. During Lent special books were assigned for reading.

As death approached, Benedict had already made his great contribution to the monastic synthesis, although in his own mind he never considered himself a great founder. Indeed, his houses numbered only three: Subiaco, Monte Cassino, and Terracino. His way was moderate, cenobitical, banning severe austerities and individualism, emphasizing manual labor and the Work of God within a family under the abbot. Gradually during the coming centuries, Benedict's rule would spread throughout the West.

Benedict had no intention of founding a religious order in the modern sense of the term. Rather each foundation was a separate family, autonomous, not leaning on the others, although

5. **Monks and Civilization,** p. 228.

following the same rule. Benedict's family was not founded as most modern religious orders and congregations to meet a particular need in the church. In general, the early monks did not feel called to particular apostolates, rather they were renunciants come to the monkish life with an eschatological goal to be attained by *metanoia, conversatio morum,* purifying and sanctifying their souls and worshipping God in community. Particular works such as teaching, calligraphy, farming, are assigned to the monk with respect to his individual background and aptitudes. But they are secondary and not essential to his monastic vocation. The monastic life is more than anything else a systematization or regulation of good Christian family life by the evangelical counsels under the *bonus et diligens pater familias.* Certainly the Christian monks through the ages due to their organized life under an abbot have been able to tackle whatever jobs came their way, filling the social, educational and missionary needs of the church. For example, the Egyptian monks counseling sinners; Basilian educators; Palestinian hostelers; Irish teachers, confessors, missioners and illuminators. But, at least in the beginning, one did not become a monk for any of these reasons. Rather through his conversion he entered a new eschatalogical way seeking to live the evangelical counsels in a most perfect way in community.

B. *Cassiodorus* (485-580)

Although Benedict who had little education put some stress on learning in his monastery, the emphasis was to change as more highly educated men joined the movement. Cassiodorus is a landmark in monastic education. A member of Theodoric's court at Revenna, he was also a relative of Symmachus and Boethius. In 535 he had planned to start a school in Rome similar to that of Origen in Alexandria. But war in 550 chased him to Constantinople. On his return in 555 he set up a monastic foundation on his own estate, the Vivarium in Calabria, erecting a monastery and a chapel to S. Martin. Cassiodorus himself did not join the community, preferring to live in his own home as a *conversus*, that is, a pious layman.

The emphasis in Cassiodorus' monastery was on study and the intellectual life rather than on manual labor as in Benedict's foundations. Scripture had the primary place, but secular literature also was studied. Whereas Benedict desired to build a house of the Lord according to the monastic tradition, Cassiodorus wished also to make it a house of learning, drawing up a manual called *Institutiones Divinarum et Humanarum Lectionum*. In two parts, it first explains sacred literature preparing the reader for an intelligent study of the bible through the commentaries and histories of the fathers. The second part treats of the liberal arts as an aid to a better understanding of the bible. Far from the minimal literary requirements of the early monks, Cassiodorus wanted his brethren to have a good Roman education including the Trivium (grammar, rhetoric and dialectic) and the Quadrivium (mathematics, music, geometry, and astronomy). Once trained in the liberal arts, the monks are better able to move on into scriptural studies. DeCarreux[6] maintains that this program may only have been reserved for the elite of the monastery whereas the bulk of the monks needed only to be skilled in the arts of manuscript copying.

Cassiodorus had a more liberal attitude towards secular literature than some other Christian leaders. He knew that the giants of Christian thought such as Origen, Evagrius, Basil, Ambrose, Augustine and Jerome had used their secular learning for the development of Christian theology.

As his Irish monk contemporaries Cassiodorus was interested in the copying of manuscripts, sometimes using professional copyists (*notarii*), book binders and translators. For the monks of the Vivarium as for the Jewish monks of Qumran, the scriptorium was a kind of second sanctuary. The MSS and codices were housed in the library in closed cases (*armoria*). Cassiodorus had had fine libraries both at Revenna and at Rome. At the Vivarium besides his own personal library with many volumes

6. **Monks and Civilization,** p. 239.

on medicine, there was the monks' library filled with books on the Bible, history and the Fathers, plus practical works including the liberal arts and Greek literature. Cassiodorus was a pioneer in monastic calligraphy, education and library science. Although Benedict seems to have been interested in learning only as an aid to the *Opus Dei* and the *lectio divina*, his sons would follow the lead of Cassiodorus as copyists, men of learning, preserving classical and Christian traditions as the foundation stones of Western civilization.

C. *Gregory the Great* (540-604)

Another important man to influence the Benedictine tradition was Gregory the Great. From a patrician family, he had been prefect of Rome, but withdrew from public life to Clivus Scauri, his paternal mansion on the Coelian Hill where he founded the monastery of S. Andrews under the rule of S. Benedict. He also built six other foundations in Sicily. Pope Pelagius II (579), needing Gregory's services, ordained him a deacon, sending him to Constantinople as an envoy.

In 568 the Long Beards (Lombards) had swept down the Italian peninsula, throwing out the Byzantine officials and destroying as they went. But with Gregory's help Rome held out, maintaining Byzantine links till the time of Charlemagne (774). When Gregory became pope in 590 he had to balance the Lombards against the Byzantines. At the time the church of Rome was rich and powerful with holdings in Italy, Gaul, Dalmatia, Sardinia, Corsica, Sicily, and Africa, all administered by papal rectors.

When Gregory accepted the papacy, he never gave up his predilection for the monastic way (L 1). The council of Rome (595) under his leadership solemnly confirmed the rule of S. Benedict.

Chalcedon (451) had given the bishops power over the monasteries. Since some bishops and civil officials were dominating the monasteries, confiscating their revenues, Gregory fought to restore the independence of the monks. The church of the monks had been born apart from the church of the bishops and to exist any other way would vitiate its historical tradition. Under Gregory's leadership in the council of Rome (601) the monks were again assured of their freedom.

> The charge which we formerly fulfilled as head of a monastery has taught us how necessary it is to provide for the tranquility and security of the monks; and as we know that most of them have had to suffer much oppression and injustice at the hands of the bishops, it concerns our fraternal feeling to provide for their future repose.[7]

In the name of Jesus Christ and Saint Peter, Gregory forbids bishops and seculars to confiscate the revenues of monasteries. Abbots are to be elected by the monks and not to be removed except for canonical reasons and the monks are not to be forced to assume the duties of secular priests. If any monk is ordained with the permission of the abbot, he must leave the monastery in order to preserve its lay aura. In general, bishops are not to interfere in the operation of the monasteries. This is the beginning of the long papal protection of the monks and their exemption from local episcopal control, underlining the essential distinction between monks and clerics. Any priest or deacon who joins the monastery must leave off his clerical functions (Bk, 5, L 1). It seems that some clerics joined up out of ambition for the abbotship. And as time went on it became customary for the abbot to be a priest (Council of Rome [826]). But Gregory felt that a monk called to the clerical life should leave the monastery, making his choice for the church of the bishops over that of the monks. Since each of these vocations is so great, it is difficult enough to lead one properly without trying to mix the two. Far from being complementary, they tended to injure each other (Bk 6, L 21). Yet in time of need as on the English missions, Gregory saw the necessity of filling bishoprics with monks.

7. From DeMontalembert, **Monks of the West,** 1, p. 369.

Monastic discipline had become lax by Gregory's time. Poverty was slipping and monks wandering. With the help of abbots, some bishops and *Defensores,* procurators of the Roman church that Gregory kept in each province, he deposed immoral abbots (Bk 3, L 23; Bk 5, L 3 & 6), and forbade the bishops to shelter wandering or excommunicated monks (Bk 7, L 35). Gregory knew the danger of monks being drawn from the monastery by alluring women. So he insisted on strict cloister with as little contact with women as possible, even to the ordering of the removal of all women from the monastic isles along the Italian coast. Yet he mercifully sought out those who, fed up with the monastic life, had fled to marry, incurring excommunication according to Chalcedon. To one ex-monk, his friend Venantius, he wrote, reminding him of the punishment of Ananias in the Acts of the Apostles (5:1-6). "If then, he was deserving of the penalty of death who withdrew the money which he had given God, consider of how great penalty you will be deserving in the divine judgment, who have withdrawn, not money, but yourself, from Almighty God, to whom you had devoted yourself in the monastic state" (Bk 1, L 34). Right up to Venantius' death Gregory kept in touch with him trying to persuade him to come back, and caring for his daughters as his own after the death of their father.

Any hankering after personal property is incompatible with the family life of the monastery. "If private property is held there by the monks, it will not be possible for either concord or charity to continue in this same congregation. What, indeed, is a monk's life, if not a despising of the world. But how can they despise the world, while still seeking after gold?" (Bk 12, L 24).

One of Gregory's chief interests was the protection and reform of the monks, even giving of his patrimony for the founding of new monasteries and giving over to the charge of the monks several ancient churches. But he was also solicitous of older foundations such as Lérins, Luxeuil and in the East.

Gregory remained essentially a monk till his death, surrounding himself with monks from his old monastery of S. Andrews and trying to live the daily life of a monk in prayer, study and liturgy. He contributed much to the development of church liturgy and music.

Gregory was concerned about the place of the papacy in the church, using his monks to promote papal policies and to keep an eye on the papal properties spread throughout Europe. From the very beginning the monks distrusted the bishops, who sought to control them along with their increasing wealth. So the monks, as Columban in Gaul, appealed to the pope for protection. As Workman comments,[8] "Little, therefore, was needed of papal encouragement to turn the monks into watchdogs in every land for the pope, ever ready to pick a quarrel with the bishop and to proclaim against him the supremacy of their papal overlord."

The bishops often tended to be individualists, emphasizing their local autonomy, whereas the monks, originally also local and autonomous, are now ecumenical, going into far distant lands under papal protection, sometimes with instructions to bring independent bishops into line with Roman practice. Thus Workman[9] describes the bishop as basically the king's man, whereas the monk is the pope's man. Columban is a case in point. In trouble with the Gaulic bishops, he appeals to Pope Gregory (Bk 9, L 127), who places him and his fellow monks under the protection of Lérins.

The origins of Benedictine monasticism are shadowy in Gaul. A tradition says that Maur, a disciple of Benedict founded a monastery at Glanfeuil, on the banks of the Loire not far from Marmoutier. But, as Butler writes[10] if the Life of Maur is discarded, then the first trace of the Benedictine rule in Gaul is around 620 when Donatus of Besancon used it as a basis of a rule for nuns. During the seventh century the Benedictine rule

8. **The Evolution of the Monastic Ideal,** p. 168. D. Knowles, however, in his introduction (xiii) feels that Workman exaggerates the monastic role as papal watchdogs.

9. **Ibid.**

10. **Benedictine Monasticism,** p. 355.

seems to have been introduced progressively throughout Gaul even into the ancient Lérinsian monasteries and their Celtic cousins. In some places several rules were used, for example, those of Caesarius, Columban and Benedict. But by the end of the seventh century Benedict had won out over Columban.

Why was the rule of Columban rejected in favor of that of Benedict? Less than fifty years after Columban's death, the Benedictine rule was adopted at Luxeuil and Bobbio and their satellites. Eligius of Limousin used both rules.

At the council of Autun (670) in Burgundy, the bishops gave formal approval to the rule of S. Benedict, commenting that if the rule of Benedict and the church canons are followed, an increase of vocations would surely follow (C 15). No mention is made of Columban's rule even though he had been gone less than half a century. Was his rule too difficult for the Gauls? Too harsh? Were the Celtic customs, tonsure, etc., too strange? Probably the Celtic monastic tradition had little more hope of survival in Gaul than the Latin tradition in Palestine. Certainly the papal and imperial approval of Benedict's rule helped to make it the supreme monastic law in the West.

But even apart from its patronage, Benedict's rule was more advanced, more moderate, prudent. Later reforms by Benedict of Aniane and at Cluny reflect a return to Irish severity. Irish monasticism was to last in its native land for seven centuries, eventually giving way to the Cistercians.

D. Augustine of Canterbury (d. 604)

Concerned about the Anglo-Saxons who were being ignored by the native British clergy, Gregory sent his prior Augustine with forty monks from S. Andrews to Britain in 597. Converting King Ethelbert along with 10,000 of his subjects, Augustine received the royal palace of Canterbury for a monastic foundation. And he built a cathedral on the site of an old Roman church, afterwards known as Christ Church, the metropolitan church of England, with Augustine as its first archbishop and abbot. He erected another monastery nearby dedicated to Peter and

Paul, later called S. Augustine's. His patron Gregory sent him
the pallium as a sign of his primacy over all the British bishops
(Bk 11, L 65).

Augustine was puzzled by the different church customs he
found practiced in Rome, Gaul and Britain. How can these
customs differ, if the faith is one? Gregory responded.

> Your brotherhood knows the custom of the church of Rome,
> in which you remember that you were brought up. But it
> pleases me, if you have found anything (Be it either in the
> church of Rome, of France or any other, that may more
> please almighty God) that you zealously choose and spread
> in the church of the English (which as yet is but late come
> to the faith) by the best order you can choose — the things
> that you have been able to gather from many churches. For
> the things are not to be loved for the place, but the place
> is to be loved for the good things that are in it. Choose then
> out of each church that which is godly, religious and which
> is right in any of them. These being gathered as it were in
> a bundle, deliver unto them and inure the minds of the
> English thereunto (Bk 11, L 24; Bede, *History* 1:27).

Gregory himself had introduced Byzantine customs into Rome,
saying, "He is but a fool who could make his primacy a reason
for disdaining to learn whatever good can be learned" (Bk 10,
L 12).

Augustine had brought a largely Roman tradition to Britain
including the Roman psalter. He tried to set up Roman type
dioceses and discourage native customs. But he soon found that
many of the British bishops resented his interference, refusing
to accept his primacy. At the synod of Augustine's Oak (602-
603) he requested some British priests to help convert the
Anglo-Saxons. He also wanted them to bring their customs in
line with Roman practice. In the legendary miracle contest,
Augustine bested the local priests by healing a blind man (Bede,
History 2:2). But the British preferred to hold a second synod
after consulting with their own people.

Meanwhile, seven British bishops plus a large number of learned monks from Bangor Iscoed consulted a wise anchorite to decide their next move. Should they leave off their native customs to follow Augustine? He replied, "If he be a man of God, follow him." A true man of God is as humble as Christ and not proud. But when the bishops found Augustine was too proud to rise to greet them, they wisely refused to cooperate, knowing that if he failed this initial courtesy, he would despise them all the more after they submitted to him. Augustine predicted their downfall as punishment for their disobedience. And in 613 Bangor Iscoed was destroyed along with 1200 souls many of whom were monks.

For one hundred fifty years the two churches, the British and Celtic monastic church with its native traditions on the one hand, and the Anglo-Saxon Roman church on the other, were to exist in a state of mutual hostility. Augustine went on founding churches, for example, the monastic cathedral of S. Paul in London on the ancient site of the temple of Apollo and an early Christian church, the monastery of S. Peter known as Westminster Abbey or the Western Monastery.

When Augustine died (604), his successor Lawrence (609), continued his program of uniting all the Britons and Celts under Rome. He was particularly angry when the Scottish bishop Dagan refused to eat with him. As much as a century later the Welsh Christians still refused to join the Latins in prayer or at meals. And anyone having contact with a Roman might have to do penance. Moreover, anything a Roman touched such as food or utensils had to be thrown away or destroyed.

Although the Roman monks had converted some of the Northumbrians, they soon lapsed. And when their king Oswald was converted by the Celtic monks of Iona, he asked them to come as missionaries to Northumbria. So Aidan, the monk-bishop of Iona went to Bernicia in the northern part of Northumbria, founding a monastery on the island of Lindisfarne, which reminded him of Iona. Using this as a base, his monks had converted most of the territory by the end of Aidan's death (651).

Meanwhile Roman monks had converted the south, but were still determined to bring all of Britain under Roman rule.

A key event was the synod of Whitby (664), under the presidency of King Oswy of Celtic practice and his son Alchfrid of Roman persuasion. Colman, Aidan's successor at Lindisfarne, defended his Celtic customs especially their celebration of Easter in the tradition of John the Apostle. On the other hand, Wilfrid, a former monk of Lindisfarne, trained in the Roman ways at Rome and Lyons and now abbot of Ripon, defended the Roman practice as the tradition of Peter and Paul. In a sense we have here a clash between the eastern Johannine tradition by way of Egypt and Lérins with the emphasis on local autonomy and closer to Jewish tradition (for example, Easter is more closely allied to the Passover) — and the western Pauline traditions stressing the universal church under the Roman apostle.

Wilfrid responded that the Scots, Red-shanks (Picts) and the Britons were against the practice of the whole world. He admitted that John and the early church had followed Jewish customs, but only to avoid scandal. But the western tradition of Peter and Paul declared Easter to be the Sunday after the Passover (14 Nisan) and not begin on the evening of the fourteenth of Nisan whatever day of the week it might fall on as in the Johannine tradition.

King Oswy chose Peter over Columba, for Peter is the heavenly porter who looks askance at those who thwart his traditions. The defeated Colman retired to Ireland with a few monks. He died there in 675. Whitby ended the Celtic customs in general although a few pockets of resistance remained. Iona surrendered in 716 and the Welsh in the eighth century. Yet the transition was probably gradual as in Gaul with the monasteries combining the rules of Columba and Benedict.

Of Wilfrid DeCarreux writes: [11]

By bursting open the too carefully guarded doors of the

11. **Monks and Civilization,** p. 270.

9

Celtic monasteries and introducing into them the rule of
S. Benedict, he made it possible for the spirit of Monte
Cassino to reach out to remote places, the very existence
of which the Patriarch had never suspected. After the work
of preparing the ground and missionary efforts was over,
these monasteries were to become even more gloriously than
they had under the Celts, centers of culture, as well as prayer
and praise, where literature, singing, the illumination of fine
manuscripts, and schools were to develop during the centuries as the endowments of the Benedictines.

The synthesis of the Celtic and Roman traditions flowered
into a monastic garden in which the Celtic foundations as Glastonbury, Menia, Llandaff, Bangor, and Iona were complemented
by Anglo-Saxon monasteries either of Benedictine or of mixed
observance, for example, Canterbury, Westminster, Malmebury,
Lindisfarne, Ripon, Peterborough, Melrose, Wearmouth, Jarrow,
Croyland and the school of York. The monastic tradition of learning blossomed in Bede and Alcuin, while its missionary zeal is
exemplified in Boniface.

10. Conclusion

onasticism as a heresy, a way of life or a religious sect, is found in many different religions. In fact, there is evidence that it is a rather normal procedure. Often it is an attempt to recapture the primordial spirit of the founder which has become lost by the third or fourth generation. Initially found in individual hermits, it is more often a communistic sharing of goods, meals, prayers, rules, etc.

Samgha

The Samgha followers of Buddha are an early example of monasticism. Their founder, forsaking the world at age twenty-nine, spent seven years living as an ascetic while seeking the

223

solution to the problem of evil, at last finding an escape from the problems of the world in Nirvana. He instructed his disciples in the basics of meditation, enlightenment and Nirvana and the control of desire, Tanha. Sending his men as frugal and compassionate missionaries, Buddha followed the ancient Indian custom of peripatetic holy men. Initially his Samgha included all his followers, but later only the elite monks.

When one entered Samgha, he left the world, was instructed and took vows. Although they started as single begging monks, as their numbers grew, the monks began to live in community. These were the elite of Buddhism, leading a high spiritual life away from the world, seeking enlightenment and aiming to destroy Atman, the root of all desire. Besides obeying the moral law and the monastic rule, they hoped to quell all earthly desires in order to pave the way to enlightenment.

Poverty, celibacy and inoffensiveness were the hallmarks of the Buddhist monks. Living frugally, supported by the laity, they in turn presented the Buddhist ideal to the laity by word and example, opening up a window for them to look out of their humdrum world into the spiritual and mythological.

With various ups and downs, reforms and divisions, Buddhist monasticism has persevered down to the present day, with its monasteries dominating the local villages. The people come to the monks for inspiration and send their children for education. What effect the Buddhist monastic tradition had on the later Jewish and Christian monks is hard to say, as no direct line of contact can at present be traced. But the casual observer will readily see that they have much in common.

Jewish Monks

Although asceticism has not been strong in Jewish tradition, we do find reforming heresies arising especially in apocalyptic times, for example, from the second century before Christ to the second century after. Of special note are the Qumran monks who fled to the desert in the second century B.C. from the Hellenizing of the Seleucids and of Jonathan, the High Priest.

Descendants of the Hasidim, their leader, the Teacher of Righteousness, led their messianic search to the desert of Judah.
With a novitiate, communism and strict levitical purity, their
theology reflected the times, messianic, apocalyptic, eschatological and dualistic.

Another group of Jewish monks were the Therapeuts of
Egypt, described by Philo. These were strict contemplatives
in contrast to the more active Qumran people. They lived a semi-
hermitic life with both male and female members, fasting, contemplating in the solitude of their monasteries, coming together
for the Sabbath synagogue service. They so resembled the later
Christian monks of lower Egypt that Eusebius and Jerome confused the two. The Therapeuts along with contemporaneous
Jewish heresies as the Essenes, Baptists, and the Christian "Way,"
all were reforming and seeking perfection. Both the communists
of Qumran and the semi-hermits of the Mareotis Lake were
to have counterparts among the Christian monks. In the very
beginning the Jerusalem Christians made an attempt at communist living, but it did not seem to last long. There remained
an ascetical thread which was to be woven into the warp and
woof of the Christian monasticism of the fourth century.

Early Christians

When compared with the Pharisees, the Baptists, or Essenes,
the Christian "Way" seemed the road of moderation. It is true
that Jesus, following the example of his cousin John, fasted and
prayed in the desert. And although he did not demand this of his
disciples, he required them to leave all to follow him. His advice
to the rich young man became the shibboleth of Christian monasticism. The common life of the disciples persisting even after
Jesus' death, did not survive long, although it provided the seeds
of later monasticism.

Virginity played a small part in early Christianity as it did
in Judaism, despite the example of John and Jesus and the
counsels of Paul. Yet a thin line of references to celibacy and
virginity winds through the Apostolic Fathers. Heterodox groups

began to demand continence for all in the new eschatological life of Baptism. In the beginning Christian virgins lived privately in their own homes and were honored in the Liturgy as the Roman Vestals. But as yet there were no organized convents. Male ascetics, the predecessors of the Christian monks, wandered from town to town. In Egypt Clement of Alexandria and Origen combining Gnostic and Stoic principles prepare the ground for the gnostic way of lower Egypt of Evagrius and his followers.

The Peace of Constantine and the Church's privileged position brought a reforming ascetical migration to the desert in search of the eschaton. Contemporary asceticism of the pagan cults may have been an influence.

The Monks of the Desert

Beginning with the hermits, whose followers soon began living as communists, Egyptian monasticism was to be the model of future generations of monks. Antony, the father of monks was made famous by Athanasius' *Life*. Disciples flocked to his solitary hut. Pilgrims came from afar, some staying, others returning to found monasteries in their native lands.

Although the hermits were succeeded by the communists, Christian monasticism always dreamed of the solitary as the ideal. Pachomius is generally considered as the father of Christian cenobite life. A contemporary of Antony, he developed Christian communism into an acceptable way of life with work, craft guilds, frugal diet, communal prayer and liturgy. This was strictly a lay heresy and as it spread Pachomius wrote a rule of conduct for his satellite communities. In lower Egypt a hybrid developed mixing communist and anchorite, not unlike the Therapeuts.

As Pachomius' foundations grew, the inevitable laxness ensued with the subsequent severity of reform. A famous Pachomian reform was that of Shenoute of Atripe, whose simple, severe, anti-intellectual anthropomorphic piety was to meet the intellectual Evagrians full force by the end of the fourth century.

Evagrius, Shenoute's contemporary, developed a type of monastic spirituality based on Origen's Gnostic and Stoic thought where through *apatheia* one can approach the *gnōsis*. Evagrius saw the active and contemplative lives as successive states with the latter the superior one. His teachings on spirituality and asceticism had great impact on East and West. Popular in lower Egypt, his Greek approach was never accepted by the anthropomorphic Copts and his followers were eventually chased from Egypt to Palestine, Constantinople, and Europe, spreading his doctrine as they went.

Although Egyptian monasticism faded fast, it remained the prototype, a lay heresy or church alongside of or even outside of the church of the bishops. The liturgy of the word was emphasized along with physical work and a rigorous asceticism. Spread by exiles and pilgrims, Egyptian monasticism flowed to East and West, but moderated and better organized as it went.

Basil and Jerome

The monastic heresy soon spread from Egypt to Syria and Palestine. Even before this there had been ascetics in the East, some were heterodox as the Montanists, demanding that all Christians lead a life of high asceticism. Others were solitaries or wanderers. When monasteries became common in the fifth century, the Syrians and Palestinians continued to place the solitary life on a pedestal both literally and figuratively.

Basil of Caesarea, founder of Eastern monasticism, came from a pious, educated family. Following his Baptism and a tour of the monks of the desert, he founded a monastery near his family home at Annesi, writing a rule which balanced prayer, work, and frugality. Avoiding the dangers of the anchorite and the huge Pachomian establishments, Basil preferred a moderate rule with a family spirit. His tradition has remained to this day as the principal monasticism of the East.

Palestinian monasticism had its origins in Egypt, Syria and Rome. Hilarion and Chariton were trained in Egypt; Euthymius from Armenia founded the semi-hermitic laurae which became the pattern of Palestine and to which the cenobium remained subordinate. The Roman pilgrimage of ascetics in the fourth and fifth centuries was spurred by the Barbarian invasions. Many started as family convents in Roman palaces, with Jerome and Pelagius as their guides. Transferring to Palestine, they brought along Roman customs and liturgy. Roman monasticism in the Holy Places waned by the second half of the fifth century and was replaced by the Greek. Euthymius took over as leader of his laurae along with his disciples Theodosius and Sabas.

The decisions of Chalcedon against Monophysitism and the independence of the monks were not well received in Palestine, but there was an eventual reconciliation. Certain monasteries as S. Sabas and Mt. Sinai were to carry the eastern monastic tradition right up to modern times despite invasions and persecutions.

Augustine

Monasticism in western Africa also owed its origins to Egypt but more indirectly insofar as its founder, Augustine, was influenced by the *Life of Antony* and by the Italian monks he had observed. Prior to Augustine, African asceticism dates back to second century Montanism and the virgins of Tertullian and Cyprian, but not yet on an organized basis.

Excited by the *Life of Antony* and by his experiences with monasticism in Milan and Rome after his conversion, Augustine determined to gather a group of Servants of God in his old home at Thagaste, then in Hippo. As bishop, he led his clerics in a communal life. A clerical monastery, it violated the basic tenet of monasticism, namely, that it is a lay heresy. Yet the form would persist and eventually affect the whole western clergy with their monastic office and celibacy.

Augustine governed his clerics with moderation, sketching a rule. In his *On the Work of the Monks,* he chastised aberrations in African monasticism and with his attacks on Pelagian asceticism caused not a little consternation in African and Gaulic monasteries, built in the semi-stoical Egyptian tradition.

Augustine's big contribution to Western monasticism was

his clerical communism, his rule, his moderation and emphasis on the Divine over against the Pelagian ascetical self-sufficiency.

John Cassian

Many of the Egyptian-influenced monks of Gaul disagreed with Augustine's theology of predestination and his deemphasis of man's part in salvation.

Martin, father of Gaulic monks and patron of all western monasticism, founded a monastery at Ligugé near Poitiers and at Marmoutier near Tours. His monasteries served as seminaries of clerics as did that of Lérins in southern Gaul.

The second founder of Gaulic monasticism was John Cassian. Trained in Palestine and Egypt, he had first hand knowledge of the desert traditions. In particular he was influenced by Evagrius and the Origenist stream. Founding the monastery of St. Victor near Marseilles, he wrote his *Institutes* to guide beginning souls, modifying severe Egyptian customs to fit the Gaulic temperament. He firmly resisted the Lérinsian trend in which monks served as clerics in local churches and on the missions. As the Egyptian fathers, he taught renunciation, obedience, lay-orientation, moderation.

Many Evagrian themes are found in John Cassian, for example, the active and contemplative life, purity of heart leading to contemplation, the interrelationship of the virtues and vices. He argued against Augustine's original sin and predestination, reflecting Eastern asceticism, which prepares the way for God.

Although John Cassian's influence is not that of Antony, Basil, Martin, or even Augustine, his work swayed Benedict, Cassiodorus and later monastic founders. With his Origenist-Evagrian tradition, he is the founder of the science of the spiritual life.

The Irish Monks

Monasticism in Britain and Ireland seems to be a descendent of the Gaulic monasteries. Patrick, possibly trained in Gaul, formed an Irish episcopal church, although fostering the monastic spirit. The founder of the First Order of Irish Saints, he had a clerical family at Armagh. After his death monk-missionaries as Finnian, Ciaran, and others came from Britain. So by the middle of the seventh century the Irish church was largely monastic, ruling the clan *paruchia*.

Columba of the royal Nialls was an important monk-missionary of Ireland and Caledonia in the seventh century, with headquarters on the island of Iona. Columban, trained at Bangor, sought the Gaulic missions, bringing the Gaulic monastic influence full circle. His independence of the bishops and civil rulers and his strange Irish customs, led to his exile eventually at Bobbio in Italy. When he died he left a string of foundations in Gaul, Switzerland, and Northern Italy, to be superceded by the Benedictine stream.

From the seventh century the monks dominated the Irish church, with the monk-bishops under the abbot. Educators, they taught students from Britain and the continent; fine manuscripts and libraries added to their fame. Irish monasticism was founded along family or clan lines. Although generally loyal to Rome, when cut off by the Anglo-Saxon invasions, they remained faithful to older traditions. Mission-minded, they converted Caledonia, Northumbria, the islands, parts of Gaul, Germany, etc. Their independence of bishops was in the monastic tradition. And their penitentials developed the practice of private confession, while their learning kept the intellectual life alive during the so-called Dark Ages. And although the Benedictine tradition would eventually dominate, Irish monasticism made an important contribution to the history of the monks.

Benedict

Benedict, organizing previous traditions into a workable system which was to rule for the next millenium, marks a turning point in the history of monasticism. When Benedict was born, Italian monasticism was on the decline, a mix of various rules and customs, dating from the time of Ambrose, Jerome and Pelagius.

First at Subiaco then at Monte Cassino Benedict gathered his lay brothers in a family spirit. Synthesizing previous traditions, he wrote a rule, simple and moderate, for beginners in the spiritual life, soldiers of Christ. Benedict favored the communist life over that of the hermits or road-runners. The abbot was the *bonus et diligens pater familias*, with his monastery reflecting the qualities of a good Christian family. New members are admitted with caution. Stable, humble, obedient, conversant in morals, the monk is a *filius familias* and as such has no personal property nor can he marry. The *Opus Dei* is his main act of worship, along with Mass, prayer and *divina lectio*. Manual work supports the family. Benedict had no idea of founding a monastic order in the modern sense. Rather each monastery was an independent family seeking salvation and union with God rather than dedicated to a particular apostolate.

Gregory the Great, monk-pope, assured the independence of monks from episcopal interference, preserving the lay hue of the monastic heresy and reforming the slipping discipline. With Gregory the alliance of the monks with the papacy began which was to prosper both. With papal and imperial approval, the Rule of Benedict eventually dominated the Irish traditions in Gaul and Britain.

Benedict to Francis

The history of the monks is a cycle of successes and failures and often it is the very monkish renunciation that leads to corporate wealth and subsequent collapse. In the history of the Benedictines a series of reforms tried to quell the tendencies to laxness, for example, Benedict of Aniane (9c), and William IX of Aquitaine at Cluny (10c). Hildebrand (Gregory VII) (11c) felt that the monastic ideal had value for the whole church and not just the chosen few, stamping out clerical marriages, simony, and insisting on obedience to the Holy See.

With Cluny came the third stage of monastic development (the first two were the anchorites and cenobites). The third stage is called connexiality by Workman (236), namely, an affiliation of communities in a common rule, in an international organization under the pope. Certainly there were vestiges of connexiality before in the Pachomian, Irish, and even in the foundations directed by Gregory the Great.

Further reforms came at Citeaux (11c) whose white monks spread over Europe and England, settling in remote and isolated places. Although the Cistercian abbeys were independent, they maintained a connexial spirit by unity of rule, annual conferences and the leadership of the abbot of Citeaux. Independent of the bishops, the Cistercians bound themselves to the pope by an oath of obedience. Workman sees in this papal alliance a reason for the decline of medieval monasticism (244).

When the monk became the auxiliary of Rome with the control of its organization centered in the pope, it was plain to all that monasticism had outlived its first purpose. She no longer held up an ideal of renunciation higher than that of the church, to some extent even outside of the church.

The church which had glorified the monastic ideal, says Workman (244), was now using it for its own ends. So the battle lines were drawn up between the bishops and the seculars with a national consciousness on the one hand and the pope and the regulars reflecting the imperial or supranational scope, on the other.

Withdrawing from the world, the Cistercians left education to the public, cathedral schools and colleges, leading to the rise of the universities at the end of the twelfth century. While the Cistercians sought the perfect observance of Benedict's rule in cenobitical isolation, others such as the Camalduli were semihermits similar to the laurae of Egypt, Palestine and some Irish foundations.

Another development in the medieval church was the clerical canons, following a tradition going back to Augustine. By sixth and seventh century Gaul it was common for clerics to live in communities under their bishops for purposes of economy, discipline and training. By the twelfth century many followed the rule of Augustine. Although they declined at the end of the Middle Ages, military and hospitaler orders grew out of them.

Friars and Regular Clerics

In the early part of the thirteenth century Francis and Dominic founded groups of friars. To counteract the monastic tendency to accumulate corporate wealth, they insisted that their houses should not own material goods, but be supported by alms or work. A lack of monastic stability left them free for apostolic work. Thus the members do not belong so much to an individual house but rather to the whole order. Dominic, adapting Augustine's rule, insisted on a good education in order to prepare his men for preaching. The friars became active in the life of the new universities producing such giants as Bonaventure, Albert the Great, Thomas Aquinas, Roger Bacon. Independent of the bishops and centralized in Rome, they became the watch dogs of the papacy. Whereas before the lay monks had lived under papal protection, now the papal church has its own clergy as well.

As monasticism dwindled in the later Middle Ages, with the Reformation and the Council of Trent came the rise of the clerks regular, who, giving up much of the common life, more closely resembled secular priests. These were the pope's clerks who were free to move in any direction at his command. The Jesuits, founded by Ignatius of Loyola, were an immediate success. Another departure from monastic practice instituted by the Jesuits was the admission of lesser members with only simple vows, which practice was to become normative for future groups of clerics, sisters and brothers, engaged in teaching, social work, missions, hospitals, etc. In more recent times secular institutes have been a further adaptation promising service to the church and wearing secular garb.

Although at the time of the Reformation religious orders were at a low state, nevertheless, the spirit of monasticism may be seen within Protestantism, namely, a reforming, protesting, prophetic, lay heresy outside the organization of the clerical church

and stressing the liturgy of the Word. Calvin's emphasis on industry and moral strictness could reflect other monastic trends. However, Renaissance individualism and egalitarianism militated
against a separate and elite monastic communism. In general,
Protestants did not consider the counsels of perfection distinct
from the precepts of the Christian code. Cannon Hannay has
stated that the Protestant ideal embodies a well-ordered use of
the good things of life and so any view of renunciation or asceticism must keep this in mind. (Appendix on Counsels and Precepts, *The Spirit and Origin of Christian Monasticism*, 1903).

Periodically Protestantism has made attempts at communism.
Most of the groups were millenarians as the followers of Kelpius,
Ephrata, Rappites, Zoarites, Shakers, etc. and didn't last long.
Recent ecumenical foundations at Taizé and in Chicago give
promise for the future.

Today and Tomorrow

The monastic heresy found in many religions is based on
man's inner desire to live a more perfect life, often away from
the rest, seeking closer union with God, and untroubled by the
material cares of the world. Yearning for the ideal within a larger
religious tradition, monasticism has always maintained an eschatological and millenial hue. This explains its success in apocalyptic times and its tailing off during periods of normalcy. Witness
the Essenes, the early Christians and the monks at the time of
the Barbarian invasions. Historically times of strife and poverty
have been kinder to monasticism than prosperity has. Recent
affluence has, no doubt, had some adverse effect on the monastic
way. Also today the ancient taunt thrown by the Romans is still
leveled at the monks. "You are escaping from reality, from those
who need your help, from where the action is?" However, the
monks were probably right when they came to the conclusion
that it is far easier to build a new city in the desert based on
solid ascetical and moral principles than to try to reconstruct
the old decadent urban order. In fact, as Augustine comments
in his *City of God* (2:21), because of its flagrant injustice and

consequent disorder, Rome had long ceased to be a society at all, if it ever had been. Well aware of this, the people fled injustice, sorrow, and the impending collapse of the empire to seek the solace of the monks. And the monks, in their turn, went among the people as clerks and missionaries even when this went contrary to their traditions.

Since Vatican II the drop off in religious and monastic vocations has been alarming. Some say that Vatican II itself may have been a negative influence insofar as it leveled religious life so that it is no longer a "better way" but a "special way" to serve God. (*Constitution on the Church*, 40).

To one familiar with the cyclical nature of monasticism, this is obviously a *low*. Historically the causes of waning monasticism have been many. First of all, we see man's concupiscence, or whatever word you may want to use to describe his tendency to go down hill, accompanied by a slipping discipline and lax poverty. Moreover, a frantic activism has often smothered the monastic *hēsychia* or tranquility so attractive to those harried and frustrated in their every day world of business, family, war, politics, crime, etc. The secular spirit of prosperous times has been another factor, tending to place present visible but ephemeral values ahead of future invisible eschatological ones. And the tendency to accumulate corporate wealth has been a long standing danger despite rules and canons to the contrary.

The very monastic foundation of asceticism is being challenged today. The old Gnostic, Stoic, Origenist, Evagrian line of *apatheia*, separation of body and soul, conquest of the passions, particularly sex and pride, in order to free the soul for a gnostic union with God, walling a person away from the world, prayer and fasting to attain perfection, has little appeal today. Modern man, as his Roman predecessors, asks: should I flee to this pious enclosed eschatological environment, or rather seek to influence the world around me? Some would wonder with Augustine whether a reformable society exists in many areas of the world today. But there is a real danger in the self-enclosed ascetical life and it is basically the Pelagianism which grew out of it, namely, that one can through certain exercises attain perfection. Of course, in itself this is doomed to failure, for without God, man can do nothing.

Another essential tool of monasticism is being challenged today, namely, its communism. The early Christians tried communism for a while in the first fervor of their millenial hopes. Monastic communism is based on that of the family which is the primordial type of cenobitic living. Community of goods and property is basic to monasticism. And all religious founders placed it as their cornerstone. Modern Marxism may trace its communism to the many Christian communal movements of the last century, and imperfect though it is, is fundamentally millenarian and eschatological. Perhaps due to the influence of existentialism, recent trends have been towards the personal and subjective over the institutional and the communal. But when the individual is placed over the family, the very root of monasticism is cut. An interesting contemporary mutation is the increasingly popular youth commune offering refuge to those turned off on established society. It seems to have something in common with monasticism.

Monastic commitment is another anomaly today. Modern emphasis on the existential, freedom, process and becoming has militated against long term commitment, out of fear of closing off options or being put in a box. Correlative to freedom is the yen for independence in opposition to monastic dependence, in which the monk, is, in a sense, a perpetual child, a *filius familias*, unable to marry, possess property or rule as a *pater familias*. Yet dependence on the *pater familias* has been the foundation of both family and monastery and a chief source of the humility required for the cenobium.

Paradoxically it is only through true commitment and self-giving dependence that genuine freedom can be attained. But this self-offering is not predetermined by a vow or a promise. Rather the goal is only partially achieved in the daily life of the monk and fully attained at death, the final self-gift.

Monasticism has traditionally been a lay heresy, based on the good Christian lay family. Workman (343) sees monasticism as a lay protest against encroaching sacerdotalism, placing personal holiness higher than ecclesiastical succession. The monks broke away as a non-sacerdotal reforming heresy and this they have in common with other more heterodox groups. Instead of a mediated communion of the soul and God through priests and sacraments, they sought a direct union through *apatheia* and *gnōsis*.

Because of man's natural tendency to weakness and sin either individually or corporately, the church has always needed and still needs idealistic reforming lay heresies. As Workman writes (333).

> Monasticism has always enabled her (Rome) to retain the norm in the church itself conveniently low — we use the term without disrespect — so as to suit the many, while yet providing for those elect spirits who were minded to reach a higher standard.

Similarly the Buddhist Samgha gives the laity a window into the transcendent to look out from their closed-in material existence.

The church has been able through the years to channel the enthusiasm of its idealists and reformers into monastic groups and religious foundations. Many Protestant sects would perhaps at another time and in different circumstances have become religious orders. If all Christians are equally ministers, as some of the Reformers claimed, what basis is left for monasticism? If we can only admit that some receive a special spirit driving them to sell all, give to the poor and follow Christ in a communistic way, then monasticism is not only possible, but essential to the existence of Christianity.

What does the future hold for the monastic spirit? We have seen its evolution through thousands of years of religious tradition. The Christian monks, starting out as hermits, quickly moved into the cenobite family then into larger connexial organizations paralleling the ecumenical church. In more modern times we have seen the paradox of regular clerics, foreign to the lay ideal of monasticism, but nevertheless, fulfilling a vital task as the Pope's clergy especially adapted to missions at the Pope's command.

What form will religious and monastic life take in the future? Possibly the emphasis on lay status will increase with a decline of the clerical orders, especially if a married priesthood is returned to Western practice and the monastic spirit of the Western secular clergy is decreased. Also the decentralization of the church government, may lessen the connexiality and Rome-centripetality, and increase the local autonomy of religious orders. With the papacy relinquishing power to the local bishops, what will become of the Pope's clergy?

This author feels that the future of monasticism may lie in the independent lay family, communist, poor, celibate, obedient, humble, under a father, leading a balanced life of the Opus Dei, work, frugality, laboring alongside the clerical church, under papal protection, giving a healthy pluralism to church structure. All the monks must be equal under the father. Therefore, no divisive clerical-lay or professed-non-professed dichotomies can be tolerated. As all the early abbots taught, although seniority should be honored, any gradation of monks would destroy family unity. The postulant will not join the family to do a particular work, but rather to seek with the support of others his own salvation, worshipping God and loving his neighbor. Although no monastic family would be irrevocably commited to a particular apostolate, the long monastic tradition in education, scholarship, liturgy, charitable works and missions should be their guide.

But what about the bishops? The whole history of the monastic heresy has been a struggle for independence from the church of the bishops. The Council of Chalcedon (451) struck a blow for episcopal control. Yet papal protection was to ensure the essential independence of the monks. Although the two independent streams, clerical and monastic, benefit the church, nevertheless, a measure of liaison is necessary perhaps through an archimandrite or vicar of religious, who preferably should be a monk or a religious. The monks and religious depend on the bishop for permission to build in his diocese, for the ordination of monks, as an outside insurance against internal corruption and as a court of appeals. In return, the monks and religious should cooperate in diocesan works as far as possible, at the same time guarding their independence.

Will vocations to the monastic and religious life resume? Since this is the life of the spirit, it cannot die, although it may suffer a period of detumescence. Many orders at present consist largely of old men or women. Barring a miracle, these groups will die, for as families they have failed to reproduce themselves. Present monastic traditions could phase out or remain vestigially as the Egyptian and Irish monastic streams, supplanted by new reforming idealists founding families more adapted to the times.

Since the idea of a life-long commitment seems repugnant to many today, perhaps the door should be left open, as in the Buddhist tradition, for a return to the secular community after a short or longer term of service in the monastery. The large number of solemnly professed religious and monks defecting today makes the future seem brighter for less spectacular and perhaps less Pelagian simple vows and promises. The Egyptian Fathers feared solemn vows for they often spelled pride or perjury.

Constantly adapting, reforming, waxing and waning, the spirit of monasticism hopes to persevere as an ideal type of life, inspiring the church with a vision of eschatological hopes in the midst of a world sometimes far removed from the eschaton.

Bibliography

I. SAMGHA

Allen, G., **The Buddha's Philosophy,** New York, Grove Press, 1952.

Burtt, E., **The Teachings of the Compassionate Buddha,** New York, Mentor, 1963.

Conze, E., **Buddhism, Its Essence and Development,** New York, Harper, 1959.

——————, ed., **Buddhist Texts Through the Ages,** New York, Harper, 1964.

——————, **Buddhist Thought in India,** University of Michigan Press, 1967.

Coomaraswamy, A., **Buddha and the Gospel of Buddhism,** New York, G. P. Putnam's Sons, 1916.

Dutt, S., **Buddhist Monks and Monasteries of India,** Fernhill, 1962.

Hamilton, C., ed., **Buddhism, A Religion of Infinite Compassion,** New York, The Liberal Arts Press, 1952.

Humphrey, S. C., **The Wisdom of Buddhism,** London, Michael Joseph, 1960.

Jacobsen, N., **Buddhism, the Religion of Analysis,** New York, Humanities Press, 1965.

King, W., **In the Hope of Nibbana,** Lassale, Ill., Opencourt Press, 1964.

Kitagawa, J., **Religions of the East,** Philadelphia, Westminster, 1960.

Pfanner, D., "The Buddhist Monk in Rural Burmese Society," in **Anthropological Studies in Theravada Buddhism, Cultural Report,** Series 13, Southeast Asia Studies, Yale Univ. Press, 1966, pp. 77-96.

Smith, F., **The Buddhist Way of Life, Its Philosophy and History,** London, Hutchinson's Univ. Library, 1951.

Suzuki, D., **The Training of the Zen Buddhist Monk,** New York, University Books, 1965.

Thomas, E., **The Life of Buddha as Legend and History,** London, Routledge and Kegan Paul, 1960.

II. JEWISH MONKS

Baron, S., and J. Blau, **Judaism, Postbiblical and Talmudic Period,** Indianapolis, Bobbs-Merrill, 1954.

Brownlee, W., **The Meaning of the Qumran Scrolls for the Bible,** Oxford Univ. Press, 1964.

Carmignac, J., **Christ and the Teacher of Righteousness,** Baltimore, Helicon Press, 1962.

Driver, G., **The Judaean Scrolls,** New York, Schocken Books, 1951.

Dupont-Sommer, A., **The Essene Writings of Qumran,** Cleveland, World, 1962.

Gaster, T., **The Dead Sea Scriptures,** Garden City, N. Y., Doubleday, 1964.

Josephus, **Antiquities** and **Jewish War,** Loeb Series, H. Thackeray, tr., Harvard Univ. Press, 1926-1965.

Murphy, R., **The Dead Sea Scrolls and the Bible,** Westminster, Md., Newman, 1961.

Philo, **On the Contemplative Life or Suppliants,** Loeb Series, F. Colson, tr., Harvard Univ. Press, 1941.

Ploeg, J., Van Der, **The Excavation at Qumran,** London, Longmans Green, 1958.

Ruiggen, H., **The Faith of Qumran; Theology of the Dead Sea Scrolls,** Philadelphia, Fortress Press, 1963.

Schubert, K., **The Dead Sea Community, Its Origin and Teaching,** New York, Harper and Row, 1959.

Sutcliffe, E., **The Monks of Qumran,** London, Burns and Oates, 1960.

III. GENERAL WORKS ON CHRISTIAN ASCETICISM AND MONASTICISM

Bouyer, L., The Meaning of Monastic Life, London, Burns and Oates, 1955.

Cousin, P., Precis d'histoire monastique, 1959.

DéCarreaux, J., Monks and Civilization, London, G. Allen and Unwin, 1964.

Dupont, J., "L'union entre les premiers chretiennes," NRT 9 (1969), pp. 897-915.

Hannah, I., Christian Monasticism, New York, Macmillan, 1925.

Hannay, J. O., The Spirit and Origin of Christian Monasticism, London, Methuen, 1903.

Harnack, A. Von, Monasticism: Its Ideals and History, London, Williams and Norgate, 1901.

Hefele, C. J., and H. Leclercq, Histoire des Conciles, Paris, Librairie Letouzey et Ane, 1938, 10 vols.

Knowles, D., From Pachomius to Ignatius, Oxford, Carendon, 1966.

————, Christian Monasticism, New York, McGraw-Hill, 1969.

Leclercq, H., "Cenobitisme" DACL 2, 3047-3248; "Monachisme" DACL 11, 1774-1947.

Malone, E., The Monk and the Martyr, Washington, Catholic Univ. Press, 1950.

Martinez, F., L'ascéticisme Chrétien pendant les trois primiers siecles de l'eglise, Paris, 1913.

Montalembert, Count De, The Monks of the West, 2 vols, Boston, T. Noonan & Co., 1860.

Morin, G., The Ideal of the Monastic Life Found in the Apostolic Age, 1914.

Mourre, M., Histoire vivante des moines des Pères du désert à Cluny, 1965.

Nigg, W., Warriors of God, New York, Knopf, 1959.

Quasten, J., Patrology, 3 vols, Westminster, Md., Newman, 1950.

Rousseau, O., Monachisme et vie religieuse d'apres l'ancienne tradition de l'eglise, 1957.

Smith, E. G., Christian Monasticism, London, 1892.

Théologie de la vie monastique, Etudes sur la tradition patristique, 1961.

Tillard, J. M. R., "Le fondement évangélique de la vie religieuse," NRT, Nov., 1969, pp. 916-955.

Workman, H., The Evolution of the Monastic Ideal, Boston, Beacon, 1962.

Zockler, O., Askese und Monchtum, Frankfurt, 1897.

IV. MONKS OF THE DESERT

General

Aetheria, Itinerarium, SC 12.

Apophthegmata Patrum, PG 65, PL 73.

E. Budge, **The Wit and Wisdom of the Christian Fathers of Egypt**, Oxford, 1934.

J. C. Guy, **Recherches sur la tradition Grecque des Apophthegmata Patrum**, Subsidia Hagiographica 36, Brussels, Société des Bollandistes, 1962.

Bell, H., **Jews and Christians in Egypt**, British Museum, 1924.

Budge, E., **The Book of Paradise II**, London, 1904.

Chitty, D., **The Desert a City**, Oxford, Blackwell, 1966.

Draguet, R., **Les pères du désert**, Paris, 1949.

Eusebius of Caesarea, **The Ecclesiastical History**, Loeb Series.

Evelyn-White, H. G., **The Monasteries of the Wâdi Natrûn.** Part II, The Monasteries of Nitria and Scetis. Part III, The Architecture and Archeology, New York, 1932-33.

Farag, F. R., **Sociological and Moral Studies in the Field of Coptic Monasticism**, Leiden, Brill, 1964.

Festugière, A-J., **Les moines d'orient I, culture ou sainteté**, Paris, Cerf, 1961.

Hardy, E. R., **Christian Egypt: Church and People**, Oxford, 1962.

Heussi, K., **Der Ursprung des Mönchtums**, Tübingen, 1936.

Historia Monachorum in Aegypto, E. Presuchen, ed., Palladius and Rufinus, Geisen, 1897.

Edition critique du texte Grec, A-J., Festugière, Subsidia Hagiographica 34, Societé des Bollandistes, Brussels, 1961.

Enquête sur les moines d'Egypte (Historia Monachorum in Aegypto) A-J., Festugière, Paris, Cerf, 1964.

Lacarrière, J., **Men Possessed by God**, Garden City, Doubleday, 1964.

Macarii, **Anecdota**, Mariott, ed., Harvard Univ. Press, 1918.

Fifty Spiritual Homilies of S. Macarius the Egyptian, London, SPCK, 1921.

Mackean, W. H., **Christian Monasticism in Egypt**, London, 1920.

Palladius, **The Lausiac History**, ACW 34.

Resch, P., **La doctrine ascetique des primiers mâitres egyptiens du quatrième siècle**, Paris, 1931.

Socrates, **History of the Church**, (PG 67), London, G. Bell, 1874.

Sozomen, **History of the Church** (PG 67), London H. Bohn, 1855.

Waddell, H., tr., **The Desert Fathers**, London, Constable & Co., 1954. From Rosweyde's **Vitae Patrum**.

Antony

Seven Letters, PG 40.

Athanasius, **Opera**, PG 25-28.

Serapion of Thmius, **Epistola ad Monachos**, PG 40.

"Letter on the Death of Antony," Museon 64 (1951), pp. 1-25.

Antonius Magnus Eremita, ed. B. Steidle, SA 38 (Rome, 1956).

Bouyer, L., **Vie de S. Antoine**, Saint-Wandrille, 1950.

Pachomius

Pachomius, Theodore and Horsieus, **Opera**, CSCO, Scr. Copt. Vols. 23-24.

Les moines d'orient, 4:2, **La première Vie Grecque de saint Pachôme**, A-J., Festugière, tr., Paris, Cerf, 1965.

S. **Pachomii, Vitae Graecae**, ed., F. Halkin, Subsidia Hagiographica 19, Brussels, Societé des Bollandistes, 1932.

Pachomiana Latina, A. Boon, ed., Louvain, 1932.

Bacht, H., "L'importance de l'ideal monastique chez S. Pachôme pour l'histoire du monachisme chretien," **RAM** (1950), 308-326.

————, "Antonius und Pachomius," SA 38 (1956), 66-107.

Evagrius

Opera, PG 40, 79.

Balthasar, H. U., Von, "Die Hiera des Evagrius," ZKT 63 (1939), pp. 86-106, 181-206.

————, "Metaphysik und Mystik des Evagrius Pontikus," ZAM 14 (1939).

Frankenberg, W., **Evagrius Pontikus**, Berlin, 1921.

Guillaumont, A., **Les Kephalia Gnostica d'Evagre le Pontique**, Patristica Sorbonensia 5, Paris, 1962.

Hausherr, I., "Le traité des l'oraison d'Evagre le Pontique," (Pseudo-Nil), RAM 15 (1934), pp. 34-91, 113-130.

Muyldermans, J., "Evagriana," **Muséon**, 44 (1931), pp. 37-68, 369-383; 51 (1938), 191-226.

Saudreau, A., "La spiritualité d'Evagre le Pontique," VSS (1936), pp. 180-190.

V. SYRIA AND PALESTINE

Syria

Amand, D., **L'ascèse monastique de S. Basile, essai historique**, Maredsous, 1949.

Bardy, G., "Basile (Saint) évêque de Césaree de Cappadoce," DSAM, 1:1273-1283; 2:1276-1283.

Basil, **Opera**, PG 29-32; FOC 9, 13, 28; NPNF, S. 2, V. 8; Loeb Series.

Clarke, W., S. **Basil the Great**, A Study in Monasticism, Cambridge, 1913.

Connolly, R., "Some Early Rules for Syrian Monks," **Downside Review**, 25 (1906), pp. 152-162, 300-306.

Dawes, E. and N. Baynes, **Three Byzantine Saints**, Oxford, Blackwell, 1948.

Festugière, A.-J., **Antioche païenne et chrétienne**, Libanius, Chrysostom et les moines de Syrie, Paris, de Boccard, 1959.

————, **Les moines d'orient II, Les moines de la région de Constantinople**, Paris, Cerf, 1961.

Gregory of Nazianzus, **Opera**, PG 35-38, NPNF, S. 2, V. 7.

Gregory of Nyssa, **Opera**, PG 44-46, FOC 58, NPNF, S. 2, V. 5, ACW 18.

Humbertclaude, P., **La doctrine asétique de S. Basile de Césarée**, Paris, 1932.

John Chrysostom, **Opera**, PG 47-64, NPNF, S.1, Vols. 9-14.

Morison, E., S. **Basil and His Rule**, Oxford, 1912.

Murphy, M., S. **Basil and Monasticism**, Washington, 1930.

Newman, J. H., **Historical Sketches**, Vol. 2, New York, Longmans, 1899.

Theodoret of Cyrus, **Opera**, PG 80-84.

Palestine

Chariton, **Vita Charitonis**, ed. Garitte, **Bulletin de l'Institut Historique Belge de Rome**, 1941, 5-50.

Cyril of Sythopolis, **Vitae SS Euthymii, Sabae et al.**, ed. Schwarz, T&U, 49, 2 (1939).

Les moines d'orient III, Les moines de Palestine, Cyril of Sythopolis, A-J. Festugière, Paris, Cerf, 1962-1963.

Gerontius, **Vita S. Melaniae Junioris**, SC 90.

Jerome, **Opera**, PL 22-30; ACW 33; NPNF S.2, V.6.

VI. AUGUSTINE

Ambrose, **Opera**, PL 14-17; CSEL 32, 62, 64, 74, 78, 79; FOC 26.

Augustine, **Opera**, PL 32-47; CSEL 12, 25, 28, 33, etc; NPNF, S.1, V. 1-8; FOC 2, 4, 5, 8, 14, 15, etc.

Brown, P., **Augustine of Hippo**, University of California Press, Berkeley, 1967.

Cillervelo, P-L., **El Monacato de San Agustin y su Regla**, Valladolid, 1947.

Evans, R., **Four Letters of Pelagius**, New York, Seabury, 1968.

————, **Pelagius: Inquiries and Reappraisals**, New York, Seabury, 1968.

Folliet, G., "Les moines Euchites à Carthage en 400-401," **Studia Patristica** 2, T&U 64 (1957), 386-399.

————, "Aux origines de l'ascétisme et du cénobitisme africain," **Studia Anselmia** 46 (1961), 25-44.

————, " 'Deificari in otio,' Augustin, Epistola X:2," **Revue des Études Augustiniennes**, 2(1962), 225-236.

Frend, W. H., "Circumcellions and Monks," JTS 20 (Oct. 1969), 542-549.

Humpfner, W., "Die Mönchsregel des heilegen Augustinus," **Augustinus Magister**, Paris, 1954, Vol. 1, 241-254.

Lambot, C., "La règle de saint Augustin et saint Césaire," **Revue Benedictine** 41 (1929), 333-341.

————, "Saint Augustine a-t-il rédigé la règle pour moines qui porte son nom?" RB 53 (1941), 41-58.

————, "La monachisme de saint Augustin," **Augustinus Magister**, Paris, 1954, Vol. 3, 64-69.

Manrique, A., **La Vida monastica en San Agustin**, Enchiridion Historicodoctrinal y Regla, El Escorial, 1959.

Marrou, H. S. Augustin et la fin de la culture antique, Paris, editions E. de Bollard, 1958.

Meer, F. Vander, Augustine the Bishop, New York, Sheed and Ward, 1961.

Merlin, N., S. Augustin et la Vie monastique, Albi, 1935.

O'Meara, J., The Young Augustine, Staten Island, Alba House, 1965.

Plinval, G. De, Pélage, ses écrits, sa vie et sa réforme, Lausanne, 1943.

Pope, H., S. Augustine of Hippo, Garden City, N. Y. Doubleday, 1961.

Portalié, E., A Guide to the Thought of S. Augustine, Chicago, Regnery, 1960.

Possidius, Life of Augustine, FOC 15.

Sage, A., La Règle de S. Augustin, commentée par ses écrits, Paris, La Vie Augustinienne, 1961.

Souter, A., Pelagius' Expositions of the Thirteen Epistles of S. Paul, Vol. 1, Texts and Studies, Cambridge, 1922.

Vaca, C., La Vida Religiosa en San Agustin, 2 Vols., Madrid, 1956.

Vega, A. C., La Regla de San Agustin, El Escorial, 1933.

VII. JOHN CASSIAN

Opera, PL 49-50; CSEL 13, 17; SC 42, 54, 64, 109-111; NPNF S.2, Vol. 11; LCC 12.

Chadwick, N., Poetry and Letters in Early Christian Gaul, London, Bowes and Bowes, 1955.

Chadwick, O., John Cassian, A Study in Primitive Monasticism, Cambridge Univ. Press, 1950.

Chrisophe, P. Cassien et Cesaire, Predicateurs dela morale monastique, Gemblou: Ducolot, 1969.

Concilia Gauliae, 314-506, CC 148.

Cristiani, L., Jean Cassien, la spiritualité du désert, Abbaye S. Wandrille, 1946.

Guy, J. C., Jean Cassien, vie et doctrine spirituelle, 1961.

Laugier, J., Jean Cassien et sa doctrine sur la grâce, Lyons, 1968.

Marrou, H. I., "Jean Cassien à Marseille," RMAL, I (1945), 5-26.

Marsili, S., Giovanni Cassiano ed Evagrio Ponto o, Studia Anselmiana 5, Rome, 1936.

Mènager, A., "La doctrine spirituelle de Cassien, la contemplation," VS 8 (1923), 183-212.

————, "Cassien et Clement d'Alexandrie," VS 9(1923), 138-152.

————, "A propos de Cassien," VS 46 (1936) Supp., 73-109.

Olphe-Galliard, M., "Vie contemplative et vie active d'après Cassien," RAM (July, 1935), 252-288.

————, "La pureté de coeur d'après Cassien," RAM (Jan. 1936) 28-60.

————, "La science spirituelle d'apres Cassien," RAM (Apr. 1937).

Paulinus of Nola, **Letters,** ACW 35, PL 61, CSEL 29-30.

S. **Martin et son temps, memorial du XVIe centenaire des debuts du monachisme en Gaul** (361-1961) SA 46.

Sulpicius Severus, **Opera,** PL 20; BDK 20; SC 133-134; FOC 7; NPNF, Series 2, Vol. 11.

VIII. IRISH MONKS

General

Acta Sanctorum Hiberniae, J. Botha, Edinburgh, Blackwood, 1888.

Bede, **History,** PL 90-95, Loeb Series.

Bieler, L., **Ireland, Harbinger of the Middle Ages,** Oxford Univ. Press, 1963.

————, **The Irish Penitentials,** Dublin, IAS, 1963.

Bryant, J., **Liberty, Order and Law Under Native Irish Rule,** London, Harding and More, 1923.

Chadwick, N., ed., **Studies in the Early British Church,** Cambridge Univ. Press, 1958.

————, **The Age of the Saints in the Early Celtic Church,** Oxford Univ. Press, 1961.

Haddan, A., and W. Stubbs, **Councils and Ecclesiastical Documents Relating to Great Britain and Ireland,** Oxford, Clarendon Press, 1869-1878.

Hughes, K., **The Church in Early Irish Society,** London, 1966.

Kenney, J., **The Sources for the Early History of Ireland,** I, New York, Columbia, 1929.

Lanigan, J., **An Ecclesiastical History of Ireland,** 4 vols., Dublin, Graisberry, 1822.

Ryan, J., **Irish Monasticism,** Dublin, Talbot, 1931.

————, ed., **Essays and Studies Presented to Professor Eoin MacNeill,** Dublin, At the Sign of the Three Candles, 1940.

Williams, H., **Christianity in Early Britain,** Oxford, 1912.

Zwicker, J., ed., **Fontes Historiae Religionis Celticae,** pars altera, Bonn, 1935.

Patrick

Opera, PL 53, ACW 17.

Confessio et Epistola, ed. J. D. White, London, SPCK, 1918.

Bieler, L., **Life and Legend of S. Patrick,** Dublin, 1948.

Blair, P. H., **Roman Britain and Early England,** Edinburgh, 1963.

Book of Armagh, ed. E. Gwynn, Dublin, 1937.

Bulloch, J., **The Life of the Celtic Church,** Edinburgh, 1963.

Bury, J. B., **The Life of S. Patrick,** London, 1961.

Carney, J., **The Problem of S. Patrick,** Dublin, 1961.

Hanson, R. P. C., **S. Patrick, His Origins and Career,** Oxford, 1968.

MacNeill, L., **Life and Legend of S. Patrick**, ed. J. Ryan, 1964.
O'Rahilly, T. F., **The Two Patricks**, Dublin, 1942.
Stokes, W., **The Tripartite Life of Patrick and Other Documents Relating to the Saint**, London, 1887.
White, N. J. D., **S. Patrick, His Writings and Life**, London, 1920.

Columba
Adomnan's Life of Columba, eds., A. and M. Anderson, New York, Nelson, 1961.
Bullough, D. A., "Columba, Adomnan and the Achievement of Iona," **Scottish Hist. Rev.**, 43 (Oct. 1964), 112-130; 44 (Apr. 1965) 17-33.
Chadwick, N., ed., **Celtic and Saxon**, Cambridge, 1963.
————, **Celtic Britain**, London, 1963.
Duke, J. A., **The Columban Church**, Edinburgh, 1957.
Fowler, J., **Prophecies, Miracles and Visions of S. Columba**, London, 1895.
Kenney, J., "The Earliest Life of S. Columcille," **Cath Hist. Rev.** New Series 5 (1926), 636-644.
Meyer, K., "Rule of Columcille," ZCP 3, 28-30.

Columban
Opera. G. S. M. Walker, ed. & tr., **Scriptores Latini Hiberniae II**, Dublin, Institute for Advanced Studies, 1957.
Le pénitentiel de S. Columban, ed. J. Laporte, Monumenta Christiana Selecta 4, New York, Desclée, 1958.
Concilia Galliae, 511-695, CC 148A.
Dubois, M. M., **S. Columban, a Pioneer of Western Civilization**, 1961.
The Irish Penitentials, SLH 5, ed. L. Bieler, Dublin, Institute for Advanced Studies, 1963.
Macmanus, F., **S. Columban**, New York, Sheed and Ward, 1961.
Metlake, G., **The Life and Writings of S. Columban**, Philadelphia, Dolphin, 1914.

IX. BENEDICT

Benedicti Regula, CSEL 75.
S. Benedicti, **Regula Monachorum** (Sangall 914), Concordantia, eds. P. Schmitz and C. Mohrmann, 1955.
The Holy Rule of Our Most Holy Father S. Benedict, ed., The Benedictine Monks of S. Meinrad Abbey, Grail Publications, 1956.
The Rule of S. Benedict, P. DeLatte, ed., Latrobe, Pa. The Archabbey Press, 1950.
Butler, C., **Benedictine Monachism**, Cambridge, 1961.
Cassiodorus, **Opera**, PL 69-70; CC 97-98; RC 40; CSEL 71.
Chapman, J., **S. Benedict and the Sixth Century**, London, 1929.

Daly, L., **Benedictine Monachism**, New York, Sheed & Ward, 1965.

Gregory the Great, **Opera**, PL 75-79; FOC 39; NPNF 12-13; ACW 11.

Jones, C., **Saints Lives and Chronicles in Early England**, Ithaca, N. Y. Cornell Univ. Press, 1947.

Knowles, D., **The Benedictines**, London, Sheed & Ward, 1929.

——————, **Great Historical Enterprises**, London, Nelson, 1963.

A Monk of Douai Abbey, **The High History of S. Benedict and His Monks**, London, Sands and Co. Ltd., 1945.

La Règle du mâitre, SC 105-107.

Zeller, H. Van, **The Benedictine Idea**, London, Burns and Oates, 1959.

— — ——, **The Holy Rule**, New York, Sheed & Ward, 1958.

Indices

Person Index

Aidan of Iona, 220f.
Alaric, 97, 134, 198.
Alcuin, 222.
Alypius, 110, 111, 113, 114, 117, 118, 136.
Ambrose, 110, 114, 119, 127, 130, 145, 171, 213, 230.
Ammonas, Bishop, 51.
Amoun of Nitria, 49, 59.
Antony, the Anchorite, 45ff, 64, 66, 69, 78, 90, 91, 105, 109, 111f, 113, 134, 164, 201, 226, 229. Life, 45, 47, 50, 109, 111, 139, 143, 198, 228.
Aphrahat, 78.
Athanasius, 45, 47, (n. 1), 49, 50, 51, 58, 66, 74, 78, 87, 91, 134, 164, 198, 226.
Augustine of Canterbury, 218ff.
Augustine of Hippo, xvi, xvii, 33, 109ff, 141, 143, 146, 161ff,

Augustine of Hippo (cont.), 169, 171, 194, 201, 213, 228f, 233, 234.

Basil of Caesarea, xvi, xvii, 58, 65, 74, 79ff, 90, 91, 102, 106, 114, 115, 134, 150, 152, 164, 169, 190, 198, 200, 201, 213, 227, 229.
Bede, 173, 182, 219, 222.
Benedict of Aniane, 133, 218, 231.
Benedict of Nursia, xvi, xvii, 37, 58, 61, 88, 133, 134, 164, 165, 186, 189, 197, 199ff, 213, 214, 218, 229, 231.
Brendan of Birr, 175, 179.
Brendan of Clonfert, 175, 178.
Brigit, 173, 176f, 181, 190.
Brown, P., 135, 138f.
Buddha (Gautama), 2ff, 223f.
Butler, C., 202, (n. 3), 217.

Subject Index

Abbot, 54, 84, 116, 151, 176, 182, 183, 202ff, 205, 208. See also **Pater Familias**, Superior.

Accidie, 73, 156, 208.

Active (Practical) and Contemplative (Theoretical) Lives, 66, 154f, 159f, 227, 229, 235. See also Contemplation, **Thēoria**.

Admissions, 11, 18f, 53, 84, 118, 147, 151, 190, 205f. See also Novitiate, Vocation, Vows.

Agapē, 40, 66, 155, 159. See also Charity.

Alexandria, 39ff, 68, 70, 103f.

Anaisthēsia, 66.

Anchorites, 37f, 51, 62, 69, 70, 95, 147, 164, 201. See also Hermits, Solitaries.

Semi-, 150, 164, 232. See also Laurae, Nitria, Scetis.

Angels, 23, 26, 63, 72.

Annals, 168, 178, 182.

Annesi, 79, 81, 227. See also Basil.

Anthropomorphists, 63, 68f, 148f, 226, 227. See also Coptic Monks, Shenoute of Atripe.

Anti-Augustinians, 161ff. See also Massilians; John Cassian, Prosper of Aquitaine.

Apathy (**Apatheia**), xviii, 40, 41, 60, 65, 66, 68, 83, 133, 139, 152, 155, 159, 228f, 235, 237. See also Asceticism, Gnosticism, Mortification, Purity of Heart, Stoics; Evagrius, John Cassian.

Apophthegmata Patrum, 76, 148, 201.

Aratta, 3.

Archimandrite, 51, 100, 102, 104, 106, 107, 238. See also Bishops, Lay Heresy.

Arians, 49, 51, 88, 91, 106, 142.